MW00441362

The Christian
Book of Lists

RANDY PETERSEN

Tyndale House Publishers, Inc.
Wheaton, Illinois

Visit Tyndale's exciting Web site at www.tyndale.com

Designed by Hee Chong Lee

Edited by Rick Blanchette

Library of Congress Cataloging-in-Publication Data

Petersen, Randy.

  The Christian book of lists / Randy Petersen.
    p. cm.
    ISBN 0-8423-0365-0 (pbk.)
    1. Christianity—Miscellanea. 2. Bible—Miscellanea. I. Title.
  BR96.P48 1997
  230—dc21   97-26578

Printed in the United States of America

03   02   01   00   99   98   97

10 9 8 7 6 5 4 3 2 1

LIST OF LISTS

PART 4: SPECIAL INTEREST

Section Two: The Church

INTRODUCTION

Things You Can Do with a *Christian Book of Lists*

1. Laugh at it.
2. Learn a few things.
3. Find yourself strangely warmed.
4. Add items I've missed.
5. Play a Christian version of Outburst or The $20 Zillion Pyramid.
6. Use with your daily devotions.
7. Amaze your friends with your grasp of trivia.
8. Bore your friends with your grasp of trivia.
9. Give copies to all your (remaining) friends for Christmas.
10. Let it remind you what a wacky but winsome subculture we live in.

It is the nature of an amusing book like this to poke fun. Please don't be offended. I love the Bible, which is why I keep finding interesting (and sometimes entertaining) things in it. And I love the church, though I sometimes agonize over it, as you probably do, too. Please don't take anything in a cruel or blasphemous way. That would miss the point.

I want to thank a number of people who have helped with this book. My parents, Bill and Ardythe Petersen, not only brought me into this world and shared their offbeat chromosomes with me but they provided me with many of these lists. My dear friends Deb Austin and Lauree Padgett also provided a number of lists or list ideas. Thank you much. (If you don't like something, it's obviously one of theirs.)

Now, grab a list and enjoy.

The Bible

PART 1

THE LONG AND SHORT OF IT

The 10 People in the Bible with the Longest Names

☛ Note: The calculations in this chapter are based on the spellings used in the NIV. Names may differ slightly between translations.

1. Maher-Shalal-Hash-Baz. A son of Isaiah (Isaiah 8:1, 3).
2. Pokereth-Hazzebaim. The head of an Israelite family (Ezra 2:57).
3. Cushan-Rishathaim. A king of Mesopotamia (Judges 3:8).
4. Josheb-Basshebeth. One of David's mightiest men (2 Samuel 23:8).
5. Merodach-Baladan. The son of a king of Babylon in the time of Hezekiah (2 Kings 20:12).
6. Zaphenath-Paneah. An Egyptian name given to Joseph (Genesis 41:45).
7. Nebuchadnezzar. A king of Babylon in the time of Daniel (Daniel 1–4).
8. Nergal-Sharezer. A Babylonian official (Jeremiah 39:3).
9. Shethar-Bozenai. A Persian official who opposed the rebuilding of the Jerusalem temple (Ezra 5:3).
10. Magor-Missabib. A name Jeremiah gave to Pashhur the priest (Jeremiah 20:3).

The People in the Bible with the Shortest Names

1. Er. There were three Ers in the Bible, and they were all very hesitant. (Just a little joke there.) The first-mentioned Er was a son of Judah (Genesis 38:2-7).
2. Ir. Mentioned in Benjamin's family line (1 Chronicles 7:12), an ancestor of the Huppites and Shuppites (from whom, of course, we get Hush Puppies).

3. Og. Amorite king defeated by the Israelites. He was a bad Og (Deuteronomy 3:1-13).
4. On. Joined in Korah's revolt against Moses (Numbers 16:1-2) and presumably was swallowed up by the earth with the rest of the rebels. That's right: On was under.
5. So. A king of Egypt whom the king of Israel asked for help (2 Kings 17:4). Apparently he replied, "So, what?"
6. Ur. Father of one of David's mighty men (1 Chronicles 11:35). You can make up your own joke.
7. Uz. Who was Uz? There were three of them, including a nephew of Abraham (Genesis 22:21). His brother's name was Buz. (Really!)

And there are 41 people with three-letter names in the Bible. Here are some of the more familiar ones:

+ Asa. A king of Judah (1 Kings 15:9-33), whose feet were killing him, literally (see verse 23).
+ Dan. A son of Jacob and patriarch of an Israelite tribe (Genesis 30:6). Archaeologists have been unable to find the tribe of Dave.
+ Eli. Priest in the tabernacle, mentor to Samuel (1 Samuel 1–4). When his sons died, he went off his rocker (4:18).
+ Eve. Your great-great-great . . . grandmother (Genesis 1–3).
+ Gad. Another son of Jacob and tribal patriarch (Genesis 30:11). And no, his first initial was not E.
+ Gog. Prince of Meshech and Tubal in the land of Magog, he figures into Ezekiel's prophecies (Ezekiel 38–39).
+ Ham. Son of Noah who got into trouble when he saw his dad naked (Genesis 9:22-25). There is no evidence that he later went into acting.
+ Job. The sufferer who lost everything, got it all back, and landed a great book deal.
+ Lot. A nephew of Abraham who made a bad real-estate decision and had to flee Sodom before it became a *real* hot property (Genesis 13; 19). (His wife, however, became a pillar of the community.)
+ Nun. Joshua's father (Exodus 33:11), which must have made it tough for young Josh in job interviews: "Who's your father?" . . . "Nun." . . . "You must have a father, son." . . . "I have Nun."

Shortest People in the Bible

1. Zacchaeus (Luke 19:2-3)
2. The spies who "seemed like grasshoppers" (Numbers 13:33)

3. Bildad the Shuhite (Job 8:1—shoe-height! Get it?)
4. The Roman soldiers who slept on their watch (see Matthew 28:11-15)

Trivia Tester

The longest chapter in the Bible is only a couple chapters away from the shortest chapter. Where can you find them? (Answer on page 8.)

The Places in Scripture with the Longest Names

One-Word Names

1. Philadelphia. City in Asia Minor; home of one of the seven churches of Revelation (Revelation 3:7-13).
2. Thessalonica. City in Macedonia visited by Paul on his second journey (Acts 17:1).
3. Adramyttium. A port city in Asia Minor (Acts 27:2-5).
4. Gederothaim. Variant name for a town in the foothills of Judah (Joshua 15:36).
5. Jehoshaphat. A valley where the Lord will judge the nations, according to Joel 3:2. May be a symbolic name; it means "the Lord judges."

Multiple-Word Names

1. Eglath Shelishiyah. A site in Moab named after a cow (Isaiah 15:5).
2. Harosheth Haggoyim. Hometown of Sisera, a general opposed to Israel (Judges 4:2).
3. Solomon's Colonnade. A porch in the outer court of the Jerusalem temple, where the early Christians met (Acts 5:12).
4. Ashteroth Karnaim. A town conquered in Abram's time (Genesis 14:5).
5. Caesarea Philippi. A city near Mount Hermon where Peter made his famous statement, "You are the Christ" (Matthew 16:13, 16).
6. Gibeath Haaraloth. A hill where Joshua had the Israelite men circumcised (Joshua 5:3). And that's just what it means.
7. Kibroth Hattaavah. A place in the wilderness where the Israelites stopped and demanded meat. Quail came, but many of the people took sick and died. The place-name means "graves of craving" (Numbers 11:34).
8. Sela Hammahlekoth. The "rock of parting" in the Judean desert where Saul stopped chasing David (1 Samuel 23:28).
9. Shaveh Kiriathaim. A plain near Moab where a battle took place in Abram's time (Genesis 14:5).

The Places in Scripture with the Shortest Names

1. Ai. Canaanite city the Israelites attacked after Jericho (Joshua 7–8).
2. Ar. A city in Moab (Numbers 21:15).
3. On. An ancient city of Egypt (Genesis 41:45).
4. Ur. Abraham's hometown, probably in ancient Babylonia (Genesis 11:28-31).
5. Uz. Where Job lived (Job 1:1).

There are 27 places in the Bible with three-letter names. Here are some of the most familiar:

+ Dan. The term for two places, really. Originally the tribe of Dan was to settle in central Palestine, but they couldn't defeat the Philistines. So most of the tribe moved north, establishing the city of Dan near Mount Hermon (Joshua 19:40-48).
+ Gad. The territory settled by the tribe of Gad, east of the Jordan (Numbers 32:20-36).
+ Lod. A crossroads town on the Plain of Sharon, near modern-day Tel Aviv (1 Chronicles 8:12).
+ Put. An African nation, often linked with Egypt and Ethiopia; it might refer to parts of Libya (Jeremiah 46:9).
+ Sin. The desert near Mount Sinai (Exodus 16:1).

Longest Books of the Bible

By Chapters

1. Psalms—150
2. Isaiah—66
3. Jeremiah—52
4. Genesis—50
5. Ezekiel—48
6. Job—42
7. Exodus—40
8. Numbers—36
9. 2 Chronicles—36
10. Deuteronomy—34

By Verses

1. Psalms—2,461
2. Genesis—1,533
3. Jeremiah—1,364
4. Isaiah—1,292
5. Numbers—1,288
6. Ezekiel—1,273

7. Exodus—1,213
8. Luke—1,151
9. Matthew—1,071
10. Job—1,070

By Words*

*Exact totals differ among different translations.

1. Psalms
2. Jeremiah
3. Ezekiel
4. Genesis
5. Isaiah
6. Numbers
7. Exodus
8. Deuteronomy
9. 2 Chronicles
10. Luke

The Best Verses in the 10 Shortest Books of the Bible

1. 2 John (13 verses, approx. 300 words). *Verse 6*—"And this is love: that we walk in obedience to his commands. As you have heard from the beginning, his command is that you walk in love."
2. 3 John (14 verses, approx. 300 words). *Verse 11—"Dear friend, do not imitate what is evil but what is good."*
3. Philemon (25 verses, approx. 450 words). *Verse 6*—"I pray that you may be active in sharing your faith, so that you will have a full understanding of every good thing we have in Christ."
4. Jude (25 verses, approx. 600 words). *Verse 21*—"Keep yourselves in God's love as you wait for the mercy of our Lord Jesus Christ to bring you to eternal life."
5. Obadiah (21 verses, approx. 650 words). *Verse 12*—"You should not look down on your brother in the day of his misfortune."
6. Titus (46 verses, approx. 900 words). *3:5*—"He saved us, not because of righteous things we had done, but because of his mercy. He saved us through the washing of rebirth and renewal by the Holy Spirit."
7. 2 Thessalonians (47 verses, approx. 1,050 words). *3:13*—"And as for you, brothers, never tire of doing what is right."
8. Haggai (38 verses, approx. 1,150 words). *2:4*—"'Be strong, all you people of the land,' declares the Lord, 'and work. For I am with you,' declares the Lord Almighty."
9. Nahum (47 verses, approx. 1,300 words). *1:7*—"The Lord is

good, a refuge in times of trouble. He cares for those who trust in him."

10. Jonah (48 verses, approx. 1,300 words). *2:9*—"But I, with a song of thanksgiving, will sacrifice to you. What I have vowed I will make good. Salvation comes from the Lord."

Answers to Trivia Tester

Psalm 119 is the longest chapter, with 176 verses.
Psalm 117 is the shortest, with 2.

CHAPTER AND VERSE

Ten Favorite Psalms

1. Psalm 19. *The heavens declare the glory of God.* . . . This psalm has three glorious sections: the paean to God's creation (19:1-6); the celebration of God's law (19:7-11); and the prayer of personal dedication (12-14). If you don't know verse 14, learn it—and pray it throughout the day.

2. Psalm 40. *I waited patiently for the Lord.* . . . The poetry here is rich, rooted in concrete images. Haven't you ever felt that you were in a "slimy pit" (40:2) and God pulled you out of the "mud and mire" (40:2)? Note: The "pierced" ear of verse 6 is not a fashion statement but an indication of one's voluntary servitude.

3. Psalm 51. *Create in me a pure heart.* . . . It's the label that makes this psalm great, telling us what David did that he was now sorry for. We know that feeling, too—David gives us words for it.

4. Psalm 73. *My feet had almost slipped.* . . . Haven't you ever felt trapped between verses 1 and 2? Yeah, yeah, God is good, *but as for me,* those assurances don't seem to apply. Why do the bad guys keep winning? The psalm turns a corner in verse 17 when the psalmist enters "the sanctuary" and sees the light. It's the bad guys who are walking in slippery places.

5. Psalm 98. *Sing to the Lord a new song.* . . . This jubilant psalm calls for creativity in worshiping God. Why do so many churches insist on being so dull?

6. Psalm 118. *Blessed is he who comes in the name of the Lord.* . . . This is a joyous processional psalm packed with messianic prophecy. Jesus used verse 22 himself, implying that he was "the stone the builders rejected."

7. Psalm 131. *My heart is not proud.* . . . Humility. Simplicity. The end of a long, hard day. Just hope in the Lord.

8. Psalm 133. *How good and pleasant it is.* . . . I remember singing this psalm in Hebrew *(Hineh mah tov)* with a study group in Israel. We had seen Mount Hermon and Mount Zion and were getting along just great. It *is* good and pleasant.

9. Psalm 139. *You have searched me and you know me. . . .* This is my pastor's favorite psalm, and he's a good friend, so I've added it. When you think no one understands, you're wrong. God knows you inside and out.
10. Psalm 150. *Praise him with tambourine and dancing. . . .* I remember the great scene in the movie *Footloose* when the preacher's daughter shows Psalm 150:4 to the dancing hero. "This is great!" he says. He had never realized the Bible was this much fun. It is. This psalm urges us to pull out the stops in glorifying our great God.

Ten Favorite New Testament Chapters

1. Matthew 6. It's hard to pick one part of the Sermon on the Mount, but this chapter is rich: The Lord's Prayer; cautions about money and worrying; "Seek first [God's] kingdom." If we ever put this chapter into practice, we'd change the world.
2. Luke 15. Jesus' "Lost" trilogy. A lost sheep, a lost coin, a lost son. In simple story form, this is the gospel. God sent Jesus to look for the lost and bring them back into relationship with him.
3. John 9. Let yourself laugh at this story of the blind man's healing and you'll realize it's one of the funniest chapters in the Bible. The Pharisees are practically Keystone Cops as they interview the don't-get-involved parents and the overzealous ex-beggar.
4. Acts 17. Glimpses of three distinct types of ministries, which could represent three types of churches today: the suffering church (Thessalonica); the studying church (Berea); and the seeker church (Athens). Paul gives a great model for seeker ministry in his Athens sermon, using their language, their philosophy, their poetry. Hey, maybe *we* could communicate with our culture like that!
5. Romans 8. From "no condemnation" to "more than conquerors," this chapter is packed with memory verses. Why not just learn the whole thing? Paul is describing the life of the believer guided by God's Spirit. This is challenging and reassuring at the same time.
6. Romans 12. After his heartfelt theological musings about the fate of Israel, Paul is back to talking about the church. As Christians we must offer our bodies as "living sacrifices," being "transformed" by God's Spirit and not being too proud of ourselves. This results in mutual ministry within the church and revolutionary love toward enemies.
7. Philippians 4. Practical guidelines for the Christian life. Don't worry, be happy. Let God's peace guard you as you focus on

what's true, noble, right, etc. Through Christ's strength, be
content.

8. 1 Timothy 6. The problem with money. Paul warns his
    protégé about the dangers of being rich. No, folks, the Bible
    doesn't say it's wrong to be rich, just that it's very difficult to
    embrace God when you're holding onto your money. It's a
    trap, Paul says. Watch out!

9. 1 John 1. The prologue is a stirring personal testimony of
    John's life with Jesus (the Word). Then John launches into a
    heresy-fighting discussion of sin and forgiveness. Yes, we sin.
    Don't deny it. But Jesus offers complete forgiveness. Claim it.

10. Revelation 4. Heaven's curtains part for a moment, and we
    see a worship service in progress. Glorious!

Other chapters that almost made the cut: Matthew 22; 23; Luke 2; 24;
John 4; Acts 2; Romans 3; 1 Corinthians 13; Galatians 5; Ephesians 2;
Hebrews 10; 1 Peter 2.

Ten Favorite Old Testament Chapters (besides the Psalms)

1. Exodus 15. The "Song of Moses," praising God for the mirac-
    ulous Red Sea crossing. Poetic, exultant, full of joyous energy.

2. Deuteronomy 6. The Lord lays down the law—in terms of
    love. Following the declaration of God's oneness ("Hear, O
    Israel," 6:4) is the command Jesus called the greatest: Love
    God with all of who you are (6:5).

3. 1 Samuel 17. For sheer drama, irony, and intriguing characters,
    it's hard to beat the story of David and Goliath.

4. 1 Kings 19. Elijah's bout with depression after his victory on
    Mount Carmel. God speaks to him not in an earthquake,
    wind, or fire but in a "gentle whisper."

5. Job 38. After the philosophizing of Job and his friends, God
    finally speaks—and in brilliant poetry. "Can you make a con-
    stellation? Then don't tell me what to do" (or words to that
    effect). Don't stop here; read the next three chapters, too.

6. Proverbs 3. The basics of wisdom. "Trust in the Lord . . . ac-
    knowledge him."

7. Song of Songs 2. Love talk between the two characters. As a
    picture of God's relationship with his people, it's inspiring.
    "My lover is mine and I am his" (2:16).

8. Isaiah 40. Beginning with "comfort" and ending on "wings
    like eagles," this chapter will stir the soul of anyone who feels
    forgotten by God.

9. Isaiah 53. The Suffering Servant bears the sins of the people.
    A stunning prophecy fulfilled in Jesus Christ.

10. Daniel 6. This Bible book is chock-full of great stories. The tale of Daniel in the lions' den is a classic expression of courageous faith in adversity.

Other chapters that almost made the cut: Numbers 22; 1 Samuel 26; 2 Kings 5; Nehemiah 8; Proverbs 8; 31; Isaiah 55; 58; Daniel 3; Hosea 11; 14.

The 10 Dullest Chapters of the Bible

Please don't consider me irreverent here. I believe in the inspiration of all Scripture. But let's just say, in your read-the-Bible-straight-through plan, it's natural to get bogged down in Leviticus. The fact is, the Bible is a lot of different *kinds* of books—history books and poetry books, but also record books and law books. There's value in all of the above, to be sure, but some parts make better bedtime reading than others.

1. Leviticus 13 (and 14 and 15). Dermatologists may disagree, but the lengthy discussion of skin diseases and mildew doesn't give me shivers of joy.
2. Numbers 1 (and 2). When you're dying to know whether the tribe of Simeon had more fighting men than Naphtali, check out this census data.
3. Numbers 7. Eighty-nine (count 'em) verses detailing the gifts of the Israelites' big donors.
4. Numbers 26. After a disastrous plague, they took another census. (Why do you think they call it Numbers?)
5. Numbers 33. The travelogue of the wandering Israelites. Here's a sample: "They left Hor Haggidgad and camped at Jotbathah. They left Jotbathah and camped at Abronah. They left Abronah and camped at Ezion Geber" (33:33-35). *And it goes on.*
6. Joshua 14 (and 15 through 19). Just when you thought it was safe—Deuteronomy is pretty good, and Joshua starts off with that Jericho story—we're divvying up the Promised Land. That means counting up the towns and assigning them to different tribes. Another pronunciation nightmare for those who read Scripture in church.
7. 1 Chronicles 1 (and 2 through 9). Begats. Who sired whom. From the beginning of time. Here's an idea: During a testimony service, stand up and quote 1 Chronicles 1:12 as your "life verse": "Pathrusites, Casluhites (from whom the Philistines came) and Caphtorites."
8. Ezra 2. More census data, but this time the Jews returning from exile are being numbered, along with their livestock. It was a

dramatic moment, of course, but you may want to skip the "435 camels and 6,720 donkeys" (2:67) and jump to chapter 3.

9. Ezekiel 40 (and 41 and 42). It's promising at first—in a vision Ezekiel is shown a massive temple complex in Jerusalem. But then his guide starts measuring everything. For me, this confirms what women have known for a long time: When a guy takes out his tape measure, you'd better leave the room because nothing interesting is going to happen. I know some prophecy enthusiasts really dig this stuff, but there are just too many cubits for me.

10. Obadiah. But it's short.

Ten Proverbs That Will Make You Smile

1. Proverbs 6:27. "Can a man scoop fire into his lap without his clothes being burned?"
2. Proverbs 10:10. "He who winks maliciously causes grief, and a chattering fool comes to ruin."
3. Proverbs 11:22. "Like a gold ring in a pig's snout is a beautiful woman who shows no discretion." (All right, all right! Remember that Proverbs was written by older men to young men. If women wrote it, we might hear more about indiscreet men.)
4. Proverbs 13:7. "One man pretends to be rich, yet has nothing; another pretends to be poor, yet has great wealth."
5. Proverbs 20:14. "'It's no good, it's no good!' says the buyer; then off he goes and boasts about his purchase."
6. Proverbs 25:16. "If you find honey, eat just enough—too much of it, and you will vomit."
7. Proverbs 25:21-22. "If your enemy is hungry, give him food to eat; if he is thirsty, give him water to drink. In doing this, you will heap burning coals on his head, and the Lord will reward you."
8. Proverbs 26:9. "Like a thornbush in a drunkard's hand is a proverb in the mouth of a fool."
9. Proverbs 26:18-19. "Like a madman shooting firebrands or deadly arrows is a man who deceives his neighbor and says, 'I was only joking!'"
10. Proverbs 27:14. "If a man loudly blesses his neighbor early in the morning, it will be taken as a curse."

Ten Favorite Verses from the Gospels

These are my favorite verses. I know there are guys in the end-zone bleachers campaigning for John 3:16, but I left that out. Sorry.

1. Matthew 6:33. "But seek first his kingdom and his righteousness, and all these things will be given to you as well."
2. Matthew 11:28-30. "Come to me, all you who are weary and burdened, and I will give you rest. Take my yoke upon you and learn from me, for I am gentle and humble in heart, and you will find rest for your souls. For my yoke is easy and my burden is light."
3. Mark 8:36. "What good is it for a man to gain the whole world, yet forfeit his soul?"
4. Mark 10:42-45. "You know that those who are regarded as rulers of the Gentiles lord it over them, and their high officials exercise authority over them. Not so with you. Instead, whoever wants to become great among you must be your servant, and whoever wants to be first must be slave of all. For even the Son of Man did not come to be served, but to serve, and to give his life as a ransom for many."
5. Luke 2:14. "Glory to God in the highest, and on earth peace to men on whom his favor rests."
6. Luke 6:27-28. "But I tell you who hear me: Love your enemies, do good to those who hate you, bless those who curse you, pray for those who mistreat you."
7. John 1:14. "The Word became flesh and made his dwelling among us. We have seen his glory, the glory of the One and Only, who came from the Father, full of grace and truth."
8. John 5:39. "You diligently study the Scriptures because you think that by them you possess eternal life. These are the Scriptures that testify about me."
9. John 15:12-13. "My command is this: Love each other as I have loved you. Greater love has no one than this, that he lay down his life for his friends."
10. John 16:33. "I have told you these things, so that in me you may have peace. In this world you will have trouble. But take heart! I have overcome the world."

Ten Favorite Verses from the New Testament Epistles

1. Romans 1:22. *(Of those who refuse to worship God)* "Although they claimed to be wise, they became fools."
2. Romans 7:15. "I do not understand what I do. For what I want to do I do not do, but what I hate I do."
3. Romans 14:13. "Therefore let us stop passing judgment on one another. Instead, make up your mind not to put any stumbling block or obstacle in your brother's way."
4. 2 Corinthians 5:17. "Therefore, if anyone is in Christ, he is a new creation; the old has gone, the new has come!"

5. 2 Corinthians 10:3-4. "For though we live in the world, we do not wage war as the world does. The weapons we fight with are not the weapons of the world."
6. Philippians 1:6. "Being confident of this, that he who began a good work in you will carry it on to completion until the day of Christ Jesus."
7. Colossians 1:17. "[Christ] is before all things, and in him all things hold together."
8. Titus 2:11-14. "For the grace of God that brings salvation has appeared to all men. It teaches us to say 'No' to ungodliness and worldly passions, and to live self-controlled, upright and godly lives in this present age, while we wait for the blessed hope—the glorious appearing of our great God and Savior, Jesus Christ, who gave himself for us to redeem us from all wickedness and to purify for himself a people that are his very own, eager to do what is good."
9. 1 John 1:9. "If we confess our sins, he is faithful and just and will forgive us our sins and purify us from all unrighteousness."
10. Jude 1:24-25. "To him who is able to keep you from falling and to present you before his glorious presence without fault and with great joy—to the only God our Savior be glory, majesty, power and authority, through Jesus Christ our Lord, before all ages, now and forevermore! Amen."

Ten Favorite Old Testament Verses

1. Genesis 50:20. *(Joseph to his brothers)* "You intended to harm me, but God intended it for good to accomplish what is now being done, the saving of many lives."
2. 1 Samuel 16:7. *(Samuel anointing David)* "But the Lord said to Samuel, 'Do not consider his appearance or his height, for I have rejected him. The Lord does not look at the things man looks at. Man looks at the outward appearance, but the Lord looks at the heart.'"
3. 2 Samuel 6:14. *(While bringing the ark back to Jerusalem)* "David, wearing a linen ephod, danced before the Lord with all his might."
4. Job 19:25. *(The sufferer expresses his faith)* "I know that my Redeemer lives, and that in the end he will stand upon the earth."
5. Psalm 115:1. "Not to us, O Lord, not to us but to your name be the glory, because of your love and faithfulness."
6. Song of Songs 8:7. "Many waters cannot quench love; rivers cannot wash it away. If one were to give all the wealth of his house for love, it would be utterly scorned."

7. Isaiah 1:18. "'Come now, let us reason together,' says the Lord. 'Though your sins are like scarlet, they shall be as white as snow; though they are red as crimson, they shall be like wool.'"

8. Isaiah 40:31. "But those who hope in the Lord will renew their strength. They will soar on wings like eagles; they will run and not grow weary, they will walk and not be faint."

9. Isaiah 55:1-2. "Come, all you who are thirsty, come to the waters; and you who have no money, come, buy and eat! Come, buy wine and milk without money and without cost. Why spend money on what is not bread, and your labor on what does not satisfy? Listen, listen to me, and eat what is good, and your soul will delight in the richest of fare."

10. Zechariah 4:6. *(God to Commander Zerubbabel)* "'"Not by might nor by power, but by my Spirit,"' says the Lord Almighty."

Great Verses Often Overlooked Because They Follow Other Great Verses

1. **We know . . .** Proverbs 1:7—"The fear of the Lord is the beginning of knowledge, but fools despise wisdom and discipline."
   . . . but read on: Proverbs 1:8—"Listen, my son, to your father's instruction and do not forsake your mother's teaching."

2. **We know . . .** Proverbs 3:5-6—"Trust in the Lord with all your heart and lean not on your own understanding; in all your ways acknowledge him, and he will make your paths straight."
   . . . but read on: Proverbs 3:7—"Do not be wise in your own eyes; fear the Lord and shun evil."

3. **We know . . .** Jeremiah 31:3—"I have loved you with an everlasting love; I have drawn you with loving-kindness."
   . . . but read on: Jeremiah 31:4—"I will build you up again and you will be rebuilt, O Virgin Israel. Again you will take up your tambourines and go out to dance with the joyful."

4. **We know . . .** Matthew 6:33—"But seek first his kingdom and his righteousness, and all these things will be given to you as well."
   . . . but read on: Matthew 6:34—"Therefore do not worry about tomorrow, for tomorrow will worry about itself. Each day has enough trouble of its own."

5. **We know . . .** John 3:16—"For God so loved the world that he gave his one and only Son, that whoever believes in him shall not perish but have eternal life."

. . . **but read on:** John 3:17—"For God did not send his Son into the world to condemn the world, but to save the world through him."

6. **We know . . .** John 14:6—"Jesus answered, 'I am the way and the truth and the life. No one comes to the Father except through me.'"

. . . **but read on:** John 14:7—"If you really knew me, you would know my Father as well. From now on, you do know him and have seen him."

7. **We know . . .** Romans 3:23—"For all have sinned and fall short of the glory of God."

. . . **but read on:** Romans 3:24-26—"And are justified freely by his grace through the redemption that came by Christ Jesus. God presented him as a sacrifice of atonement, through faith in his blood. He did this to demonstrate his justice, because in his forbearance he had left the sins committed beforehand unpunished—he did it to demonstrate his justice at the present time, so as to be just and the one who justifies those who have faith in Jesus."

8. **We know . . .** 2 Corinthians 5:17—"Therefore, if anyone is in Christ, he is a new creation; the old has gone, the new has come!"

. . . **but read on:** 2 Corinthians 5:18-20—"All this is from God, who reconciled us to himself through Christ and gave us the ministry of reconciliation: that God was reconciling the world to himself in Christ, not counting men's sins against them. And he has committed to us the message of reconciliation. We are therefore Christ's ambassadors, as though God were making his appeal through us. We implore you on Christ's behalf: Be reconciled to God."

9. **We know . . .** Ephesians 2:8-9—"For it is by grace you have been saved, through faith—and this not from yourselves, it is the gift of God—not by works, so that no one can boast."

. . . **but read on:** Ephesians 2:10—"For we are God's workmanship, created in Christ Jesus to do good works, which God prepared in advance for us to do."

10. **We know . . .** 2 Timothy 2:15—"Do your best to present yourself to God as one approved, a workman who does not need to be ashamed and who correctly handles the word of truth."

. . . **but read on:** 2 Timothy 2:16-17—"Avoid godless chatter, because those who indulge in it will become more and more ungodly. Their teaching will spread like gangrene."

Ten Bible Verses People Don't Quote Much

1. Exodus 4:13. "But Moses said, 'O Lord, please send someone else to do it.'" *Well, people actually say it all the time; they just don't know they're quoting Scripture.*

2. Psalm 3:7. "Arise, O Lord! Deliver me, O my God! Strike all my enemies on the jaw; break the teeth of the wicked." *Send them to the orthodontist! Make them pay for massive dental work!*

3. Ecclesiastes 7:16. "Do not be overrighteous, neither be over-wise—why destroy yourself?" *Not a problem for some of us.*

4. 1 Kings 18:27. "At noon Elijah began to taunt them. 'Shout louder!' he said. 'Surely he is a god! Perhaps he is deep in thought, or busy, or traveling. Maybe he is sleeping and must be awakened.'" *The term for* busy *is probably a polite term for "going to the bathroom."*

5. 2 Thessalonians 3:10. "For even when we were with you, we gave you this rule: 'If a man will not work, he shall not eat.'" *But what if we applied this to church suppers?*

6. Proverbs 17:8. "A bribe is a charm to the one who gives it; wherever he turns, he succeeds." *Warning: The book of Proverbs often just tells us what is true about life, rather than what we should do. This is not a nugget of moral instruction.*

7. Leviticus 11:20. "All flying insects that walk on all fours are to be detestable to you." *For many of us, this is not a difficult command to follow.*

8. Amos 4:1. "Hear this word, you cows of Bashan on Mount Samaria, you women who oppress the poor and crush the needy and say to your husbands, 'Bring us some drinks!'" *If it's any consolation, Amos was equally insulting to men.*

9. 1 Timothy 5:23. "Stop drinking only water, and use a little wine because of your stomach and your frequent illnesses." *I know this was written at a time when wine had fewer impurities than water, but it's still a neat verse to tease teetotalers.*

10. Leviticus 19:27. "Do not cut the hair at the sides of your head or clip off the edges of your beard." *Why wasn't I aware of this verse back in the '60s?*

PART 3

ABOUT JESUS

Twenty-six Old Testament Prophecies Fulfilled in Jesus

1. Numbers 24:17. "I see him, but not now; I behold him, but not near. A star will come out of Jacob; a scepter will rise out of Israel." *As a Jew, Jesus was a descendant of Jacob (Matthew 1:2).*

2. Genesis 49:10. "The scepter will not depart from Judah, nor the ruler's staff from between his feet, until he comes to whom it belongs and the obedience of the nations is his." *Jesus was of the tribe of Judah (Luke 3:33).*

3. Isaiah 9:7. "Of the increase of his government and peace there will be no end. He will reign on David's throne and over his kingdom, establishing and upholding it with justice and righteousness from that time on and forever." *Jesus was a descendant of David (Matthew 1:6).*

4. Micah 5:2. "But you, Bethlehem Ephrathah, though you are small among the clans of Judah, out of you will come for me one who will be ruler over Israel, whose origins are from of old, from ancient times." *Jesus was born in Bethlehem (Luke 2:4-7).*

5. Isaiah 7:14. "Therefore the Lord himself will give you a sign: The virgin will be with child and will give birth to a son, and will call him Immanuel." *Jesus was born of the Virgin Mary (Luke 1:26-27). Though his name was not Immanuel (which means "God with us"), his subsequent ministry made clear that he was God in human form (John 1:14).*

6. Hosea 11:1. "When Israel was a child, I loved him, and out of Egypt I called my son." *Clearly Israel itself had been called out of captivity in Egypt, but the baby Jesus was also carried there to escape Herod's threats (Matthew 2:14-15).*

7. Malachi 3:1. "'See, I will send my messenger, who will prepare the way before me. Then suddenly the Lord you are seeking will come to his temple; the messenger of the covenant, whom you desire, will come,' says the Lord Almighty." *Jesus was preceded by a messenger, John the Baptist (Matthew 3:1).*

8. Psalm 2:7. "I will proclaim the decree of the Lord: He said to me, 'You are my Son; today I have become your Father.'" *At*

Jesus' baptism, God's voice thundered from heaven, declaring Jesus his Son (Matthew 3:17).

9. Isaiah 9:1. "Nevertheless, there will be no more gloom for those who were in distress. In the past he humbled the land of Zebulun and the land of Naphtali, but in the future he will honor Galilee of the Gentiles, by the way of the sea, along the Jordan—The people walking in darkness have seen a great light; on those living in the land of the shadow of death a light has dawned." *Jesus conducted most of his ministry in the region of Galilee (Matthew 4:13-16).*

10. Isaiah 61:1. "The Spirit of the Sovereign Lord is on me, because the Lord has anointed me to preach good news to the poor. He has sent me to bind up the brokenhearted, to proclaim freedom for the captives and release from darkness for the prisoners." *Jesus' ministry focused on the poor and needy as he healed them, offered them access to God, and railed against the abuses of the elite (Luke 4:18-21).*

11. Daniel 9:25-26. "Know and understand this: From the issuing of the decree to restore and rebuild Jerusalem until the Anointed One, the ruler, comes, there will be seven 'sevens,' and sixty-two 'sevens.'. . . After the sixty-two 'sevens,' the Anointed One will be cut off." *Interpretations differ, but these numbers can be finagled to compute 69 periods of 7 years (483 years) between Artaxerxes' edict to restore Jerusalem and the early A.D. 30s—when Jesus was ministering in and around Jerusalem and died (was "cut off") there.*

12. Isaiah 53:3. "He was despised and rejected by men, a man of sorrows, and familiar with suffering. Like one from whom men hide their faces he was despised, and we esteemed him not." *Though Jesus had some popular acclaim, in the end he was rejected by the crowds, who preferred to see a criminal released (Luke 23:18).*

13. Zechariah 9:9. "Rejoice greatly, O Daughter of Zion! Shout, Daughter of Jerusalem! See, your king comes to you, righteous and having salvation, gentle and riding on a donkey, on a colt, the foal of a donkey." *In the Triumphal Entry, Jesus rode into Jerusalem on a donkey (Mark 11:7).*

14. Psalm 41:9. "Even my close friend, whom I trusted, he who shared my bread, has lifted up his heel against me." *Jesus was betrayed by Judas, one of his closest 12 disciples (Luke 22:47-48).*

15. Zechariah 11:12. "I told them, 'If you think it best, give me my pay; but if not, keep it.' So they paid me thirty pieces of silver." *Judas arranged to betray Jesus for the sum of 30 silver pieces, which he later returned (Matthew 26:14-15; 27:3).*

16. Psalm 35:11. "Ruthless witnesses come forward; they question me on things I know nothing about." *Jesus was accused by false witnesses (Mark 14:57-58).*

17. Isaiah 53:7. "He was oppressed and afflicted, yet he did not open his mouth; he was led like a lamb to the slaughter, and as a sheep before her shearers is silent, so he did not open his mouth." *Jesus remained silent during his trial (Mark 15:4-5).*

18. Isaiah 50:6. "I offered my back to those who beat me, my cheeks to those who pulled out my beard; I did not hide my face from mocking and spitting." *Jesus was beaten and spat upon (Matthew 26:67).*

19. Isaiah 53:9. "He was assigned a grave with the wicked, and with the rich in his death, though he had done no violence, nor was any deceit in his mouth." *Jesus was crucified with thieves and buried in a rich man's tomb (Mark 15:27; Matthew 27:57-60).*

20. Zechariah 12:10. "They will look on me, the one they have pierced, and they will mourn for him as one mourns for an only child, and grieve bitterly for him as one grieves for a first-born son." *Jesus was pierced with nails through his hands and feet and a sword in his side, his wounds observed not only by a few faithful at the cross but also later by Thomas and the other disciples (John 19:34; 20:27).*

21. Psalm 69:21. "They put gall in my food and gave me vinegar for my thirst." *On the cross, Jesus was given vinegar and gall (Matthew 27:34).*

22. Psalm 22:7-8. "All who see me mock me; they hurl insults, shaking their heads: 'He trusts in the Lord; let the Lord rescue him. Let him deliver him, since he delights in him.'" *On the cross, Jesus was mocked by passersby (Luke 23:35).*

23. Psalms 22:17; 34:20. "I can count all my bones; people stare and gloat over me. . . . He protects all his bones, not one of them will be broken." *Though victims of crucifixion routinely had their bones broken, the soldiers did not break Jesus' bones (John 19:33).*

24. Psalm 22:18. "They divide my garments among them and cast lots for my clothing." *Soldiers divided Jesus' clothing and cast lots for his robe (Matthew 27:35-36).*

25. Psalms 16:10; 49:15. "You will not abandon me to the grave, nor will you let your Holy One see decay. . . . But God will redeem my life from the grave; he will surely take me to himself." *Jesus rose from the dead (Mark 16:6).*

26. Psalm 68:18. "When you ascended on high, you led captives in your train; you received gifts from men, even from the

rebellious—that you, O Lord God, might dwell there." *Jesus ascended into heaven (Acts 1:9).*

Fifteen Witty Things Jesus Said

1. Mark 2:17. "It is not the healthy who need a doctor, but the sick. I have not come to call the righteous, but sinners." *Criticized for hanging out with "sinners," Jesus acknowledged his true mission.*

2. Mark 3:25. "If a house is divided against itself, that house cannot stand." *Accused of being in league with the devil, Jesus took that charge to the point of absurdity. If it were true, his casting out of demons would be a bad strategy indeed.*

3. Matthew 16:6. "Be on your guard against the yeast of the Pharisees and Sadducees." *The disciples didn't get it. They thought he wanted some bread. But Jesus was warning them about the way these leaders expanded God's law and corrupted it.*

4. Luke 18:25. "It is easier for a camel to go through the eye of a needle than for a rich man to enter the kingdom of God." *Some commentators suggest that there was a "Needle's Eye" gate in Jerusalem that a camel could get through but only without baggage. Whether or not that's true, it's a funny picture.*

5. Luke 20:3-4. "I will also ask you a question. Tell me, John's baptism—was it from heaven, or from men?" *Jesus escaped a catch-22 question by launching one of his own and catching the Pharisees in their own politics. If they said John had a merely human message, they'd disappoint the people, who saw John as a prophet. But if they admitted that John's message was divine, they'd have to obey that message—and that would lead them to faith in Jesus, which they were stubbornly resisting.*

6. Mark 12:17. "Give to Caesar what is Caesar's and to God what is God's." *Jesus wriggled out of another jam. In this politically charged environment, he managed to stay true to Israel without advocating rebellion against Rome.*

7. Matthew 5:46-47. "If you love those who love you, what reward will you get? Are not even the tax collectors doing that? And if you greet only your brothers, what are you doing more than others? Do not even pagans do that?" *There's nothing special about reciprocal demonstrations of love. God's people need to go the extra mile.*

8. Matthew 6:24. "No one can serve two masters. Either he will hate the one and love the other, or he will be devoted to the one and despise the other. You cannot serve both God and Money." *In his typical fashion, Jesus started with a situation from*

everyday life—servants and masters—and then used it to challenge his listeners.

9. Matthew 6:34. "Therefore do not worry about tomorrow, for tomorrow will worry about itself. Each day has enough trouble of its own." *This is wall-plaque stuff.*

10. Matthew 7:3-5. "Why do you look at the speck of sawdust in your brother's eye and pay no attention to the plank in your own eye? How can you say to your brother, 'Let me take the speck out of your eye,' when all the time there is a plank in your own eye? You hypocrite, first take the plank out of your own eye, and then you will see clearly to remove the speck from your brother's eye." *This was like a vaudeville routine in the first century, taking a simple premise to an absurd degree.*

11. Luke 11:11-13. "Which of you fathers, if your son asks for a fish, will give him a snake instead? Or if he asks for an egg, will give him a scorpion? If you then, though you are evil, know how to give good gifts to your children, how much more will your Father in heaven give the Holy Spirit to those who ask him!" *A classic argument Jesus made often: If humans do this, imagine how much more God does.*

12. Matthew 15:14. "They are blind guides. If a blind man leads a blind man, both will fall into a pit." *Those Pharisees bore the brunt of Jesus' wit. What a great word picture here!*

13. Matthew 23:24. "You strain out a gnat but swallow a camel." *Is there a better way to describe the Pharisees' pickiness amid their wholesale corruption?*

14. Matthew 23:27. "Woe to you, teachers of the law and Pharisees, you hypocrites! You are like whitewashed tombs, which look beautiful on the outside but on the inside are full of dead men's bones and everything unclean." *Ouch!*

15. John 10:34-36. "Is it not written in your Law, 'I have said you are gods'? If he called them 'gods,' to whom the word of God came—and the Scripture cannot be broken—what about the one whom the Father set apart as his very own and sent into the world? Why then do you accuse me of blasphemy because I said, 'I am God's Son'?" *Jesus was always pretty coy about his claims of divinity because he knew he'd be charged with blasphemy. But here he found a psalm (82) that called the rulers of the people "gods." Ironically, Psalm 82 challenges the rulers (the "gods") to care for the needy, something the Jewish leaders of Jesus' day were not doing.*

The Seven Major "I Ams" of Jesus

1. Bread. "I am the bread of life. He who comes to me will never go hungry, and he who believes in me will never be thirsty" (John 6:35; see also John 6:41, 48, 51).
2. Light. "I am the light of the world. Whoever follows me will never walk in darkness, but will have the light of life" (John 8:12; see also John 9:5).
3. Gate (Door). "I am the gate; whoever enters through me will be saved. He will come in and go out, and find pasture" (John 10:9; see also John 10:7).
4. Good Shepherd. "I am the good shepherd. The good shepherd lays down his life for the sheep. . . . I am the good shepherd; I know my sheep and my sheep know me" (John 10:11, 14).
5. Resurrection and Life. "I am the resurrection and the life. He who believes in me will live, even though he dies" (John 11:25).
6. Way, Truth, and Life. "I am the way and the truth and the life. No one comes to the Father except through me" (John 14:6).
7. Vine. "I am the true vine, and my Father is the gardener. . . . I am the vine; you are the branches. If a man remains in me and I in him, he will bear much fruit; apart from me you can do nothing" (John 15:1, 5).

Seventeen Other "I Am" Gems

1. Before Abraham. "'I tell you the truth,' Jesus answered, 'before Abraham was born, I am!'" (John 8:58).
2. Willing to heal. "Jesus reached out his hand and touched the man. 'I am willing,' he said. 'Be clean!' Immediately he was cured of his leprosy" (Matthew 8:3).
3. Gentle and humble. "Take my yoke upon you and learn from me, for I am gentle and humble in heart, and you will find rest for your souls" (Matthew 11:29).
4. Son of God. "But Jesus remained silent and gave no answer. Again the high priest asked him, 'Are you the Christ, the Son of the Blessed One?' 'I am,' said Jesus. 'And you will see the Son of Man sitting at the right hand of the Mighty One and coming on the clouds of heaven'" (Mark 14:61-62). "He trusts in God. Let God rescue him now if he wants him, for he said, 'I am the Son of God'" (Matthew 27:43). "They all asked, 'Are you then the Son of God?' He replied, 'You are right in saying I am'" (Luke 22:70). "Why then do you accuse me of blasphemy because I said, 'I am God's Son'?" (John 10:36).

5. With you. "And surely I am with you always, to the very end of the age" (Matthew 28:20). "For I am with you, and no one is going to attack and harm you, because I have many people in this city" (Acts 18:10).

6. Servant. "But I am among you as one who serves" (Luke 22:27).

7. From above. "You are from below; I am from above. You are of this world; I am not of this world" (John 8:23).

8. Lifted up. "But I, when I am lifted up from the earth, will draw all men to myself" (John 12:32).

9. Teacher and Lord. "You call me 'Teacher' and 'Lord,' and rightly so, for that is what I am" (John 13:13).

10. In the Father. "Believe me when I say that I am in the Father and the Father is in me; or at least believe on the evidence of the miracles themselves" (John 14:11).

11. King. "You are right in saying I am a king" (John 18:37).

12. Root/Offspring of David. "I, Jesus, have sent my angel to give you this testimony for the churches. I am the Root and the Offspring of David, and the bright Morning Star" (Revelation 22:16).

13. Sending you. "I am sending you out like sheep among wolves. Therefore be as shrewd as snakes and as innocent as doves" (Matthew 10:16). "Peace be with you! As the Father has sent me, I am sending you" (John 20:21).

14. Here. "Here I am! I stand at the door and knock. If anyone hears my voice and opens the door, I will come in and eat with him, and he with me" (Revelation 3:20).

15. First and Last (Alpha/Omega). "'I am the Alpha and the Omega,' says the Lord God, 'who is, and who was, and who is to come, the Almighty'" (Revelation 1:8). "When I saw him, I fell at his feet as though dead. Then he placed his right hand on me and said: 'Do not be afraid. I am the First and the Last'" (Revelation 1:17). "He said to me: 'It is done. I am the Alpha and the Omega, the Beginning and the End. To him who is thirsty I will give to drink without cost from the spring of the water of life'" (Revelation 21:6). "I am the Alpha and the Omega, the First and the Last, the Beginning and the End" (Revelation 22:13).

16. Alive. "I am the Living One; I was dead, and behold I am alive for ever and ever! And I hold the keys of death and Hades" (Revelation 1:18).

17. Coming soon. "He who testifies to these things says, 'Yes, I am coming soon.' Amen. Come, Lord Jesus" (Revelation 22:20).

Four "I Am *Nots*" of Jesus

1. Possessed. "'I am not possessed by a demon,' said Jesus, 'but I honor my Father and you dishonor me'" (John 8:49).
2. Glory seeking. "I am not seeking glory for myself; but there is one who seeks it, and he is the judge" (John 8:50).
3. Alone. "But a time is coming, and has come, when you will be scattered, each to his own home. You will leave me all alone. Yet I am not alone, for my Father is with me" (John 16:32).
4. Of the world. "They are not of the world, even as I am not of it" (John 17:16).

Ten Surprises about Jesus

Philip Yancey wrote a fine book called *The Jesus I Never Knew* (Zondervan). In *Christianity Today* (June 17, 1996), he talks about some surprising things he learned in the process.

1. "Jesus was a Jew." Yancey knew that, of course, but just how Jewish—that was the surprise.
2. "Yet Jesus did not act like a Jew." That is, Jesus worked to turn the system upside down.
3. "Jesus lost the 'culture wars.'" The prevailing culture didn't seem to be affected much.
4. "Jesus was a poor salesman." By today's rules, Jesus would have failed.
5. "No one knows what Jesus looked like." But we tend to glamorize him.
6. "You might not have wanted Jesus at your backyard barbecue." He had a way of saying difficult things to listen to.
7. "Jesus is not the church." If you reject the church, don't reject Jesus.
8. "Yet the church is Jesus." We carry on his mission, in his power.
9. "Catholics are better at calendars than Protestants." Speaking as a Protestant, Yancey is saying that the Catholic observance of Good Friday, Easter Sunday, and the Saturday in between captures an important sense of spiritual reality. Protestants treat that Saturday as any other.
10. "Jesus saves my faith." When we doubt and wonder and disagree with other Christians, we need to center again on Jesus.

Ten Qualities of Jesus

1. Divine (Mark 15:39)
2. Faultless (Luke 23:14)
3. Perfect (Luke 23:41)

4. Eloquent (John 7:46)
5. Rejected (John 18:40)
6. Forsaken (Matthew 27:46)
7. Sociable (Luke 15:2)
8. Powerful (Acts 13:39)
9. Hated (John 15:18, 25)
10. Honored (John 9:33)

Christ, the Subject of Isaiah 53

Few prophetic passages give as clear a picture of what Jesus did as does Isaiah's song of the Servant's suffering in chapter 53. In verse after verse, we get a new snapshot of the One who would come to save his people.

1. Verse 2: The Sensitive One
2. Verse 3: The Sorrowing One
3. Verse 4: The Smitten One
4. Verse 5: The Suffering One
5. Verse 6: The Sin-bearing One
6. Verse 7: The Silent One
7. Verse 8: The Stricken One
8. Verse 9: The Sincere One
9. Verse 10: The Submissive One
10. Verse 11: The Satisfying One

Ten Things You Can Learn about Christ from the Old Testament

1. His genealogy (Genesis 3:15)
2. His birth (Micah 5:2)
3. His character (Isaiah 53:2, 9)
4. His ministry (Isaiah 9:1-2)
5. His entry into Jerusalem (Zechariah 9:9)
6. His suffering (Psalm 22:14-15)
7. His death (Isaiah 53:9)
8. His resurrection (Psalm 16:10)
9. His ascension (Psalm 24:7-10)
10. His everlasting reign (Psalm 45:6-7)

Jesus As a Worshiper

1. He knew his Father in a personal way (John 8:29).
2. He praised and gave thanks to his Father (John 11:41).
3. He loved and honored his Father (John 8:49).
4. He lived in dependence on his Father (Matthew 14:23).
5. He did not seek to do his own will (John 5:30).

6. He was humble and obedient to his Father (Philippians 2:8).
7. He lived to the glory of his Father (John 17:4).

Jesus' Greatest Hits: Major Discourses in the Gospel of John

1. On the new birth (3:1-21)
2. On the water of life (4:4-26)
3. On resurrection and life (5:19-47)
4. On the bread of life (6:26-59)
5. On his own deity (8:12-59)
6. On the good shepherd (10:1-21)
7. On his own deity, again (10:22-38)
8. On his role (12:20-50)
9. On his departure (13:31–14:31)
10. On his relationship with his followers (15:1–16:33)
11. On his own glorification (17:1-26)

Names and Titles of Jesus

1. Christ. The Greek word for "Anointed One"; in Hebrew, it is "Messiah."
2. Jesus. His personal name, meaning "the Lord saves."
3. Lamb of God. John the Baptist hailed him in this way, foreshadowing Jesus' self-sacrifice for our sins.
4. Lord. This was the term used in those days for God and for those with ultimate authority.
5. Master. A term of respect used by his followers.
6. Prophet. One authorized to speak God's messages to humanity.
7. Rabbi (or Teacher). Similar to today's *Reverend,* a term of respect for those with spiritual authority.
8. Shepherd. Jesus saw himself as one who led, protected, and cared for his followers as a shepherd does for sheep.
9. Son of David. A term of royalty; David's dynasty owned the throne eternally. And Jesus was, in fact, a descendant of David.
10. Son of Man. Jesus used this term to underscore his humanity, but the "Son of" may carry a "new, improved" idea. He is humanity as it was meant to be.
11. Son of God. He was careful about using this "blasphemous" term, but it did indicate both a divine identity and a loving relationship with his Father.
12. Teacher. Jesus was always teaching—in parables and with pithy comments.
13. Word. *Logos* in Greek; the logic and purpose behind the whole Creation.

Messianic Prophecies in Matthew

Yes, we've already discussed many of the prophecies concerning Christ, but Matthew seems especially interested in citing the Old Testament connections of Jesus.

Matthew	Event	Old Testament Scripture
1:23	Virgin birth	Isaiah 7:14
2:5-6	Birthplace	Micah 5:2
2:15	Egypt	Hosea 11:1
8:17	Healings	Isaiah 53:4
12:18-21	Servanthood	Isaiah 42:1-4
13:34-35	Parables	Psalm 78:2
21:5	Triumphal Entry	Zechariah 9:9
21:42	Rejection	Psalm 118:22
22:44	Deity	Psalm 110:1
26:31	Abandonment	Zechariah 13:7
26:64	Return	Daniel 7:13
27:34, 48	Crucifixion	Psalm 69:21
27:35	Crucifixion	Psalm 22:18
27:39-40	Crucifixion	Psalm 22:7
27:43	Crucifixion	Psalm 22:8
27:46	Crucifixion	Psalm 22:1
27:57-60	Burial	Isaiah 53:9

Jesus' Words from the Cross

1. Luke 23:34. "Father, forgive them, for they do not know what they are doing."
2. Luke 23:43. "I tell you the truth, today you will be with me in paradise."
3. John 19:26-27. "Dear woman, here is your son. . . . Here is your mother."
4. Matthew 27:46. "My God, my God, why have you forsaken me?"
5. John 19:28. "I am thirsty."
6. John 19:30. "It is finished."
7. Luke 23:46. "Father, into your hands I commit my spirit."

The 10 Best Parables of Jesus

Jesus told dozens of parables, and it's tough to pick the 10 "best." I may miss your favorite, but here's a purely subjective rating.

1. The Prodigal Son (Luke 15:11-32). The story of every Chris-

tian's rebellion and return. How can you forget the picture of God as a loving father looking for the son to come home?

2. Sheep and Goats (Matthew 25:31-46). There are few points that can strike us deeper than Jesus' identification with "the least of these."

3. The Good Samaritan (Luke 10:30-37). A classic story that challenges our prejudices in any age.

4. The Wheat and the Weeds (Matthew 13:24-30). As good an answer to the problem of evil as you're going to find. Let the wheat and weeds grow together—for now.

5. The Lost Sheep (Matthew 18:12-14; Luke 15:4-7). Simple and stirring: The shepherd leaves the flock to search for the one who's lost.

6. The Pearl of Great Price (Matthew 13:45-46). Short and sweet: We catch the merchant's joy over finding this precious gem.

7. The Talents (Matthew 25:14-30). It's our story once again. God has given us much. What will we do with it?

8. The Unforgiving Servant (Matthew 18:23-35). How can a forgiven one not forgive others? This is who we are.

9. Workers in the Vineyard (Matthew 20:1-16). But it's not fair! Some get paid for one hour what others get for the whole day. But grace has its own logic.

10. The Rich Man and Lazarus (Luke 16:19-31). Turnabout for the tycoon and the beggar.

SPECIAL INTEREST

Bible Verses about Writing

As a writer, I'm naturally interested in what the Bible has to say about my craft. Verses for a few other occupations follow, but I may not have included yours. When *you* write a book, you can find all the Bible verses about selling insurance or manufacturing widgets or whatever you do. Note: Boldface was added for emphasis.

Inspiration for Christian Writers

1. Deuteronomy 6:6-9. "These commandments that I give you today are to be upon your hearts. Impress them on your children. Talk about them when you sit at home and when you walk along the road, when you lie down and when you get up. Tie them as symbols on your hands and bind them on your foreheads. **Write them on the doorframes of your houses** and on your gates." But nowadays you can use computers.

2. Job 19:23-25. **"Oh, that my words were recorded,** that they were written on a scroll, that they were inscribed with an iron tool on lead, or engraved in rock forever! I know that my Redeemer lives, and that in the end he will stand upon the earth." The living Redeemer, our purpose, power, and patron.

3. Psalm 102:18-20. **"Let this be written for a future generation,** that a people not yet created may praise the Lord: 'The Lord looked down from his sanctuary on high, from heaven he viewed the earth, to hear the groans of the prisoners and release those condemned to death.'" You may be writing for future readers, telling of freedom in Christ.

4. Proverbs 3:3-4. "Let love and faithfulness never leave you; bind them around your neck, **write them on the tablet of your heart.** Then you will win favor and a good name in the sight of God and man." Do love and faithfulness characterize your writing?

5. Ecclesiastes 12:10-12. "The Teacher searched to find **just the right words,** and what he wrote was upright and true. The words of the wise are like goads, their collected sayings like

firmly embedded nails—given by one Shepherd. Be warned, my son, of anything in addition to them. **Of making many books there is no end,** and much study wearies the body." Don't just add to the endless pile of books—search for "just the right words."

6. Habakkuk 2:2. "Then the Lord replied: '**Write down the revelation** and make it plain on tablets so that a herald may run with it.'" Don't be fancy. Make it plain.

7. Luke 1:3-4. "Therefore, since I myself have carefully investigated everything from the beginning, it seemed good also to me **to write an orderly account** for you, most excellent Theophilus, so that you may know the certainty of the things you have been taught." Research, orderly presentation, so they may *know.*

8. John 20:30-31. "Jesus did many other miraculous signs in the presence of his disciples, which are not recorded in this book. **But these are written that you may believe** that Jesus is the Christ, the Son of God, and that by believing you may have life in his name." Writing from faith, to faith.

9. 1 John 2:7. "Dear friends, **I am not writing you a new command but an old one,** which you have had since the beginning." Sometimes older is better.

10. Revelation 1:19. "**Write,** therefore, what you have seen, what is now and what will take place later." Prophetic writing involves past, present, and future.

When the Writer Is Divine

1. Jeremiah 31:33. "'This is the covenant I will make with the house of Israel after that time,' declares the Lord. 'I will put my law in their minds and **write it on their hearts.** I will be their God, and they will be my people.'" A strong theme throughout Scripture—God's law written on people's hearts.

2. Daniel 5:5, 8. "Suddenly the fingers of a human hand appeared and wrote on the plaster of the wall, near the lampstand in the royal palace. The king watched the hand as it wrote. . . . Then all the king's wise men came in, but **they could not read the writing** or tell the king what it meant." MENE, MENE, TEKEL, PARSIN! Is that so hard to understand?

3. John 8:6. "Jesus bent down and **started to write on the ground** with his finger." What was he writing? We don't know. Some say he was listing the sins of the people who were about to stone the adulterous woman. No wonder they walked away.

4. 2 Corinthians 3:1–3. "Are we beginning to commend ourselves again? Or do we need, like some people, letters of recommendation to you or from you? You yourselves are our letter, written on our hearts, known and read by everybody. You show that **you are a letter from Christ,** the result of our ministry, written not with ink but with the Spirit of the living God, not on tablets of stone but on tablets of human hearts." Given our status in God's family, we could be considered "heir mail."

5. Revelation 21:5. "He who was seated on the throne said, 'I am making everything new!' Then he said, **'Write this down,** for these words are trustworthy and true.'" The one who makes things new still needs people to write down his trustworthy words.

Variations on the Theme

1. Songwriter? Deuteronomy 31:19, 22: "'Now **write down for yourselves this song** and teach it to the Israelites and have them sing it, so that it may be a witness for me against them.' . . . So Moses wrote down this song that day and taught it to the Israelites."

2. Speechwriter? Psalm 45:1: "My heart is stirred by a noble theme as I recite **my verses for the king;** my tongue is the **pen of a skillful writer.**"

3. Contract writer? Exodus 34:27: "Then the Lord said to Moses, **'Write down these words,** for in accordance with these words I have made a **covenant** with you and with Israel.'"

4. Travel writing? Joshua 18:4: "Appoint three men from each tribe. I will send them out to make a survey of the land **and to write a description of it.**"

5. Writer of job descriptions? 1 Samuel 10:25: "Samuel explained to the people **the regulations of the kingship. He wrote them down** on a scroll and deposited it before the Lord."

6. Spin doctors? Jeremiah 8:8: "How can you say, 'We are wise, for we have the law of the Lord,' when actually the **lying pen of the scribes** has handled it falsely?"

7. Editors? John 19:21: "The chief priests of the Jews protested to Pilate, 'Do not write "The King of the Jews," but that this man **claimed** to be king of the Jews.'"

8. Stubborn authors replying to editors? John 19:22: "Pilate answered, **'What I have written, I have written.'**"

9. Ghostwriter? 1 Peter 5:12: **"With the help of Silas,** whom

I regard as a faithful brother, **I have written** to you briefly, encouraging you and testifying that this is the true grace of God. Stand fast in it."

10. Book reviewer? 2 Peter 3:15-16: "Bear in mind that our Lord's patience means salvation, just as our dear brother Paul also wrote you with the wisdom that God gave him. **He writes the same way in all his letters,** speaking in them of these matters. **His letters contain some things that are hard to understand,** which ignorant and unstable people distort, as they do the other Scriptures, to their own destruction."

Bible Verses about Teaching

Whether you teach in a public school, a Christian school, or a Sunday school, whether you train workers at your job or lead a Bible study at church, the Bible has plenty to say about what you do. Note: Boldface was added for emphasis.

Challenges for Teachers

1. Exodus 18:20. **"Teach them** the decrees and laws, and **show them the way to live** and the duties they are to perform." God's lesson plan for Moses works well for modern teachers, too.

2. Deuteronomy 32:2. **"Let my teaching fall like rain and** my words descend like dew, like showers on new grass, like abundant rain on tender plants." It may come as a surprise to some, but this has nothing to do with spitting on your students as you teach.

3. Proverbs 6:23. "For these commands are a lamp, this teaching is a light, and **the corrections of discipline are the way to life."** Try telling that to the kid you just sent to the principal's office.

4. Proverbs 9:9. "Instruct a wise man and he will be wiser still; teach a righteous man and he will **add to his learning."** Support for advanced classes? The fact is, true learners never stop learning.

5. Proverbs 13:14. "The teaching of the wise is a fountain of life, **turning a man from the snares of death."** Did you know that your teaching is a life-or-death issue?

6. Matthew 5:19. "Anyone who breaks one of the least of these commandments **and teaches others to do the same** will be called least in the kingdom of heaven, but whoever practices and teaches these commands will be called great in the

kingdom of heaven." Teachers have twice the pressure—and perhaps twice the blessing.

7. Romans 2:21. "You, then, who teach others, **do you not teach yourself?** You who preach against stealing, do you steal?" Practice what you prea—er, *teach!*

8. 2 Timothy 3:16-17. "All Scripture is God-breathed **and is useful for teaching,** rebuking, correcting and training in righteousness, so that the man of God may be thoroughly equipped for every good work." Notice the list of activities associated with teaching—and the ultimate purpose.

9. Titus 2:7-8. "In everything set them an example by doing what is good. **In your teaching show integrity,** seriousness and soundness of speech that cannot be condemned, so that those who oppose you may be ashamed because they have nothing bad to say about us." Your life teaches more than your words do.

10. James 3:1. "Not many of you should presume to be teachers, my brothers, because you know that **we who teach will be judged more strictly."** *Gulp.*

The Lord as Master Teacher

1. Job 36:22. "God is exalted in his power. **Who is a teacher like him?"** No argument here.

2. Isaiah 48:17. "This is what the Lord says—your Redeemer, the Holy One of Israel: 'I am the Lord your God, **who teaches you what is best for you,** who directs you in the way you should go.'" Even when God teaches, though, the students don't always realize it's "what is best" for them.

3. Mark 1:22. "The people were amazed at his teaching, **because he taught them as one who had authority,** not as the teachers of the law." When you're confident in the truth, people listen.

4. Mark 4:2. "He taught them many things by **parables."** Teacher, tell us another story!

5. Luke 20:21. "So the spies questioned him: 'Teacher, we know that you speak and teach what is right, and that you do not show partiality but **teach the way of God in accordance with the truth.'"** Watch out for partiality in your classroom. If you want to teach in accordance with the truth, make sure you value *all* your students.

Acknowledging the Unique Gift

1. Exodus 35:34. **"And he has given [Bezalel and Oholiab] the ability to teach others."** These master craftsmen were divinely gifted teachers, too.

2. Romans 12:6-7. "We have different gifts, according to the grace given us. If a man's gift is . . . teaching, **let him teach.**" Duh.
3. 1 Corinthians 12:29. "Are all apostles? Are all prophets? **Are all teachers?** Do all work miracles?" No. But sometimes you have to work miracles to be a good teacher.

Variations on the Theme

1. Biology teacher? 1 Kings 4:33: "[Solomon] described plant life, from the cedar of Lebanon to the hyssop that grows out of walls. He also taught about animals and birds, reptiles and fish." Job 12:7-8: "But ask the animals, and they will teach you, or the birds of the air, and they will tell you; or speak to the earth, and it will teach you, or let the fish of the sea inform you."
2. Discipline problem? Proverbs 5:13: "I would not obey my teachers or listen to my instructors." Jeremiah 32:33: "They turned their backs to me and not their faces; though I taught them again and again, they would not listen or respond to discipline."
3. Crossing picket lines? Acts 5:28, 42: "'We gave you strict orders not to teach in this name,' he said. 'Yet you have filled Jerusalem with your teaching.' . . . Day after day, in the temple courts and from house to house, they never stopped teaching and proclaiming the good news that Jesus is the Christ."
4. Health teachers? 2 Timothy 2:17: "Their teaching will spread like gangrene."
5. Market-driven education? 2 Timothy 4:3: "For the time will come when men will not put up with sound doctrine. Instead, to suit their own desires, they will gather around them a great number of teachers to say what their itching ears want to hear."

Bible Verses for Students

☞ Note: Boldface was added for emphasis.

General Instructions and Encouragement

1. Psalm 32:8. "I will **instruct you and teach you** in the way you should go; I will counsel you and watch over you."
2. Deuteronomy 4:5-6. "See, I have taught you decrees and laws as the Lord my God commanded me, so that you may follow them in the land you are entering to take possession of it. Observe them carefully, for **this will show your wisdom and understanding to the nations,** who will hear about all

these decrees and say, 'Surely this great nation is a wise and understanding people.'" Bragging about a good report card?

3. Proverbs 1:7. "The fear of the Lord is **the beginning of knowledge,** but fools despise wisdom and discipline."

4. Proverbs 23:12. **"Apply your heart to instruction** and your ears to words of knowledge." How many students really get their hearts into it?

5. Ecclesiastes 12:1. **"Remember your Creator** in the days of your youth, before the days of trouble come and the years approach when you will say, 'I find no pleasure in them.'" It's astonishingly easy to forget your Creator, isn't it?

6. Luke 6:40. **"A student is not above his teacher,** but everyone who is fully trained will be like his teacher." So look for good teachers to learn from—in school, in church, in the community.

7. John 14:26. "But the Counselor, the Holy Spirit, whom the Father will send in my name, **will teach you all things** and will remind you of everything I have said to you."

8. Isaiah 50:4. "The Sovereign Lord has given me an instructed tongue, to know the word that sustains the weary. He wakens me morning by morning, wakens my ear to listen like one being taught." What if you're not a morning person?

9. Deuteronomy 17:11. "Act according to the law they teach you and the decisions they give you. **Do not turn aside from what they tell you,** to the right or to the left." It's actually talking about priests and judges, but it works for good teachers, too.

10. Proverbs 2:10. "For wisdom will enter your heart, and **knowledge will be pleasant to your soul."**

The Limits of Learning

1. 1 Corinthians 1:20. "Where is the wise man? **Where is the scholar?** Where is the philosopher of this age? Has not God made foolish the wisdom of the world?"

2. 1 Corinthians 8:1-2. **"Knowledge puffs up,** but love builds up. The man who thinks he knows something does not yet know as he ought to know."

3. 1 Corinthians 13:2. "If I . . . can fathom all mysteries and all knowledge . . . , **but have not love,** I am nothing."

4. 2 Corinthians 10:5. "We demolish arguments and every pretension that sets itself up against the knowledge of God, and **we take captive every thought** to make it obedient to Christ."

5. 1 Timothy 6:20-21. "Turn away from godless chatter and the opposing ideas of **what is falsely called knowledge,** which

some have professed and in so doing have wandered from the faith."

Prayers for the Student

1. Psalm 119:73. "Your hands made me and formed me; **give me understanding** to learn your commands."
2. Philippians 1:9-11. "And this is my prayer: that your love may abound more and more in knowledge and depth of insight, **so that you may be able to discern what is best** and may be pure and blameless until the day of Christ, filled with the fruit of righteousness that comes through Jesus Christ—to the glory and praise of God."
3. Psalm 71:17. "Since my youth, O God, **you have taught me,** and to this day I declare your marvelous deeds."
4. Psalm 143:10. **"Teach me to do your will,** for you are my God; may your good Spirit lead me on level ground."
5. Job 6:24. "Teach me, and I will be quiet; **show me where I have been wrong."**

Examples of Good Students

1. Ezra. Ezra 7:10: "For Ezra had **devoted himself to the study and observance of the Law of the Lord,** and to teaching its decrees and laws in Israel."
2. Daniel and friends. Daniel 1:3-4, 17: "Then the king ordered Ashpenaz, chief of his court officials, to bring in some of the Israelites . . . young men without any physical defect, handsome, showing aptitude for every kind of learning, well informed, quick to understand, and qualified to serve in the king's palace. He was to teach them the language and literature of the Babylonians. . . . To these four young men **God gave knowledge and understanding of all kinds of literature and learning."**
3. Moses. Acts 7:22: "Moses was **educated** in all the wisdom of the Egyptians and was powerful in speech and action."
4. Apollos. Acts 18:24-25: "Meanwhile a Jew named Apollos, a native of Alexandria, came to Ephesus. He was a learned man, **with a thorough knowledge of the Scriptures.** He had been instructed in the way of the Lord."
5. Jesus. Luke 2:46: "After three days they found him in the temple courts, sitting among the teachers, **listening to them and asking them questions."**

Variations on the Theme

1. Astronomy 101? Psalm 19:1-2: "The heavens declare the glory of God; the skies proclaim the work of his hands. Day

after day they pour forth speech; **night after night they display knowledge."**

2. Advanced calculus? Psalm 139:6: "Such knowledge is too wonderful for me, **too lofty for me to attain."**

3. Learning to love a D-minus? Proverbs 12:1: "Whoever loves discipline loves knowledge, but **he who hates correction is stupid."**

4. The freshman experience? Ecclesiastes 1:13, 18: "I devoted myself to study and to explore by wisdom all that is done under heaven. **What a heavy burden God has laid on men!** . . . For with much wisdom comes much sorrow; the more knowledge, the more grief." Hosea 4:6: "My people are destroyed from lack of knowledge." 2 Timothy 3:7 (KJV): "Ever learning, and never able to come to the knowledge of the truth."

5. The sophomore experience? Isaiah 47:10: **"Your wisdom and knowledge mislead you** when you say to yourself, 'I am, and there is none besides me.'" Psalm 119:99: "I have more insight than all my teachers."

6. The junior experience? John 6:60: "On hearing it, many of his disciples said, **'This is a hard teaching.** Who can accept it?'" Ecclesiastes 12:12: "Much study wearies the body."

7. The senior experience? Acts 26:24: "'You are out of your mind, Paul!' he shouted. **'Your great learning is driving you insane.'"**

Bible Verses for Businesspeople

Most of us are "businesspeople" to some extent. We make deals, we pay bills, we manage our homes. The Bible has a great deal to say to you, whatever you do for a living. But these verses are especially chosen for those who deal with money at their jobs, those who manage employees, and those type A folks who have fancy briefcases and cellular phones. Note: Boldface was added for emphasis.

Ten Passages for General Guidance

1. Genesis 2:3. "And God blessed the seventh day and made it holy, because on it **he rested from all the work of creating that he had done."** If God needs a rest, so do you.

2. Leviticus 19:13. "Do not **defraud** your neighbor or **rob** him." Or blindside him in negotiations or overstate the value of your product or . . . You get the idea.

3. Deuteronomy 24:14–15. "Do not take advantage of a hired man who is poor and needy, whether he is a brother Israelite or an alien living in one of your towns. **Pay him his wages**

each day before sunset, because he is poor and is counting on it. Otherwise he may cry to the Lord against you, and you will be guilty of sin." Maybe you don't have to make every day payday, but be sure to treat your workers well.

4. Job 36:18. "Be careful that no one **entices you by riches;** do not let a large bribe turn you aside." Just what questionable things will you do to get a raise?

5. Ecclesiastes 2:24. "A man can do nothing better than to eat and drink and **find satisfaction in his work.** This too, I see, is from the hand of God." Of course, the writer soon found that work was meaningless, too.

6. Ecclesiastes 4:8. "There was a man all alone; he had neither son nor brother. There was no end to his toil, yet his eyes were not content with his wealth. **'For whom am I toiling,'** he asked, 'and why am I depriving myself of enjoyment?' This too is meaningless—a miserable business!" Sound familiar?

7. Colossians 3:22–4:1. "Slaves, obey your earthly masters in everything; and do it, not only when their eye is on you and to win their favor, but with sincerity of heart and reverence for the Lord. **Whatever you do, work at it with all your heart,** as working for the Lord, not for men, since you know that you will receive an inheritance from the Lord as a reward. It is the Lord Christ you are serving. . . . Masters, provide your slaves with what is right and fair, because you know that you also have a Master in heaven." Whether you are a slave (employee) or a master (boss) or both, you need to work diligently and fairly.

8. 1 Timothy 6:9-10. **"People who want to get rich** fall into temptation and a trap and into many foolish and harmful desires that plunge men into ruin and destruction. For the love of money is a root of all kinds of evil. Some people, eager for money, have wandered from the faith and pierced themselves with many griefs." You don't know anyone who really *wants* to get rich, do you?

9. James 1:11. "For the sun rises with scorching heat and withers the plant; its blossom falls and its beauty is destroyed. In the same way, the rich man will fade away **even while he goes about his business."** Watch out.

10. James 4:13-16. "Now listen, you who say, 'Today or tomorrow we will go to this or that city, spend a year there, carry on business and make money.' Why, you do not even know what will happen tomorrow. What is your life? You are a mist that appears for a little while and then vanishes. Instead, **you ought to say, 'If it is the Lord's will,** we will live and do

this or that.' As it is, you boast and brag. All such boasting is evil." If the Lord is really your CEO, you have to let him call the shots.

Ten Proverbs about Business

1. Proverbs 6:6-11. "Go to the ant, you sluggard; consider its ways and be wise! It has no commander, no overseer or ruler, yet it stores its provisions in summer and gathers its food at harvest. How long will you lie there, you sluggard? When will you get up from your sleep? A little sleep, a little slumber, a little folding of the hands to rest—and poverty will come on you like a bandit and scarcity like an armed man."
2. Proverbs 10:4. "Lazy hands make a man poor, but diligent hands bring wealth."
3. Proverbs 10:16. "The wages of the righteous bring them life, but the income of the wicked brings them punishment."
4. Proverbs 12:11. "He who works his land will have abundant food, but he who chases fantasies lacks judgment."
5. Proverbs 12:24. "Diligent hands will rule, but laziness ends in slave labor."
6. Proverbs 13:4. "The sluggard craves and gets nothing, but the desires of the diligent are fully satisfied."
7. Proverbs 14:23. "All hard work brings a profit, but mere talk leads only to poverty."
8. Proverbs 18:9. "One who is slack in his work is brother to one who destroys."
9. Proverbs 21:5. "The plans of the diligent lead to profit as surely as haste leads to poverty."
10. Proverbs 22:29. "Do you see a man skilled in his work? He will serve before kings; he will not serve before obscure men."

Variations on the Theme

1. The secret of delegation. Exodus 18:17-23: "Moses' father-in-law replied, 'What you are doing is not good. You and these people who come to you will only wear yourselves out. **The work is too heavy for you; you cannot handle it alone.** Listen now to me and I will give you some advice, and may God be with you. You must be the people's representative before God and bring their disputes to him. . . . But select capable men from all the people—men who fear God, trust-worthy men who hate dishonest gain—and appoint them as officials over thousands, hundreds, fifties and tens. Have them serve as judges for the people at all times, but have them bring every difficult case to you; the simple cases they can decide

themselves. That will make your load lighter, because they will share it with you. If you do this and God so commands, you will be able to stand the strain, and all these people will go home satisfied.'"

2. Nepotism confronted? Genesis 29:15: "Laban said to him, **'Just because you are a relative of mine,** should you work for me for nothing? Tell me what your wages should be.'"

3. Pharaoh the foreman? Exodus 5:4: "But the king of Egypt said, 'Moses and Aaron, why are you taking the people away from their labor? **Get back to your work!'"**

4. Even with a good retirement plan. . . . Ecclesiastes 2:21: "For a man may do his work with wisdom, knowledge and skill, and then he must leave all he owns to someone who has not worked for it. This too is meaningless and a great misfortune."

5. Guarding against corporate raiders? Nehemiah 4:17-18: "Those who carried materials **did their work with one hand and held a weapon in the other,** and each of the builders wore his sword at his side as he worked."

6. The archetypal supermom? Proverbs 31:10-31: "A wife of noble character who can find? She is worth far more than rubies. . . . She selects wool and flax and works with eager hands. She is like the merchant ships, bringing her food from afar. She gets up while it is still dark; she provides food for her family and portions for her servant girls. **She considers a field and buys it; out of her earnings she plants a vineyard.** She sets about her work vigorously; her arms are strong for her tasks. **She sees that her trading is profitable,** and her lamp does not go out at night. . . . She opens her arms to the poor and extends her hands to the needy. . . . Give her the reward she has earned, and let her works bring her praise at the city gate." A pretty remarkable businesswoman in any era.

7. Team building? Ecclesiastes 4:9: "Two are better than one, because **they have a good return for their work."**

8. Investment portfolio? Luke 19:13: "So he called ten of his servants and gave them ten minas. **'Put this money to work,'** he said, 'until I come back.'"

9. Management in the trenches? 2 Corinthians 1:24: "Not that we lord it over your faith, but **we work with you** for your joy, because it is by faith you stand firm."

10. Winning through humiliation? (Yes, your own.) Mark 10:42-44: "Jesus called them together and said, 'You know that those who are regarded as rulers of the Gentiles lord it over them, and their high officials exercise authority over them. **Not so**

with you. Instead, whoever wants to become great among you must be your servant, and whoever wants to be first must be slave of all.'"

11. Watch those landscapers! James 5:4: "Look! **The wages you failed to pay** the workmen who mowed your fields are crying out against you. The cries of the harvesters have reached the ears of the Lord Almighty."

12. The businessperson's prayer? Psalm 90:17: "May the favor of the Lord our God rest upon us; **establish the work of our hands for us**—yes, establish the work of our hands."

Bible Verses for Parents

There is probably no job more demanding, more emotionally charged, or more frightening than being a parent. And it's hard to get good training. These Bible verses won't answer all your questions, but they will help you focus on your priorities and choose broad strategies that will honor God. Note: Boldface was added for emphasis.

General Instructions

1. Deuteronomy 11:18-19. "Fix these words of mine in your hearts and minds; tie them as symbols on your hands and bind them on your foreheads. **Teach them to your children,** talking about them when you sit at home and when you walk along the road, when you lie down and when you get up." . . . And when you watch Saturday-morning cartoons, and when you drive to soccer practice, and when you shop at the mall, and . . .

2. Psalm 34:11. "Come, my children, listen to me; **I will teach you the fear of the Lord.**" You teach kids the fear of the Lord not by scaring them to death but by showing them that God cares about what we do.

3. Hosea 11:3. "It was I who taught Ephraim to walk, taking them by the arms; but they did not realize it was I who healed them." Oh, the things that kids forget as they grow older! It's nice to know that God understands that feeling.

4. Matthew 7:9-11. "Which of you, if his son asks for bread, will give him a stone? Or if he asks for a fish, will give him a snake? If you, then, though you are evil, **know how to give good gifts to your children,** how much more will your Father in heaven give good gifts to those who ask him!" But what if your son asks for Nintendo's latest time waster?

5. Matthew 11:25. "At that time Jesus said, 'I praise you, Father, Lord of heaven and earth, because you have hidden these

things from the wise and learned, **and revealed them to little children.**'" It's amazing how much kids can teach us.

6. Matthew 19:14. "Jesus said, 'Let the little children come to me, and do not hinder them, for **the kingdom of heaven belongs to such as these.'**" Help your kids develop their own relationship with Jesus.

7. 1 Corinthians 13:11. **"When I was a child, I talked like a child,** I thought like a child, I reasoned like a child. When I became a man, I put childish ways behind me." Paul is making a point about spiritual gifts, but there's a bonus point, too. Don't expect your kids to act like grown-ups.

8. Psalm 78:2-7. "I will open my mouth in parables, I will utter hidden things, things from of old—what we have heard and known, what our fathers have told us. **We will not hide them from their children;** we will tell the next generation the praiseworthy deeds of the Lord, his power, and the wonders he has done. He decreed statutes for Jacob and established the law in Israel, which he commanded our forefathers to teach their children, so the next generation would know them, even the children yet to be born, and they in turn would tell their children. Then they would put their trust in God and would not forget his deeds but would keep his commands." The education of your children is a crucial link in a long chain.

9. Psalm 103:13. **"As a father has compassion on his children,** so the Lord has compassion on those who fear him." Is your compassion like the Lord's?

10. Psalm 127:3-5. "Sons are a heritage from the Lord, **children a reward from him.** Like arrows in the hands of a warrior are sons born in one's youth. Blessed is the man whose quiver is full of them." So you said your kids are "sharp as a tack"?

Examples of Biblical Parenting

1. Jacob. Genesis 37:3-4: "Now Israel [Jacob] **loved Joseph more than any of his other sons,** because he had been born to him in his old age; and he made a richly ornamented robe for him. When his brothers saw that their father loved him more than any of them, they hated him and could not speak a kind word to him." Favoritism: a bad idea then; a bad idea now.

2. Hannah. 1 Samuel 1:27-28: "I prayed for this child, and the Lord has granted me what I asked of him. **So now I give him to the Lord.** For his whole life he will be given over to

the Lord." Children are gifts from God. Hannah knew she needed to give hers back.

3. David. 2 Samuel 18:33: "The king was shaken. He went up to the room over the gateway and wept. As he went, he said: 'O my son Absalom! My son, my son Absalom! **If only I had died instead of you**—O Absalom, my son, my son!'" David made some mistakes, to be sure, but the account of his reaction to his son's rebellion is heartbreaking.

The Discipline Question

1. Proverbs 22:6. "Train a child in the way he should go, **and when he is old he will not turn from it.**" That's the theory, anyway. But *how* do you train a child?

2. Proverbs 29:15. **"The rod of correction** imparts wisdom, but a child left to himself disgraces his mother." Proverbs is keen on the use of "the rod" to discipline kids, but I think the key is in the second phrase. A child "left to himself" may conclude that no one cares and thus find his own way of behaving.

3. Ephesians 6:4. "Fathers, **do not exasperate your children;** instead, bring them up in the training and instruction of the Lord." To exasperate is to discourage, to steal hope. You want to be sure your kids remain hopeful, realizing that they *can* be good kids. Sometimes severe punishment can defeat that purpose.

4. 1 Timothy 3:2-5. "Now the overseer . . . must manage his own family well **and see that his children obey him with proper respect.** (If anyone does not know how to manage his own family, how can he take care of God's church?)" In several passages, the New Testament draws this comparison: A church leader must be a good home leader, too. Which makes us wonder whether good parenting is similar to good leadership—communicating a vision, organizing the effort, valuing the gifts of the group members, demanding their best effort, being an example, etc.

Often-Overlooked Women in the Old Testament

1. Hagar. Sarah's handmaid; Sarah let Abraham father Hagar's child (Ishmael), then threw her out.

2. Rebekah. Isaac's wife; schemed with Jacob to get Isaac's blessing, then sent him off to her brother, Laban.

3. Leah. Mother of most of Jacob's sons; this is the older daughter Jacob married after being tricked.

4. Zipporah. Moses' wife; in what seems to have been a turbulent marriage.
5. Rahab. Prostitute in Jericho who opened her home (and city) to Israelite spies.
6. Orpah. Sister-in-law to Ruth; she left Naomi and went back home. (And, yes, Oprah Winfrey is sort of named after her.)
7. Hannah. Samuel's mother; she prayed for a child for years, then gave him back to God.
8. Michal. David's first wife, Saul's daughter; used as a political pawn; she frowned on David's dancing.
9. Athaliah. Queen mother who killed her opponents and ruled Judah for six years.
10. Gomer. Hosea's unfaithful wife.

Often-Overlooked Women in the New Testament

1. Elizabeth. Mother of John the Baptist; cousin and confidante of Mary.
2. Anna. Elderly woman who blessed the baby Jesus in the temple.
3. Joanna. A noblewoman who helped support Jesus' ministry.
4. Martha. Sister of Mary and Lazarus; she gets criticized for her focus on dinner preparations but shows a keen knowledge of Jesus' identity.
5. The widow of Nain. Jesus brought her only son back to life.
6. Peter's mother-in-law. Jesus healed her from a dangerous fever.
7. Pilate's wife. Counseled the governor to have nothing to do with Jesus because of a nightmare she had.
8. Lydia. Cloth merchant in Philippi; first European convert to Christianity; helped Paul establish a church there.
9. Phoebe. Paul introduces her with great respect in Romans 16:1; she may have funded his ministry and/or served as a church leader.
10. The recipient of 2 John. The "chosen lady" may have been a church leader, a patron, or just a friend. (Some scholars suggest it's a code name for the church, but there's no reason this can't be a person.)

Ten Great Things Said by Bible Women

1. Ruth (to Naomi): "Don't urge me to leave you or to turn back from you. Where you go I will go, and where you stay I will stay. Your people will be my people and your God my God. Where you die I will die, and there I will be buried. May the Lord deal with me, be it ever so severely, if anything but death separates you and me" (Ruth 1:16–17).

2. Martha (to Jesus): "Yes, Lord . . . I believe that you are the Christ, the Son of God, who was to come into the world" (John 11:27).

3. Mary, Jesus' mother (in her "Magnificat" prayer after learning she would bear the Messiah): "His mercy extends to those who fear him, from generation to generation. He has performed mighty deeds with his arm; he has scattered those who are proud in their inmost thoughts. He has brought down rulers from their thrones but has lifted up the humble. He has filled the hungry with good things but has sent the rich away empty" (Luke 1:50-53).

4. The Syrophoenician Woman (after this Gentile woman begged Jesus to exorcise a demon from her daughter, he tested her by saying, "It is not right to take the children's bread and toss it to their dogs"): "Yes, Lord . . . but even the dogs under the table eat the children's crumbs" (Mark 7:27-28).

5. Rahab (to the two Israelite spies she sheltered): "I know that the Lord has given this land to you and that a great fear of you has fallen on us. . . . We have heard how the Lord dried up the water of the Red Sea for you when you came out of Egypt. . . . When we heard of it, our hearts melted and everyone's courage failed because of you, for the Lord your God is God in heaven above and on the earth below" (Joshua 2:9-11).

6. Deborah (after a great victory): "So may all your enemies perish, O Lord! But may they who love you be like the sun when it rises in its strength" (Judges 5:31).

7. Miriam (after the crossing of the Red Sea): "Sing to the Lord, for he is highly exalted. The horse and its rider he has hurled into the sea" (Exodus 15:21).

8. Esther (preparing to ask the king for mercy for her people): "Go, gather together all the Jews who are in Susa, and fast for me. Do not eat or drink for three days, night or day. I and my maids will fast as you do. When this is done, I will go to the king, even though it is against the law. And if I perish, I perish" (Esther 4:16).

9. Abigail (to David): "Even though someone is pursuing you to take your life, the life of my master will be bound securely in the bundle of the living by the Lord your God. But the lives of your enemies he will hurl away as from the pocket of a sling. When the Lord has done for my master every good thing he promised concerning him and has appointed him leader over Israel, my master will not have on his conscience the staggering burden of needless bloodshed or of having

avenged himself. And when the Lord has brought my master success, remember your servant" (1 Samuel 25:29-31).

10. Mary Magdalene (to Peter and John, the morning of the Resurrection): "They have taken the Lord out of the tomb, and we don't know where they have put him!" (John 20:2).

Important Young People of the Old Testament

1. Isaac. Abraham's promised son; nearly sacrificed on Mount Moriah, he grew up to be a patriarch himself.
2. Ishmael. Abraham's other son, born to the handmaid Hagar; though he was not the child of God's covenant and was cast away with Hagar, he grew up to father many nations of his own.
3. Samuel. Served as a child in the tabernacle with Eli the priest; God called him one night to foretell doom for Eli's household.
4. David. As a youth, he felled the giant Goliath.
5. The first child of David and Bathsheba. Born of their adulterous union, the baby took sick and died within a week. Their next son was Solomon.
6. "The sons of the prophets." A group of young men who supported the prophetic ministry of Elisha; this may have been a seminary of sorts, making them "prophets in training."
7. Joash. Hidden as a baby from his murderous grandmother, Athaliah, Joash became Judah's king at age seven and did pretty well, guided by Jehoiada the priest.
8. Josiah. Judah's other child-king; he took the throne at age eight. Eighteen years later, the Scriptures were rediscovered and Josiah led a revival.
9. Isaiah's son. A major prefigurement of Jesus; when Isaiah prophesied about a "young woman" (the Hebrew word can also mean "virgin") giving birth, there were two fulfillments. First, when Isaiah's own son was born (and there were certain prophecies about what would happen to Judah before the child was very old); and second, of course, when Jesus was born of the Virgin Mary.
10. Shadrach, Meshach, and Abednego. Young Jews who, along with Daniel, were captured and taken to Babylon, where they served in Nebuchadnezzar's court. They stayed true to their faith, facing the fiery furnace instead of worshiping the king.

Important Young People of the New Testament

1. Jesus. We're all familiar with his birth stories, but we also see him as a 12-year-old, gabbing with rabbis in the temple.

2. The boy who brought the loaves and fish. Jesus turned his bag lunch into a banquet.
3. The child Jesus brought to himself. We don't know who it was, but Jesus used a child to teach his disciples about humility (Matthew 18:2-6).
4. Jairus's daughter. The father came to Jesus when the girl was ill. By the time Jesus got there (after stopping to heal someone else on the way), the girl was dead. Not to worry. Jesus brought the girl back to life.
5. The daughter of Herodias. Her dancing pleased King Herod so much that he offered her anything; with coaching from Mom, she asked for John the Baptist's head on a platter. And you thought kids *today* were crude.
6. John Mark. A young man who hung around the disciples and joined Paul and Barnabas on their first journey but left halfway through.
7. Timothy. Paul met his family and sort of adopted this young man; Timothy became a valuable associate of Paul's, a church leader, and a recipient of two New Testament letters.
8. Eutychus. Dozed off as Paul preached through the night. Unfortunately, he was sitting in a window. He fell and died, but Paul brought him back to life.
9. Rhoda. A servant girl who answered the door when Peter came back from prison, but left him standing there.
10. Paul's nephew. Heard of a plot against Paul's life and informed the authorities.

Artists of the Bible

1. Art design, craftsmanship—Bezalel, Oholiab (Exodus 31:2-11)
2. Music composition/lyrics—David (Psalms), Asaph (Psalms), Moses (Exodus 15; Psalm 90), Hannah (1 Samuel 2), Zechariah (Luke 1), Mary (Luke 1)
3. Music performance—David (1 Samuel 16:23)
4. Dance—David (2 Samuel 6:14)
5. Song and dance—Miriam (Exodus 15:20-21)
6. Drama—Jacob, directed by Rebekah (Genesis 27)
7. Performance art—Ezekiel (Ezekiel 2; 4; and most of the book)
8. Fashion design—Dorcas/Tabitha (Acts 9:36, 39)
9. Sculpture—Moses (Numbers 21:9)
10. Architecture—Moses; Solomon; Nehemiah; Ezekiel (overseeing construction of Jerusalem or temple)
11. Calligraphy—God (Daniel 5); Jesus (John 8:6); Paul (Galatians 6:11)
12. Instrumentals—Jubal (Genesis 4:21)

JUST WANNA HAVE FUN

Things I Wish Weren't in the Bible

1. The household clause in Acts 16:31. "Believe in the Lord Jesus, and you will be saved—**you and your household**" (emphasis added). Is the whole family saved because the father believes? This bit of patriarchal culture flies in the face of the evangelical premise that each individual must decide for Christ personally. Even if you can explain them away, these four words spoil the thunder of an otherwise splendid verse.

2. The no-win situation in Isaiah 6:9-10—"Go and tell this people: 'Be ever hearing, but never understanding; be ever seeing, but never perceiving.' Make the heart of this people calloused; make their ears dull and close their eyes. Otherwise they might see with their eyes, hear with their ears, understand with their hearts, and turn and be healed." This passage obviously says something very important because it's quoted half a dozen times in the New Testament—but what does it mean? Smack-dab in the middle of Isaiah's spectacular call to ministry, God seems to be asking Isaiah to fail. Sure, there are explanations, but it's distracting when, right in the middle of this cool missionary text, you have to break out into fisticuffs between Presbyterians and Methodists.

3. The strange goings-on in Ruth 3. "In the middle of the night something startled the man, and he turned and discovered a woman lying at his feet. 'Who are you?' he asked. 'I am your servant Ruth,' she said. 'Spread the corner of your garment over me, since you are a kinsman-redeemer'" (Ruth 3:8-9). This was Naomi's plan to get Ruth to marry the wealthy Boaz. Find him sleeping on the threshing floor and lie down at his feet. What's that about? Obviously there's some cultural custom happening here, but try explaining that to a Sunday school class of dirty-minded sixth graders.

4. The head-covering thing. "And every woman who prays or prophesies with her head uncovered dishonors her head—it is just as though her head were shaved" (1 Corinthians 11:5). The apostle Paul had this all figured out: man, woman, no cov-

ering, covering. It meant something really special in those days, I'm sure. OK, so maybe it was only prostitutes who went without hats and Christian women were already suspect because they prayed in church. So Paul is saying, Don't look like prostitutes. But then why should men not cover their heads? It's all very confusing to us modern folks. Still, Paul knocks himself out explaining it all, concluding with: "For this reason, and because of the angels, the woman ought to have a sign of authority on her head" (11:10). *And because of the angels?* Oh, thanks—that explains everything!

5. Judges 19–21, rated R. "In those days Israel had no king. Now a Levite who lived in a remote area in the hill country of Ephraim took a concubine . . ." (Judges 19:1). It starts off like a bad limerick and gets worse. When you start complaining about the nasty subject matter of modern movies, take a gander at this ancient passage—if you can stomach it. The disgusting story ends with the fitting statement: "In those days Israel had no king; everyone did as he saw fit" (Judges 21:25).

6. The begats of Matthew 1. "A record of the genealogy of Jesus Christ the son of David, the son of Abraham" (Matthew 1:1). So the brand-new believer is dying to read the New Testament. Opening to Matthew 1, however, he must think he's stumbled into the county clerk's office. There's a list of names of Jesus' ancestors. Yes, it's nice to know that people like Rahab and Ruth made the list, but somewhere around Amminadab, the plot gets a little thin. Can't we put this in 1 Chronicles somewhere and cut to the chase: "This is how the birth of Jesus Christ came about" (Matthew 1:18)?

7. The multimetal statue in Daniel 2. "The head of the statue was made of pure gold, its chest and arms of silver, its belly and thighs of bronze, its legs of iron, its feet partly of iron and partly of baked clay" (Daniel 2:32–33). For many people, this is their favorite part of Scripture, but I get tired of all the wranglings over which kingdoms are which body parts and how many toes—er, nations—are in the European Economic Community.

8. Agag me with a spoon. "But Samuel said, 'As your sword has made women childless, so will your mother be childless among women.' And Samuel put Agag to death before the Lord" (1 Samuel 15:33). This chapter presents the story of what King Saul did wrong—he didn't massacre the Amalekites. This was a rival nation that God told Saul to destroy completely. But Saul spared some of the livestock as well as the king, Agag. Not only did the prophet Samuel express God's displeasure to Saul, but he hacked Agag to death himself. Now, Agag was a bad guy, and the

Amalekites were ruthless enemies of God's people. If spared, they might have led the Israelites into idolatry or captivity. Certainly we have to let God call the shots. But still, it's tough to deal with these Old Testament massacres.

9. The vengeance of the bald guy. "As [Elisha] was walking along the road, some youths came out of the town and jeered at him. 'Go on up, you baldhead!' they said. 'Go on up, you baldhead!' He turned around, looked at them and called down a curse on them in the name of the Lord. Then two bears came out of the woods and mauled forty-two of the youths" (2 Kings 2:23-24). If you've ever been jeered by teenagers, you're probably thinking, *Where are the bears when you need 'em?* Scholars tell us the youths were making fun of Elisha's religious devotion, but still . . .

10. Jephthah's vow. "If you give the Ammonites into my hands, whatever comes out of the door of my house to meet me when I return . . . I will sacrifice it as a burnt offering" (Judges 11:30-31). He should have been a little more careful in wording that promise because his daughter was the first to greet him, "dancing to the sound of tambourines" (Judges 11:34). He must have thought she was off at college or something, because he obviously expected to be welcomed back by something a little more bovine. Still he made the sacrifice (after letting his daughter party with her sorority for a couple months). We assume that his vow was foolish, but was he right to follow through on it? Scripture is maddeningly mum.

Books of the Bible That Don't Exist but Sound Like They Should

1. Hezekiah
2. Athenians
3. Ruminations
4. First Canticles
5. Second Hesitations
6. Effluvium
7. Malchus
8. Alexandrians
9. Euripides
10. Jehoshaphat

Best Excuses in the Bible

1. Adam, on eating the forbidden fruit (Genesis 3:12): "The woman you put here with me—she gave me some fruit from the tree, and I ate it."

2. Eve, ditto (Genesis 3:13): "The serpent deceived me, and I ate."

3. Laban, on deceiving Jacob by giving him the wrong daughter in marriage (Genesis 29:26-27): "It is not our custom here to give the younger daughter in marriage before the older one. . . . We will give you the younger one also, in return for another seven years of work."

4. Aaron, on making the golden calf (Exodus 32:22-24, italics added for emphasis): "Do not be angry, my lord. . . . You know how prone these people are to evil. They said to me, 'Make us gods who will go before us. As for this fellow Moses who brought us up out of Egypt, we don't know what has happened to him.' So I told them, 'Whoever has any gold jewelry, take it off.' Then they gave me the gold, and I threw it into the fire, and *out came this calf!"*

5. Saul, on performing the prebattle sacrifice that only Samuel the priest was allowed to do (1 Samuel 13:11-12): "When I saw that the men were scattering, and that you did not come at the set time, and that the Philistines were assembling at Micmash, I thought, 'Now the Philistines will come down against me at Gilgal, and I have not sought the Lord's favor.' So I felt compelled to offer the burnt offering."

6. Saul, on not destroying the Amalekites and their livestock as God had commanded (1 Samuel 15:20-21): "But I did obey the Lord. . . . I went on the mission the Lord assigned me. I completely destroyed the Amalekites and brought back Agag their king. The soldiers took sheep and cattle from the plunder, the best of what was devoted to God, in order to sacrifice them to the Lord your God at Gilgal."

7. Elijah, on moping in the desert (1 Kings 19:10): "I have been very zealous for the Lord God Almighty. The Israelites have rejected your covenant, broken down your altars, and put your prophets to death with the sword. I am the only one left, and now they are trying to kill me too."

8. The servant, on burying the talent he'd been given (Matthew 25:24-25): "Master . . . I knew that you are a hard man, harvesting where you have not sown and gathering where you have not scattered seed. So I was afraid and went out and hid your talent in the ground. See, here is what belongs to you."

9. Jesus, as a boy, on staying behind in the temple while his parents journeyed home (Luke 2:49): "Why were you searching for me? . . . Didn't you know I had to be in my Father's house?"

10. Paul, on not visiting the Corinthians as he had promised (2 Corinthians 1:16-17, 23; 2:1): "I planned to visit you on my

way to Macedonia and to come back to you from Macedonia,
and then to have you send me on my way to Judea. When I
planned this, did I do it lightly? Or do I make my plans in a
worldly manner so that in the same breath I say, 'Yes, yes' and
'No, no'? . . . I call God as my witness that it was in order to
spare you that I did not return to Corinth. . . . So I made up
my mind that I would not make another painful visit to you."

Odd Bible Characters

Odd can be interesting, strange, or complex. The Bible is full of such
people. Here are 10 of the oddest:

1. Melchizedek. A priest who shows up out of nowhere and
   blesses Abraham (Genesis 14:18-20). Who was this "king of
   Salem"? The book of Hebrews shows him as a foreshadowing
   of Christ (Hebrews 7:1-17).
2. Laban. Jacob's uncle, father-in-law, and nemesis in trickery, this
   wealthy herdsman always seemed to be plotting something.
   He gave Jacob the wrong bride and squeezed an extra seven
   years of work out of him. Jacob finally broke free, with some
   trickery of his own (Genesis 29–31).
3. Nabal and Abigail. This wealthy landowner refused to show
   kindness to David and his army. In a rage, David nearly slaugh-
   tered Nabal's household, but Nabal's wife, Abigail, saved the
   day by bringing food for David's people. When Nabal learned
   of it, he had some sort of a stroke and later died. David then
   took Abigail as his own wife (1 Samuel 25).
4. Shimei. A relative of King Saul, Shimei cursed King David vehe-
   mently at one point (2 Samuel 16:5-13) but later apologized,
   and David spared his life (2 Samuel 19:16-23). Shimei apparently had some power in Jerusalem, though his loyalties were
   always suspect. For a time, though, he seemed to be in David's
   inner circle (1 Kings 1:8). Later, Solomon made Shimei promise
   to stay in Jerusalem, and when Shimei made a quick out-of-
   town trip, Solomon had him killed (1 Kings 2:36-46).
5. Obadiah, Ahab's other prophet. This is not the author of the
   Old Testament book by this name. This is a prophet in Elijah's
   time who managed to stay faithful to God (and alive!) in the
   court of King Ahab and Queen Jezebel. Once, when Jezebel
   was hunting down prophets and killing them, Obadiah hid a
   hundred of them (1 Kings 18:1-16).
6. David's mighty men. David had a group of 30 loyal warriors
   who formed the core of his defense force as he fled from
   King Saul and battled the Philistines. Three of them were especially worthy. On one occasion, in the heat of battle, David

mused about how great it would be to drink water from the wells of his hometown of Bethlehem. His three main mighty men broke through enemy lines to get him a cup of that water. David was so touched by their devotion that he wouldn't drink it (1 Chronicles 11).

7. Sanballat, Tobiah, and Geshem. Sounds like a law firm, doesn't it? Actually they were Mideast leaders who opposed Nehemiah's rebuilding of Jerusalem's walls. Sanballat was later governor of Samaria, Tobiah was an Ammonite official, and Geshem was an Arab. Together they teased, intimidated, and plotted against Nehemiah—but Nehemiah managed to stonewall them, so to speak.

8. Job's friends Eliphaz, Bildad, and Zophar. You have to give them credit for *being there.* They sat with Job on the trash pile for a week before anyone spoke. They should have made it a month. When they *did* speak, they kept making assumptions and accusations, and Job had to defend himself.

9. Rhoda. The prayer group was meeting at Mary's house, praying for Peter's release from prison. It was likely that Peter would be executed, as James had been. Only a miracle could save him. Then came a knock at the gate. Rhoda, the servant girl, went to answer—and heard Peter there! Shocked, she ran back in and told everyone but left Peter at the gate. The others didn't believe her at first—but fortunately Peter kept knocking (Acts 12:12-16).

10. Eutychus. It was nearing midnight and getting musty in the room where Paul was preaching. Eutychus was sitting in a window. And he fell asleep—*fell* being the operative word in that phrase. He plummeted to his death, but Paul raised him back to life—and kept preaching (Acts 20:7-12).

Fifteen Weather Conditions That Affected Bible Stories

1. Noah's flood. It rained. *A lot.*
2. The famine in Egypt. Lack of rain, and Joseph saw it coming.
3. Thunder and hail that assaulted Egypt. Just one of the 10 plagues that eventually convinced Pharaoh to let God's people go.
4. The wind that parted the Red Sea. God sent a wind at just the right time to deliver the Israelites from Egypt.
5. Thunder and lightning at Mount Sinai. God sure knows how to put on a show.
6. The bright cloud that led the Israelites. It wasn't your *normal* weather condition, but it looked like a cloud, and it led the people where God wanted them to go.

7. The sun standing still. Joshua needed another hour to defeat his foes, and this was before daylight saving time.
8. The dew that did and didn't appear on Gideon's fleece. Trying to wriggle out of an assignment, Gideon tested God by suggesting these miracles.
9. The thunder that routed the Philistines. After Samuel made a sacrifice, God sent thunder, and the Philistines were scared silly.
10. Elijah's drought. The fiery prophet predicted a drought on Israel and the rain that ended it.
11. Elijah's whirlwind. The chariot of fire appeared, but Elijah rode a whirlwind to heaven.
12. The storm that beached Jonah. If Jonah hadn't been tossed overboard, he would never have met the whale.
13. The storm that Jesus calmed. Quiet, he said, be still.
14. Darkness at Jesus' death. It was only three o'clock, but the sun gave up for the day.
15. The storm that caused Paul's shipwreck. A Mediterranean squall on the way to Rome.

Ten Common Sayings Not in the Bible

1. A bird in the hand is worth two in the bush.
2. A stitch in time saves nine.
3. Beggars can't be choosers.
4. Charity begins at home.
5. Cleanliness is next to godliness.
6. Everything that glitters is not gold.
7. God helps those who help themselves.
8. Honesty is the best policy.
9. Rob Peter to pay Paul.
10. Strike while the iron is hot.

Ten Words Surprisingly Not in the Bible

1. Advent
2. Anthem
3. Benediction
4. Bible
5. Catholic
6. Christmas
7. Denomination
8. Eucharist
9. Potluck
10. Pope

Soap Operas in the Bible?

1. *Guiding Light:* "By day the Lord went ahead of them in a pillar of cloud to guide them on their way and by night in a pillar of fire to give them light, so that they could travel by day or night" (Exodus 13:21).
2. *The Young and the Restless:* "The younger one [the Prodigal Son] said to his father, 'Father, give me my share of the estate.' So he divided his property between them" (Luke 15:12).
3. *As the World Turns:* "The Mighty One, God, the Lord, speaks and summons the earth from the rising of the sun to the place where it sets" (Psalm 50:1).
4. *All My Children:* "Yet to all who received him, to those who believed in his name, he gave the right to become children of God" (John 1:12).
5. *One Life to Live:* "Man is destined to die once, and after that to face judgment" (Hebrews 9:27).
6. *Another World:* "Jesus said, 'My kingdom is not of this world. If it were, my servants would fight to prevent my arrest by the Jews. But now my kingdom is from another place'" (John 18:36).
7. *The City:* "For he was looking forward to the city with foundations, whose architect and builder is God" (Hebrews 11:10).
8. *Dynasty:* "If you do whatever I command you and walk in my ways and do what is right in my eyes by keeping my statutes and commands, as David my servant did, I will be with you. I will build you a dynasty as enduring as the one I built for David and will give Israel to you" (1 Kings 11:38).

Popular Songs That (with a Little Imagination) Could Refer to Bible Characters

1. **"Matthew,"** by John Denver
2. **"Daniel,"** by Elton John
3. **"Jeremiah** was a bullfrog . . . ," in "Joy to the World," by Three Dog Night
4. "Hey **Jude,"** by the Beatles
5. *Joshua Judges Ruth,* an album by Lyle Lovett
6. "Take this **Job** and Shove It," by Johnny Paycheck
7. **"Hosea,** can you see . . . ?" in "The Star-Spangled Banner"

Nine Books of the Bible That End with the Letter *H*

1. Ruth
2. Nehemiah
3. Isaiah

4. Jeremiah
5. Jonah
6. Micah
7. Obadiah
8. Zephaniah
9. Zechariah

Extra Credit

Fifteen books of the New Testament are named for individuals. The names of 13 New Testament books end in the letter *s*. Two books are named for individuals whose names end in *s*. Only one New Testament book that is not named for an individual doesn't end in *s*. What is it? (Answer at the end of this section.)

Ten Books Referred to in the Old Testament That Have Never Been Found

1. Book of the Wars of the Lord (Numbers 21:14)
2. Book of Jashar (Joshua 10:13)
3. Records of Nathan the prophet (1 Chronicles 29:29)
4. Records of Gad the seer (1 Chronicles 29:29)
5. Prophecy of Ahijah the Shilonite (2 Chronicles 9:29)
6. Visions of Iddo the Seer (2 Chronicles 9:29)
7. Records of Shemaiah the prophet (2 Chronicles 12:15)
8. Annals of Jehu (2 Chronicles 20:34)
9. Annotations of the prophet Iddo (2 Chronicles 13:22)
10. Records of Samuel the seer (1 Chronicles 29:29)

People in the Bible Who Had Trouble with Water

1. Noah. Forty days and nights' worth
2. Naaman. Didn't want to dip in the muddy Jordan
3. Peter. Walked on it—for a while
4. Moses. Hit the rock to get water instead of asking it politely
5. Isaac. Had a controversy over water rights—well, well, well
6. David's mighty men. Crossed enemy lines to get David a drink, then David spilled it
7. Elijah. God told him to predict a drought that made Ahab and Jezebel steaming mad.
8. Pharaoh's army. The seabed was dry when the Israelites crossed it, but the water crashed down on the Egyptians, making them Sea Red.
9. Mary (water to wine). When the wedding reception needed wine, she told Jesus about it—he used water to do the trick.

10. The Samaritan woman. Where would Jesus get this "living water" he was talking about?
11. Elisha's seminarians. They dropped their prize axhead into the river, but the prophet made it float.

Beautiful Women in the Bible

1. Sarah (Genesis 12:11)
2. Rebekah (Genesis 24:16)
3. Rachel (Genesis 29:17)
4. Abigail (1 Samuel 25:3)
5. Bathsheba (2 Samuel 11:2)
6. Tamar (2 Samuel 13:1)
7. Abishag (1 Kings 1:3)
8. Esther (Esther 1:11)
9. Job's daughters (Job 42:15)
10. The Beloved (Song of Songs 1:5)

Biblical Names Beginning with Z

1. Zacchaeus
2. Zebulun
3. Zechariah
4. Zedekiah
5. Zephaniah
6. Zerubbabel
7. Zilpah
8. Zimir
9. Zipporah
10. Zophar

Familiar Phrases Taken from Scripture

1. Turn the other cheek
2. Weaker vessel
3. Voice crying in the wilderness
4. To the pure all things are pure
5. A time to be born, a time to die
6. Thorn in the flesh
7. The spirit is willing, the flesh is weak
8. Strain at a gnat and swallow a camel
9. See through a glass darkly
10. Salt of the earth
11. The powers that be
12. Pearls before swine

Pro-Sports Teams That Could Have Played in the Bible League

(And the people who'd play for them)

1. **John the Baptist** would play for the **Trailblazers.**
2. **Saul** would play with the **Kings,**
3. chasing **David,** on the **Dodgers.**
4. **Goliath,** of course, would be with the **Giants.**
5. You'd find **Noah** on the **Mariners,**
6. and **Jonah** on the **Whalers,**
7. with fishermen **James and John** on the **Nets.**
8. (But late in his career **John** gets sent to the **Islanders.**)
9. **Jacob and Esau?** The **Twins.**
10. (Though **Esau** might be traded to the **Reds.**)
11. You'd expect to see **Herod** on the **Royals,**
12. **Simon the Zealot** on the **Patriots,**
13. and **Achan,** Jericho's thief, on the (forgive me) **Steelers.**
14. **Peter** would be with the **Rockies.**
15. Though, forgiving people 70-times-seven times, he might also end up with the **49ers.**
16. **Gabriel, Michael, and a host of others** would be **Angels.**
17. And a whole bunch of folks, of course, are **Saints.**

Bible Tongue Twisters

1. Samuel sasses Saul for spoiling the sacrifice.
2. Paul probably passed on preaching in Pergamum.
3. Can Corinth keep calm, considering crucial questions?
4. Nebuchadnezzar knew nearly no one north of Nuzi.
5. Paul pestered Peter for paltry prejudice.
6. Tired Timothy told 10 thrilling things to 13 top teachers.
7. Ruth and Rahab rerouted Israel's royal race.
8. Herod hated holy happenings.
9. We rarely wonder why wary Rachel wanted Reuben right away.
10. Thessalonica.

Bible Palindromes

A palindrome is a word or phrase that reads the same backward and forward.

1. An introduction in the Garden of Eden?
   "Madam, I'm Adam."
2. Something Cain might have said to Eve?
   "Ma, is Adam mad as I am?"
3. What the manna-eating Israelites might have been?
   Stressed for a jar of desserts.

4. What Hiram might have said after negotiating a price for the cedars used in temple construction?
   "No, wise Sol loses. I won!"
5. What Ruth might have said after seeing Boaz?
   "I moan, Naomi."
6. What Ezekiel's foe (Ezekiel 38:2) might say to the mirror?
   "Gog, am I Magog?"
7. Moses' prayer for his brother?
   "Do, God, honor Aaron. Oh, do, God!"

The Bible's Best Fights

We're talking not about national wars and battles but about disagreements, arguments, feuds. Even some of your favorite characters had such disputes, and sometimes with *other* favorite characters.

1. Paul vs. Peter in Antioch. Peter had pioneered the outreach to the Gentiles, but here he was hanging out with the legalistic Jewish believers and refusing to eat with Gentiles. Paul let him have it (Galatians 2:11-21).
2. Saul vs. David in Judah. King Saul was on the downslope of his reign. David, the court musician, was also a valiant warrior loved by thousands. When Saul interrupted David's harp playing by flinging a spear at him, David knew his gig was up. He spent several years scampering through caves in the Judean desert, with Saul in hot pursuit.
3. The Judaizers vs. the missionaries in Jerusalem. Acts 15 records the church council that convened to consider the terms under which the Gentiles would be welcomed into the previously all-Jewish church. We don't know all the political maneuvering that went on. Presumably Paul made a strong case for freedom, but it was Peter who won the day for the Gentiles. Still, the legalists managed to slide in a few restrictions.
4. Caleb and Joshua vs. the other spies at Kadesh Barnea. Twelve had been sent to scout out the Promised Land. They returned with visions of milk and honey—but the 10 spies thought the Canaanite opposition was too steep. "We're like grasshoppers next to them," was the majority opinion. Only Caleb and Joshua dared to differ, lobbying for a swift entry into the land, trusting in God's power. God rewarded them by making them the only two Israelites to survive the 40-year sojourn in the desert (Numbers 13–14).
5. Paul vs. Barnabas in Antioch. They made their first missionary journey together, along with Barnabas's cousin Mark. But Mark bailed out halfway through. Preparing for their second journey, Barnabas wanted to give the kid another chance. Paul

said no. So the two friends split up—Barnabas taking Mark with him to Cyprus and Paul taking Silas and Timothy to Asia Minor (Acts 15).

6. Miriam and Aaron vs. Moses in the desert. It was a brief dispute probably fueled by jealousy. Moses' brother and sister attacked his interracial marriage and questioned how he got to be so special. "Does the Lord only speak through Moses?" they challenged. Well, yes. The Lord chastised the siblings and struck Miriam with leprosy (Numbers 12).

7. Isaac vs. the well diggers in Canaan. Isaac was turning the other cheek long before the Sermon on the Mount. He dug a well. The locals came and claimed it. Instead of fighting, he dug another well. The locals claimed that, too. The third time was a charm. All's well that ends well.

8. Paul vs. the "superapostles" in Corinth. Paul was a feisty chap, wasn't he? Apparently some other preachers (possibly the legalists Paul was battling all along) came to Corinth after Paul had left and started bad-mouthing the apostle. They trumpeted their own credentials and may have called themselves "superapostles." In 2 Corinthians 10–12, Paul coyly responds to their charges, boasting not in his strengths but in his weaknesses.

9. Isaiah vs. Ahaz in Jerusalem. Isaiah was probably a court prophet, so King Ahaz cared about what he had to say. But Isaiah had a way of saying what this king of Judah didn't want to hear, especially about the geopolitical climate of the times. Ahaz was considering an alliance with the superpower Assyria to gain protection from his pesky neighbors Syria and Israel (the northern kingdom). Bad idea, says Isaiah—it's like killing flies with a sledgehammer. (That's a loose translation.) In strong language, Isaiah urged the king to fear the Lord more than his foes (Isaiah 7–9).

10. Jesus' disciples vs. each other. Human nature being what it is, it's not surprising that Jesus' disciples would start elbowing each other for the best positions. Perhaps they thought Jesus would set up his earthly kingdom right away and they wanted to get dibs on some cabinet posts. Whenever he heard this bickering, Jesus scolded them and taught about humility (Luke 9 and elsewhere).

Words Used Most Often in the Bible

These 10 most common words make up about one-fourth of all the words in the Bible (NIV):

1. The (55,728 times)
2. And (29,600)

3. Of (25,210)
4. To (20,933)
5. You (13,727)
6. In (11,277)
7. Will (10,192)
8. He (9,660)
9. A (9,144)
10. I (8,747)

The Oddest Things People Did in the Bible

1. The Israelites' marching around Jericho (Joshua 6). If you attack a city, you *attack* it, right? God had a better idea—and the walls came a-tumblin' down.
2. Gideon's pruning his army to 300 men, then arming them with trumpets, torches, and pitchers (Judges 7). It turned out to be rather ingenious—the sudden light and sound terrified the enemy army—but it probably seemed very weird at the time.
3. Samson's tying foxes' tails together around torches and sending them through the enemy's fields (Judges 15:3-5). What a way to ruin their economy! Burn their crops, and let the foxes spread the fire far and wide. Brilliant! But how do you get the foxes to sit still while you tie their tails?
4. David's pretending to be insane (1 Samuel 21:12-15). Running from Saul, he wound up with a rival king. To save his skin, David ranted (and drooled) like a lunatic. It worked, prompting the king to deliver one of the great lines of Scripture: "Am I so short of madmen that you have to bring this fellow here?"
5. Elijah's pouring water on the sacrifice to be consumed by fire (1 Kings 18). Was he really that sure that God would come through—or was he suicidal?
6. Hosea's marrying the prostitute Gomer (Hosea 1–3). God told him to, and so he did, knowing full well she would break his heart.
7. Ezekiel's whole life. In chapter 3 he's eating a scroll. In chapter 4 he lies on his left side for 390 days, then on his right for 40 more. In chapter 5 he shaves his head and divides his hair into three parts. You get the idea. This guy was punk before punk was cool.
8. Jesus' spitting and healing (John 9:6). He spat on the ground, made mud, and put it on the blind man's eyes. At least the guy couldn't see what Jesus was doing.
9. Peter's walking on water (Matthew 14:28-31). It's easy to criti-

cize Peter for his lack of faith, but let's see *you* get out there
on those rolling waves, huh? What made him step out of the
boat at all?

10. Paul and Silas's singing hymns in prison (Acts 16). Deep in a
dank dungeon, what makes people want to sing—except
extraordinary faith? Or incredible wackiness. You make the call.

Ten Unusual Modes of Transportation in the Bible

The question is: What are the most interesting ways people (or other
beings) got from one place to another?

1. Stairway to heaven (Genesis 28:12). Jacob saw angels going up
and down on it.

2. A talking donkey (Numbers 22:30). Lots of people used donkeys to get where they wanted to go. Balaam's gave him direc-
tions.

3. Long poles (Exodus 25:14). This is how the ark of the covenant was carried.

4. Whirlwind (2 Kings 2:11). A chariot of fire appeared, and Elijah was carried by a whirlwind out of sight.

5. Jehu the crazy driver (2 Kings 9:20). It wasn't exactly a chariot
of fire, but close. This king was a speed demon. According to the
guy who watched his cloud of dust, "he drove like a madman."

6. The wheel within a wheel (Ezekiel 1). Ezekiel saw "living
creatures" traveling in these multiwheeled contraptions.
Hmmm? Helicopters?

7. The great fish (Jonah 1:17). Who knows how far Jonah traveled those three days and nights inside the fish's belly?

8. Chariots driven by spirits with multicolored horses (Zechariah 6:1-8). This was the prophet Zechariah's vision. The chariots scattered to the four corners of the earth.

9. The Spirit (Acts 8:39). After Philip baptized the Ethiopian,
"the Spirit of the Lord suddenly took Philip away." He
showed up in another city.

10. Basket (Acts 9:25). To escape the Jewish leaders after his conversion, Paul had to be let down in a basket through a hole in
the city wall of Damascus.

Seven Marys

Every time you turn around in the New Testament, you bump into
another Mary. Who were all these people, and how can you keep
them straight?

1. The mother of Jesus. The Virgin Mary, the one who "trea-
sured up all these things and pondered them in her heart"

(Luke 2:19) and asked Jesus to run out and get more wine for a wedding reception (John 2:3).

2. Sister of Martha and Lazarus. She sat at Jesus' feet as he taught; she once anointed those feet with perfume. A comparison of similar stories in the Gospels raises the possibility that she had "led a sinful life," perhaps as a prostitute, but there is no direct evidence of this.

3. Mary Magdalene. Once demon possessed, she became a close follower of Jesus after he cast out those demons (Luke 8:2). Despite various modern stories, there is no indication that she was ever a prostitute or ever had a romantic interest in Jesus.

4. Mother of Mark. This woman hosted a house church, where Peter went after his miraculous prison break (Acts 12:12). She was Rhoda's boss.

5. Mother of James the Younger and Joses (Joseph). This is "the other Mary" who was at the tomb on Resurrection Sunday (Matthew 27:56, 61; 28:1).

6. The wife of Clopas. This woman stood near the cross with a few other Marys (John 19:25), which makes her possibly the same as number 5. Is her husband perhaps the same as "Cleopas" (Luke 24:18)? Would this make her the second disciple on the road to Emmaus? Hmmmmmm.

7. A Roman Christian greeted in Romans 16:6. Of course, there's an outside chance, given the mobility of that era, that this was the same as one of the other Marys—but only a historical novelist would make that connection.

Biblical Pairs

1. Tigris and Euphrates (rivers of Mesopotamia)
2. Dan to Beersheba (the extent of the Promised Land; its northernmost and southernmost settlements)
3. Milk and honey (commodities in Canaan)
4. Fire and brimstone (God's judgment)
5. Sackcloth and ashes (signs of repentance)
6. Rod and staff (shepherd's tools)
7. Sheep and goats (shepherd's subjects)
8. The bread and the cup (elements of the Passover/Lord's Supper)
9. Alpha and omega (first and last letters of Greek alphabet, signifying beginning and end)
10. Heaven and hell (God's favor or disfavor)

Ten Pet Rocks of Scripture

1. Jacob had a pet rock, and he named it Bethel (Genesis 28:18-19).

2. Jacob had another pet rock, and he named this one Mizpah (Genesis 31:49).

3. Moses had a pet rock, and he named it The Lord Is My Banner (Exodus 17:15).

4. Joshua had some pet rocks, and he called them the remembering stones (Joshua 4).

5. Joshua had another pet rock that was called the "witness stone" (Joshua 24:26-27).

6. Samson hid in a pet rock that was named Etam, "the lair" (Judges 15:8).

7. Samuel had a pet rock that he named Ebenezer, "stone of help" (1 Samuel 7:12).

8. David and Jonathan had a pet rock that was named Ezel, "departure" (1 Samuel 20:19).

9. Jesus had a pet rock, and he named him Peter (Matthew 16:18; John 1:42).

10. God took a rejected rock, named him Jesus, and made him the capstone (Acts 4:11).

Dysfunctional Families in the Bible

1. The Adam Family. With all that blaming in Eden, it's no wonder Cain turned out bitter against his brother.

2. The Noah Family. They started out well enough, but after the flood there's this odd story about Ham seeing his father naked.

3. The Abraham Family. First Abraham pretends Sarah is his sister, then Sarah lets Abe father a child by Hagar, but then she kicks Hagar out. And that whole near-sacrifice thing has to leave emotional scars on Isaac.

4. The Lot Family. Greed makes him move to the big city. Bad move. At one point Lot offers his daughters to rapists. Later there's incest, and Lot's wife gets a-salted. Not a pleasant situation.

5. The Isaac Family. Isaac favors Esau, but Rebekah loves Jacob. Mom and mama's boy plot to deceive Dad. Jacob has to run away.

6. The Jacob Family. Four different mothers. Thirteen kids. Dad showing favoritism to one. Enough said.

7. The Moses Family. Aaron and Miriam get jealous, but there are also stormy times with Zipporah, Moses' wife. She never got into being Israel's first lady.

8. The Eli Family. Dad turns a blind eye as his sons rip off the people.

9. The David Family. Adultery was just the beginning. More sex

and violence occur among David's kids, culminating in Absalom's open rebellion.

10. The Job Family. Anytime your spouse tells you to "curse God and die," you know you're in trouble.

Simon Says . . . but Which Simon?

1. Simon Peter (Matthew 10:2)
2. Simon the Zealot (Matthew 10:4)
3. Simon, son of Mary and Joseph (Matthew 13:55)
4. Simon of Cyrene (Matthew 27:32)
5. Simon the Leper (Mark 14:3)
6. Simon the Pharisee (Luke 7:40)
7. Simon the sorcerer (Acts 8:9)
8. Simon the tanner (Acts 9:43)

Feet

We all know that the Bible offers heeling for our soles, but it also shoes us much more about our lowest appendages. I know there are times when the devil or his sneakers pump you to the point that you want to cry ankle. But if you truly want to sock it toe him and keep instep with other believers, read on. This collection is quite a feet.

1. At the burning bush, God told Moses to take off his sandals (Exodus 3:5).
2. King Asa died of a foot ailment (2 Chronicles 16:12).
3. God's Word is a lamp for our feet (Psalm 119:105).
4. "Keep your foot from evil" (Proverbs 4:27).
5. Peter and John strengthened a man's feet and ankles (Acts 3:7).
6. The Prodigal Son returned and got new sandals (Luke 15:22).
7. Mary sat at Jesus' feet (Luke 10:39).
8. A woman wet Jesus' feet with her tears and wiped them with her hair (Luke 7:38).
9. John the Baptist said he was not worthy to carry Jesus' sandals (Matthew 3:11).
10. Preachers have beautiful feet (Romans 10:15).
11. And you might say Samson died of fallen arches (Judges 16:30).

Ten Rest Stops

The Israelites camped out at these places on the way to Sinai (Numbers 33).

1. Succoth
2. Etham
3. Pi Hahiroth

4. Marah
5. Elim
6. Red Sea
7. Desert of Sin
8. Dophkah
9. Alush
10. Rephidim

Siblings

1. Cain and Abel were brothers. Blood brothers, you might say.
2. Shem, Ham, and Japheth were brothers, the sons of Noah. (Did Shem and Japheth feel like the bread in a Ham sandwich?)
3. Abraham had two brothers: Haran, the father of Lot; and Nahor, grandfather of Laban and Rebekah.
4. Isaac's half brother was Ishmael—and centuries of conflict have followed from that sibling rivalry.
5. Jacob and Esau were twin brothers. Jacob seemed to get the brains, Esau the brawn.
6. Rachel and Leah were sisters, both married to Jacob. (Sounds like a bad TV-talk-show theme, doesn't it?)
7. Joseph made his brothers jealous. So they almost made him dead.
8. Did you know that Joseph and his brothers had a sister? Her name was Dinah, and she caused a war of her own.
9. Joseph's two sons, Manasseh and Ephraim, each fathered powerful half-tribes of Israel. (Perhaps remembering when he stole Esau's blessing, Jacob gave the firstborn blessing to the younger one, Ephraim.)
10. Moses' brother, Aaron, and sister, Miriam, helped him lead Israel.
11. Ruth's sister-in-law, Orpah, chose not to travel back to Israel with Naomi.
12. David was the youngest of eight sons of Jesse and was nearly overlooked when Samuel came looking for a king.
13. Amnon, a son of David, fell in love with his half sister Tamar and raped her. Tamar's brother Absalom had Amnon killed.
14. God refers to Jerusalem, Samaria, and Sodom as sisters—"arrogant, overfed and unconcerned" (Ezekiel 16:49).
15. Jesus called two pairs of brothers as his disciples—Peter and Andrew, James and John. Actually, Andrew went and told Peter about Jesus.
16. King Herod took his brother Philip's wife, Herodias. John the Baptist was outraged; he lost his head.

17. Jesus had four brothers (well, half brothers)—James, Joseph, Simon, and Judas (Jude).
18. Jesus' brothers "did not believe in him" (John 7:5) but urged him to make a name for himself in Jerusalem—even when the authorities were out to kill Jesus.
19. James, the brother of Jesus, must have come to believe in Jesus, for he became a leader in the early church.
20. Paul had a sister, whose son helped him escape a death threat.
21. Seven sisters, the daughters of Philip, were all prophetesses.

Some of David's Wives

Kings married a lot of women. It was what they did in those days. We know Solomon was legendary with his 1,000 wives and concubines, but his dad, David, was no slouch in the matrimony department either.

1. Michal (1 Samuel 18:27)
2. Abigail (1 Samuel 25:42)
3. Ahinoam (1 Samuel 25:43)
4. Maacah (1 Chronicles 3:2)
5. Haggith (1 Chronicles 3:2)
6. Abital (1 Chronicles 3:3)
7. Eglah (1 Chronicles 3:3)
8. Bathsheba (1 Chronicles 3:5)

Ten of David's Sons

1. Amnon—mother: Ahinoam (1 Chronicles 3:1)
2. Absalom—mother: Maacah (1 Chronicles 3:2)
3. Adonijah—mother: Haggith (1 Chronicles 3:2)
4. Daniel—mother: Abigail (1 Chronicles 3:1)
5. Ithream—mother: Eglah (1 Chronicles 3:3)
6. Nathan—mother: Bathsheba (1 Chronicles 3:5)
7. Shammua—mother: Bathsheba (1 Chronicles 3:5)
8. Shephatiah—mother: Abital (1 Chronicles 3:3)
9. Shobab—mother: Bathsheba (1 Chronicles 3:5)
10. Solomon—mother: Bathsheba (1 Chronicles 3:5)

A.k.a.: 11 Name Changes in Scripture

1. Abram became Abraham.
2. Sarai became Sarah.
3. Jacob became Israel.
4. Joseph was known as Zaphenath-Paneah in Egypt.
5. Naomi asked to be called Mara ("bitter").
6. Esther's Hebrew name was Hadassah.

7. Daniel's Babylonian name was Belteshazzar.
8. Shadrach, Meshach, and Abednego are the Babylonian names for the Hebrew Hananiah, Mishael, and Azariah.
9. Simon Bar-Jonah was named Peter ("rock") by Jesus.
10. Saul became known as Paul in the Gentile world.
11. Joseph of Cyprus gained the nickname Barnabas ("encourager").

Answer to "Extra Credit"

Revelation

STUFF THAT MAY ACTUALLY BE USEFUL

Unsung Role Models

1. Miriam, Moses' sister. We assume that Miriam was the sister who watched the baby Moses get picked up by Pharaoh's daughter (Exodus 2:4). But later, she emerges as a leader of the Israelites. After the Red Sea crossing, she led the Israelite women in a song and dance (Exodus 15:20-21).

2. Jethro, Moses' father-in-law. When Moses was at his wits' end, leading the Israelites through the desert, Jethro suggested that he delegate some leadership to a council of elders (Exodus 18).

3. Caleb. Two of the 12 Israelites who scouted out Canaan returned with a message of faith, not fear. One was Joshua, who succeeded Moses as leader of the nation. The other was Caleb. As a result, he and Joshua were the only wilderness wanderers to enter the Promised Land (Numbers 14).

4. Jael. When the prophetess Deborah teased General Barak that the opposing general would be defeated by a woman (Judges 4:9), it was not herself she had in mind, but Jael. In a grisly scene, Jael fed the rival general and gave him a place to sleep—then drove a tent peg through his head (Judges 4:21). A brave endeavor, but *do not try this at home!*

5. The widow of Zarephath. In a terrible famine, Elijah asked her to make him some bread with the last of her oil and flour. She did, and God rewarded her with a never-ending supply. Later her son died, but she turned to Elijah for help, and God raised the son in answer to Elijah's prayers (1 Kings 17).

6. Elihu. After Job was thoroughly criticized and cajoled by his three friends, Elihu showed up and started talking sense. He didn't get everything right, but he was pretty close (Job 32–37).

7. Baruch. Jeremiah's secretary went through thick and thin with the prophet, faithfully recording and delivering his prophecies.

8. The centurion of faith. This Roman centurion asked Jesus to heal his servant. Yet, realizing that it wouldn't be kosher for Jesus to visit a Gentile's house, the Roman suggested that Jesus could do this healing long distance. Jesus praised the man's faith and healed the servant (Matthew 8:5-13).

9. Silas. This prophet and early church leader was an envoy from the Jerusalem church to the more Gentile-oriented church at Antioch (Acts 15). Joining Paul's second missionary journey, Silas found himself singing psalms with the apostle in a Philippian jail when an earthquake interrupted them (Acts 16). Later, he served as Peter's secretary (1 Peter 5:12).

10. Priscilla and Aquila. They seem to pop up everywhere in Paul's ministry: Rome, Corinth, Ephesus. They worked with Paul for a while and had a church group meeting in their home. When the brilliant preacher Apollos was lacking some key theology, this couple took him aside and taught him (Acts 18; Romans 16:3).

Ten Mighty Musts of Scripture

We must

1. die (2 Samuel 14:14).
2. be born again (John 3:7).
3. worship God in Spirit and in truth (John 4:24).
4. be clothed with immortality (1 Corinthians 15:53).
5. appear before the judgment seat (2 Corinthians 5:10).

Jesus must

1. do the work of the One who sent him (John 9:4).
2. increase, while we decrease (John 3:30).
3. be lifted up (John 3:14).
4. rise again (John 20:9).
5. reign (1 Corinthians 15:25).

Ten Bible Passages People Often Misread

1. Taking God's name in vain (Exodus 20:7, KJV). The commandment originally had to do with oath taking. Don't "swear to God" you'll do something unless you really mean to do it. I still think it's a bad idea to say, "Oh, my God!" unless you're praying, but that's not exactly what the third commandment is about.

2. Bearing false witness (Exodus 20:16, KJV). Again, the commandment refers to something specific—perjury. It was important for Israelites to have integrity in their judicial system. There are New Testament passages against lying in general, but this commandment has to do with lying in court.

3. An eye for an eye (Exodus 21:24). People quote this today as an exemplary form of justice. Two problems: (1) Originally this command served as kind of a restraint—if someone put out your eye, you were entitled only to his eye, not his life;

(2) Jesus tackles this text head-on in Matthew 5:38–39, telling people to turn the other cheek.

4. In sin my mother conceived me (Psalm 51:5, KJV). Historically some have taken this to mean that the act of conception (sex) is sinful. Wrong! David is talking about his own sin, not his mother's, though this can be taken to undergird the doctrine of original sin. The NIV translation is a good one: "Surely I was . . . sinful from the time my mother conceived me."

5. The unforgivable sin (Matthew 12:32). Blasphemy against the Holy Spirit, Jesus said, would not be forgiven—and many Christians worry that they might have unwittingly committed this sin. Stop worrying. The very fact that you care about this indicates that you are responding to the Holy Spirit and are not guilty of this sin. Jesus' statement is a tautology. Those who reject the Spirit's testimony about Jesus (like the religious leaders with whom Jesus was speaking) will not come to Jesus for forgiveness. The forgiveness awaits them, but they remain unforgiven because they don't want forgiveness.

6. All things work together for good (Romans 8:28). This is a splendid promise, but it is used too quickly to console sufferers with the idea "Someday you'll look back on this and laugh." Some do, but it doesn't always happen like that. The end of the verse provides a crucial explanation: for "those . . . who have been called according to his purpose." It is God's purpose we're in line with, not our own.

7. Wives, submit to your husbands (Ephesians 5:22). In today's politicized climate, this is a hot potato, but it doesn't have to be. Look at the previous verse and the next paragraph. Verse 21 says, "Submit to one another out of reverence for Christ." For the Christian, submission is a way of life. For men, too? Absolutely. Look at verse 25: "Husbands, love your wives, just as Christ loved the church and gave himself up for her." Jesus submitted himself for our sakes, and husbands should do the same for their wives.

8. Work out your own salvation (Philippians 2:12). Some come to think that our salvation is a joint effort, that God saves us—but we earn it, too. This is inconsistent with the general thrust of the entire New Testament. A close look at this working, however, reveals the reality of the situation: We work *after* we are saved, letting God's Spirit work his power within us as we show our gratitude to God. The next verse (13) makes this clear: "for it is God who works in you."

9. The "whatsoever" verse (Philippians 4:8, KJV). When you hear this quoted, the preacher usually goes on to say that

people should not think about things that are not true, noble, right, pure, etc. But there is no negative in this verse. Paul is not telling us *not* to think about anything; instead, he's telling us to fill our minds with good stuff wherever we find it. We live in a mixed-bag world, as did Paul. Sometimes we'll have to dig through mud to find some gems.

10. Money is the root of all evil (1 Timothy 6:10). There's a double twist here. First, many are quick to point out that it's not money that's the root of all kinds of evil but the *love of* money. This is quite true. But the haste with which people point that out makes me wonder whether it matters. We love money an awful lot, more than we realize, and that puts us in danger. Sure, money itself isn't evil, but it has a way of inspiring greed. Get some, want more. So be careful!

Ten Ways to Get into the Psalms (and Get the Psalms into You)

1. Meditate on one or two verses each day.
2. Read a psalm every morning.
3. Better yet, read the same one at night, too.
4. Underline. Go color-coded. Maybe indicate God's characteristics in blue, his commands to you in red.
5. Keep a list of notable quotables, and dip into them when you write to friends or send get-well cards.
6. Memorize meaningful verses; jot them down on three-by-five-inch index cards to help you remember them.
7. Read a psalm as if God is talking to you. (After all, he is.) And then use it as a prayer to him.
8. Write your own psalm, beginning with the first line of a biblical psalm and then making up the rest.
9. Study several psalms on related themes.
10. Paraphrase or summarize the psalms that you read.

Twelve Greek Words for English-Bible Readers to Know

1. *Agape/Philia.* Love. Christians latched onto *agape* to denote God's love, and thus Christian love. *Philia* is a strong word, too, but has to do with friendship or a family feeling. The Greek shows a distinction between these two in Jesus' post-resurrection talk with Peter (John 21).
2. *Hamartia* (also *amartia*). Sin. In ancient Greek it was simply "missing the mark," an idea underscored in Romans 3:23. Christianity added a stronger moral dimension to the word.
3. *Diakonia* (also *diaconia*). Service. A norm for Christian behavior. From this word, church officers and workers are called

deacons. This is somewhat weaker than Paul's frequent term for himself, *doulos,* bond slave.

4. *Ekklesia* (also *ecclesia*). The church. Literally, "the called-out ones." The idea is that God calls people out of the world to be his special people.

5. *Gnosis.* Knowledge. Already in the first century, the philosophy of Gnosticism was creeping into the church, claiming that certain people merited special knowledge *(gnosis)* about God. It's fascinating to see Paul try to reclaim this and other Gnostic terms in his writings—especially Colossians.

6. *Koinonia.* Fellowship. But not just gabbing at the coffee hour. The biblical word has a strong sense of sharing possessions (see Acts 2:42 in this light). The word literally means "common-ness."

7. *Kosmos* (also *cosmos*). World. Literally, "design," "appearance"—which is why we recognize it in the words *cosmos* and *cosmetics.* The Greeks believed in the orderly arrangement of the universe. But Christian writers, especially John, used it to connote the arrangement of human beings in opposition to God. It is a world system that regularly rebels against God's ways.

8. *Logos.* Word. But in Greek thought it was so much more. The *Logos* was the controlling principle of the universe, the logic by which everything functioned. Physicists today are looking for a "principle of everything." That's what *Logos* was to the Greeks. John's assertion that the *Logos* became flesh (John 1:14) was breathtaking.

9. *Marturia.* Witness. We know martyrs as those who witnessed for Christ to the point of death. But the basic word simply denotes a person who testifies about what he or she has experienced.

10. *Parakletos* (also *Paraclete*). Counselor, Comforter. Jesus used this term for the Holy Spirit (John 14:16) and it literally means "one who is called alongside." *Being there* is thus one of the Spirit's most important activities on our behalf.

11. *Parousia.* Coming. In ancient Greek it meant both "being there" and "getting there." Christians began to use it for the future presence of Christ—that is, his second coming.

12. *Sarx.* Flesh. The Greek word originally had most of the connotations we have for "flesh"—skin, meat, etc. —but Paul developed a whole new understanding. *Sarx* became that "fleshly desire" in humans that fights against the higher calling of God. It's important to know that Paul is not saying that the physical body is evil; just that our flesh-based desires lead us away from God.

Twelve Hebrew Words for English-Bible Readers to Know

1. *Baruch.* Bless. We bless the Lord and are blessed by him.
2. *El/Jah.* Names for God. *El* is the generic name for a god, and thus was attached to other terms (as in *El Shaddai,* which is probably "God of the mountains"). *Jah* was the personal name (fully *Jahveh* or *Yahweh,* though the Hebrews were shy about uttering the full name). You see both of these terms in many Old Testament names.
3. *Hesed.* Loving-kindness, mercy. A key attribute of God. "His mercy endures forever" (NKJV).
4. *Kavod.* Glory. Literally, "weight." In the '60s, people would praise something by saying it was "heavy, man." But that's as old as Moses.
5. *Nabi.* Prophet. The word probably comes from a root that means "to be called." Prophets were called by God to speak his truth about current events and the future.
6. *Olam.* Eternity, the ages. God is king of the ages, Lord for eternity.
7. *Ruach.* Spirit, breath, wind. Whenever the Old Testament speaks of God's Spirit, it has the very physical sense of God's breathing. God's breath goes out from him and accomplishes what he wants. The same meaning carries over to the Greek *pneuma* in the New Testament.
8. *Shalom.* Peace, well-being. People greeted each other saying, "Is it *shalom* with you?"
9. *Shaphat.* Judge. This refers to human judges, of course, but also to God as judge of us all.
10. *Shekinah.* Dwelling. At key times throughout Israel's history, God appeared in a fiery way—at dedications of tabernacle and temple, on the journey through the desert, on Sinai, and some would say at Pentecost. In each case, some scholars say, he was manifesting his *shekinah* glory, the radiance of his dwelling presence.
11. *Torah.* Law. The term can refer to the first five books of the Old Testament (the law of Moses), to the whole Old Testament, or to the abstract idea of God's requirements.
12. *Tov.* Good. When God looked at creation each day, he said, "*Tov,* it's good." After he made Adam, he said it was *meod tov*— very good.

Distinctives of the Gospels

Of course, many of the same stories of Jesus are presented in several of the Gospel accounts, but there are some stories that are unique to one Gospel or another. Let's look at those. Note: Mark has virtually nothing that isn't also used by Matthew or Luke.

Stories That Only Matthew Tells

1. The magi come to the baby Jesus (2:1-12)
2. Herod kills the children in Bethlehem (2:13-23)
3. Jesus heals two blind men (9:27-31)
4. Jesus pays taxes (17:24-27)
5. Parable of workers in vineyard (20:1-16)
6. Parable of 10 virgins (25:1-13)
7. Parable of sheep and goats (25:31-46)
8. Guards report the Resurrection (28:11-15)

Stories That Only Luke Tells

1. John the Baptist's birth (1)
2. The shepherds and angels at Jesus' birth (2:8-20)
3. Simeon and Anna at the temple (2:21-38)
4. The boy Jesus visits the temple (2:41-50)
5. Jesus reads Scripture in Nazareth (4:16-30)
6. Jesus raises son of widow from Nain (7:11-17)
7. The Good Samaritan (10:25-37)
8. Jesus visits Mary and Martha (10:38-42)
9. Parable of the shrewd manager (16:1-12)
10. Parable of rich man and Lazarus (16:19-31)
11. Jesus heals 10 lepers (17:12-19)
12. Parable of the persistent widow (18:2-8)
13. Parable of the Pharisee and tax collector (18:9-14)
14. Zacchaeus (19:1-10)

Stories That Only John Tells

1. Jesus changes water to wine at Cana (2:1-11)
2. Jesus meets with Nicodemus (3)
3. Jesus meets the woman at the well (4:1-42)
4. Jesus heals a nobleman's son (4:46-54)
5. Jesus heals a lame man in Jerusalem (5)
6. An adulterous woman (8:1-11)
7. Jesus announces himself as the Light of the World (8:12-20)
8. Jesus heals a man blind from birth (9)
9. Jesus raises Lazarus (11)
10. Doubting Thomas (20:19-31)
11. With Peter at breakfast (21)

Ten Prayers of Christ in Luke

1. At his baptism (3:21)
2. After healing the leper (5:16)
3. Before choosing the 12 apostles (6:12)
4. When he was alone (9:18-22)

5. Transfiguration (9:28-29)
6. With the disciples (11:1-4)
7. For Peter (22:32)
8. For himself (22:41, 44)
9. "Father, forgive them . . ." (23:34)
10. His dying prayer (23:46)

What Christ's Blood Achieves

1. Redemption (1 Peter 1:18-19)
2. Forgiveness (Ephesians 1:7)
3. Cleansing (1 John 1:7)
4. Justification (Romans 5:9)
5. Nearness (Ephesians 2:13)
6. Assurance (Exodus 12:13)
7. Peace (Colossians 1:20)
8. Participation with God (1 Corinthians 10:16)
9. Victory (Revelation 12:11)

Quick Fixes for Spiritual Sickness from the Psalms

1. In a bad mood? See 34:1-2.
2. Sad about something? See 70:4.
3. Proud of yourself? See 71:15-16.
4. Bothered by enemies? See 71:24.
5. Struggling with evil desires? See 119:9.
6. Frenzied? See 46:10.
7. Guilty? See 103:12.
8. Longing for more money? See 62:10.

Ten "Fear Nots" in the Old Testament

1. To Abram (Genesis 15:1), promising protection
2. To Hagar (Genesis 21:17), promising protection for her son
3. To Isaac (Genesis 26:24), promising blessing
4. To Jacob (Genesis 46:3), telling him to go to Egypt
5. To Moses (Numbers 21:34), assuring him of victory in battle
6. To Joshua (Joshua 8:1), reassuring him after a defeat at Ai
7. To Gideon (Judges 6:23), on his seeing God's angel
8. To Israel (Isaiah 43:1), speaking of redemption
9. To Ezekiel (Ezekiel 3:9), regarding his rebellious listeners
10. To Daniel (Daniel 10:12), as he saw a vision

Ten "Fear Nots" of Jesus

1. About persecution: "Do not be afraid of those who kill the body but cannot kill the soul" (Matthew 10:28).

2. To his followers, about their value to God: "So don't be afraid; you are worth more than many sparrows" (Matthew 10:31).

3. Walking on water, to his disciples: "Take courage! It is I. Don't be afraid" (Matthew 14:27).

4. After his resurrection, to the women: "Do not be afraid. Go and tell my brothers to go to Galilee; there they will see me" (Matthew 28:10).

5. To Jairus, after hearing that his daughter had died: "Don't be afraid; just believe" (Mark 5:36).

6. To fisherman Simon Peter after a miraculous catch: "Don't be afraid; from now on you will catch men" (Luke 5:10).

7. After encouraging his followers to seek God's kingdom: "Do not be afraid, little flock, for your Father has been pleased to give you the kingdom" (Luke 12:32).

8. Shortly before his death: "Do not let your hearts be troubled and do not be afraid" (John 14:27).

9. To Paul, in a vision: "Do not be afraid; keep on speaking, do not be silent" (Acts 18:9).

10. To John, in Revelation: "Do not be afraid. I am the First and the Last" (Revelation 1:17).

Four Christmas "Fear Nots"

1. The angel to Zechariah (Luke 1:13)
2. The angel to Joseph (Matthew 1:20)
3. The angel to Mary (Luke 1:30)
4. The angel to the shepherds (Luke 2:10)

Ten New Testament Mysteries

1. Christ (Colossians 4:3)
2. Faith (1 Timothy 3:9)
3. Marriage (Ephesians 5:31-32)
4. Resurrection (1 Corinthians 15:51)
5. Salvation (1 Peter 1:10-12)
6. The gospel (Ephesians 6:19)
7. The kingdom (Matthew 13:11)
8. The woman and the beast of Revelation (Revelation 17:7)
9. Christ in you (Colossians 1:27)
10. Grafting of Gentiles onto the tree of God's favor (Romans 11:25; Ephesians 3:3-6)

What's Better about Jesus?

Comparative Thinking in the Book of Hebrews

1. Jesus is superior to angels (1:4).

2. Moses was a servant, but Jesus is a son (3:5-6).
3. Christ is a high priest of a higher order than Aaron's (5:1-10).
4. Christians have a better hope than the law provides (7:19).
5. Jesus guarantees a better covenant (7:22).
6. Jesus has a superior ministry . . .
7. . . . founded on better promises (8:6).
8. Christ's once-for-all sacrifice is better than the old sacrificial system (9:15-28).
9. Christians have better possessions than anything the authorities can take away (10:34).
10. People of faith look for a better country (11:16).
11. The resurrection we anticipate is better than release from an earthly prison (11:35).
12. "God had planned something better for us" (11:40).
13. The blood of Christ "speaks a better word" than the blood of Abel (12:24).

Ten Activities of the Holy Spirit

1. Challenges sinners (Genesis 6:3)
2. Convicts people of sin (John 16:8)
3. Helps us in our weakness (Romans 8:26)
4. Strengthens and encourages (Acts 9:31)
5. Teaches (John 14:26)
6. Guides (John 16:13)
7. Assures us that we are God's children (Romans 8:16)
8. Glorifies Christ (John 16:14)
9. Lives within Christians (John 14:17)
10. May be grieved (Ephesians 4:30)

Ten People Who Prayed Their Way out of Trouble

1. Jacob, from his brother (Genesis 32:9-12)
2. Joshua, after the defeat at Ai (Joshua 7)
3. David, entangled by the "cords of death" (Psalm 116)
4. Elisha, encircled by the Arameans (2 Kings 6)
5. Asa, from Zerah the Cushite (2 Chronicles 14)
6. Jehoshaphat, from the Ammonites and Moabites (2 Chronicles 20)
7. Hezekiah, from Sennacherib's army (2 Chronicles 32)
8. The church, for Peter in prison (Acts 12)
9. Paul and Silas, in prison (Acts 16)
10. Paul, on his voyage to Rome (Acts 27)

Twelve People Who Cried

1. Jacob (Genesis 33:4)
2. Esau (Genesis 33:4)
3. Joseph (Genesis 43:30)
4. Moses (Exodus 2:6)
5. Naomi (Ruth 1:9)
6. Ruth (Ruth 1:9)
7. Jonathan (1 Samuel 20:41)
8. David (2 Samuel 3:32)
9. Elisha (2 Kings 8:11)
10. Peter (Matthew 26:75)
11. Mary (John 20:11)
12. Jesus (John 11:35)

Ten Terms Psalm 119 Uses for Scripture

1. Law(s)
2. Precepts
3. Statutes
4. Commands
5. Ways
6. Word
7. Decrees
8. Wonders
9. Promise
10. Truth (Way of truth or Word of truth)

Gifts Given in the Bible

1. From Jacob to Joseph: A "richly ornamented robe" (Genesis 37:3; "coat of many colours," KJV)
2. From God to people in general, especially Moses: Mouth, hearing, sight (specifically he gave Moses the eloquence he needed; Exodus 4:11)
3. From Hannah to God: Her only son, Samuel (1 Samuel 1:11)
4. From Jonathan to David: His robe, tunic, sword, bow, belt (1 Samuel 18:4)
5. From the queen of Sheba to Solomon: "120 talents of gold, large quantities of spices, and precious stones" (1 Kings 10:10)
6. From the magi to the baby Jesus: Gold, incense, myrrh (Matthew 2:11)
7. From God to the world: His one and only Son (John 3:16)
8. From Mary to Jesus: Expensive perfume (John 12:3)
9. From God to Jesus' disciples (then and now): The Holy Spirit (John 14:26; Acts 1:4-5)

Seven Gifts of God

1. Rest for the weary (Matthew 11:28)
2. Life to the dead (Romans 6:23)
3. Righteousness to Gentiles as well as Jews (Romans 9:30)
4. The Spirit to those who obey him (Acts 5:32)
5. Salvation to sinners (Luke 19:9)
6. Suffering to those who follow him (Philippians 1:29)
7. Encouragement to those who need it (2 Thessalonians 2:16)

Spiritual Gifts

Every Christian has some kind of special ability from God that, combined with the special abilities of others, will build up the church and glorify God. There are three or four New Testament passages that discuss these spiritual gifts, even listing some of those available. The lists vary, however, from passage to passage, giving the impression that these are just some of the many ways God can empower his people.

1. Administration
2. Leadership
3. Encouragement (Exhortation)
4. Teaching
5. Prophecy
6. Evangelism
7. Service (Helps)
8. Caring (Mercy)
9. Hospitality
10. Giving (Contributing)
11. Discipling
12. Healing
13. Discernment
14. Wisdom
15. Faith
16. Miracles
17. Speaking in tongues
18. Interpretation of tongues

Other possible gifts in our modern era?

1. Craftsmanship
2. Creative communication
3. Counseling
4. Praise
5. Technology

Ten Things in the Bible That Were Sold

1. Abraham bought a plot of land for Sarah's burial for 400 silver shekels (Genesis 23:16).
2. Esau sold his birthright to Jacob for some lentil stew (Genesis 25:33).
3. Joseph was sold into slavery for 20 silver shekels (Genesis 37:28).
4. Joab would have paid 10 silver shekels and a fancy belt for the killing of Absalom (2 Samuel 18:11).
5. David bought a threshing floor and oxen for 50 silver shekels (2 Samuel 24:24).
6. Solomon imported a chariot (600 shekels) and a horse (150 shekels) (1 Kings 10:29).
7. Two sparrows were sold for a penny (Matthew 10:29).
8. In Jesus' parable, workers sold a day's work for a denarius (Matthew 20:2).
9. A woman of Bethany anointed Jesus with perfume that "could have been sold at a high price" (Matthew 26:9).
10. Jesus was "sold" by Judas for 30 silver coins (Matthew 26:15).

Precious Possessions of the Lord from Psalm 100

1. His people
2. His pastures
3. His gates
4. His courts
5. His name
6. His love
7. His faithfulness

A Hive of *Be*'s Worth Keeping

1. "Be thankful" (Colossians 3:15).
2. "Be holy" (1 Peter 1:16).
3. "Be content with what you have" (Hebrews 13:5).
4. "Be joyful always" (1 Thessalonians 5:16).
5. "Be glad" (Matthew 5:12).
6. "Be joyful in hope, patient in affliction, faithful in prayer" (Romans 12:12).
7. "Be reconciled to God" (2 Corinthians 5:20).
8. "Be reconciled to your brother" (Matthew 5:24).
9. "Be kind and compassionate to one another" (Ephesians 4:32).
10. "Be devoted to one another in brotherly love" (Romans 12:10).
11. "Be patient with everyone" (1 Thessalonians 5:14).

12. "Be sympathetic, love as brothers, be compassionate and humble" (1 Peter 3:8).
13. "Be of one mind" (2 Corinthians 13:11).
14. "Be completely humble and gentle" (Ephesians 4:2).
15. "Be merciful to those who doubt" (Jude 1:22).
16. "Be willing to associate with people of low position" (Romans 12:16).
17. "Be careful to do what is right in the eyes of everybody" (Romans 12:17).
18. "Be alert" (Ephesians 6:18).
19. "Be clear minded and self-controlled so that you can pray" (1 Peter 4:7).
20. "Be careful . . . that the exercise of your freedom does not become a stumbling block to the weak" (1 Corinthians 8:9).
21. "Be on your guard" (Matthew 10:17).
22. "Be very careful, then, how you live—not as unwise but as wise" (Ephesians 5:15).
23. "Be separate" (2 Corinthians 6:17).
24. "Be baptized" (Acts 2:38).
25. "Be filled with the Spirit" (Ephesians 5:18).
26. "Be [Christ's] witnesses" (Acts 1:8).
27. "Be eager to prophesy" (1 Corinthians 14:39).
28. "Be all the more eager to make your calling and election sure" (2 Peter 1:10).
29. "Be imitators of God" (Ephesians 5:1).
30. "Be wise in the way you act toward outsiders" (Colossians 4:5).
31. "Be quick to listen, slow to speak and slow to become angry" (James 1:19).
32. "Be prepared to give an answer to everyone who asks you to give the reason for the hope that you have" (1 Peter 3:15).
33. "Be strong in the Lord and in his mighty power" (Ephesians 6:10).

Who Are We?

1. Pupils sitting at the feet of Jesus (John 11:32)
2. Soldiers putting on spiritual armor (Ephesians 6:14)
3. Runners laying aside extra weight (Hebrews 12:1)
4. Sowers scattering seed beside every stream (Isaiah 32:20)
5. Ambassadors urging peace and reconciliation (2 Corinthians 5:20)
6. Priests offering spiritual sacrifices (Romans 12:1)
7. Fishermen gathering many fish (John 21:6)
8. Architects counting the cost of a new construction (Luke 14:28)

9. Builders putting up a high-quality building (1 Corinthians 3:11-16)
10. Dancers exulting in the joy of the Lord (Psalm 150:4)

What Am I in Christ?

1. I am forgiven (Ephesians 1:7).
2. I am a new creation (2 Corinthians 5:17).
3. I am loved (Jeremiah 31:3).
4. I am alive with Christ (Ephesians 2:5).
5. I am more than a conqueror (Romans 8:37).
6. I am coheir with Christ (Romans 8:17).
7. I am free from condemnation (Romans 8:1).
8. I am hopeful (Colossians 1:27).
9. I am moving toward wholeness (Philippians 1:6).
10. I am going to have everlasting life (John 6:47).

"Be Careful!" in Scripture

1. About forgetting God (Deuteronomy 6:12; 8:11)
2. About evil and unkind thoughts (Deuteronomy 15:9)
3. About things forbidden (Judges 13:4-13)
4. About the lure of money (Job 36:18)
5. About God's anger (Acts 13:40-41)
6. About false teachers (Matthew 7:15; 16:6, 11)
7. About persecutors (Matthew 10:17)
8. About people who do evil (Philippians 3:2)
9. About falling into error (2 Peter 3:17)
10. About greed (Luke 12:15)

Eight Portraits in Genesis

1. Adam and Eve illustrate human nature.
2. Cain and Abel illustrate the carnal mind and spiritual mind at war within us.
3. Enoch illustrates communion with God.
4. Noah illustrates regeneration—saved by the ark.
5. Abraham and Sarah illustrate faith in the midst of doubt.
6. Isaac illustrates sonship.
7. Jacob and Esau illustrate the brain and brawn of human struggle.
8. Joseph illustrates suffering and glory.

"Faithful" Servants of God

1. Moses (Numbers 12:7; Hebrews 3:5). "My servant Moses . . . is faithful in all my house."
2. Daniel (Daniel 6:4). "He was trustworthy."

3. Timothy (1 Corinthians 4:17). "Faithful in the Lord."
4. Abraham (Galatians 3:9). "So those who have faith are blessed along with Abraham, the man of faith."
5. Epaphras (Colossians 1:7; 4:12). "A faithful minister of Christ."
6. Tychicus (Colossians 4:7; Ephesians 6:21). "A faithful minister and fellow servant."
7. Onesimus (Colossians 4:9). "Our faithful and dear brother."
8. Paul (1 Timothy 1:12). "Jesus . . . considered me faithful."
9. Silas (1 Peter 5:12). "I regard as a faithful brother."
10. Antipas (Revelation 2:13). "My faithful witness."

Ten Activities of Angels

Everyone knows an angel appeared to Mary, announcing that she would bear the Christ child. And about nine months later, an angel choir sang to shepherds as their lead singer gave the details of Jesus' birth. But *what else* have angels been up to?

1. Climbing Jacob's ladder (Genesis 28:12)
2. Blocking the path of Balaam and his talking donkey (Numbers 22:21-35)
3. Strengthening Elijah during a drought (1 Kings 19:5-8)
4. Touching Isaiah's lips with a burning coal (Isaiah 6:6-7)
5. Keeping Shadrach, Meshach, and Abednego cool in the furnace (Daniel 3:28)
6. Keeping the lions' mouths shut for Daniel (Daniel 6:22)
7. Announcing the birth of John the Baptist to his dumbstruck father (Luke 1:11-20)
8. Attending to Jesus after his temptation (Mark 1:13)
9. Rolling back the stone from Jesus' tomb (Matthew 28:2)
10. Springing Peter from prison (Acts 12:7-11)

The Trinity throughout Scripture

Some say the apostle Paul made up the idea of the Trinity. Don't believe it. God the Father, Son, and Holy Spirit appears throughout the Bible.

1. In Creation (Genesis 1:2, 26)
2. In God's omnipresence (Psalm 139:7)
3. In calling us to serve (Isaiah 6:8)
4. In atonement (Hebrews 9:14)
5. In giving us new life (Romans 8:11)
6. In baptism (Matthew 3:16-17; 28:19)
7. In our access to God (Ephesians 2:18)
8. In our election by God (1 Peter 1:1-2)

9. In the ongoing direction of our lives (2 Thessalonians 3:5)
10. In benediction (2 Corinthians 13:14)

Famine Values

Here's what some Bible people did during drought and hunger:

1. Abraham went down to Egypt and tried to pass off his wife as his sister (Genesis 12:10-13).
2. Isaac went down to Gerar and tried the same thing (Genesis 26:1, 7).
3. Joseph found an opportunity to rise to power in Egypt (Genesis 41:25-57).
4. Jacob sent his sons to Egypt for an unexpected reunion with Joseph (Genesis 42–45).
5. Naomi's family went to Moab, where one of her sons married Ruth (Ruth 1:1, 4).
6. King David asked the Lord what was going on (2 Samuel 21:1).
7. Elijah challenged the prophets of Baal (1 Kings 18).
8. The Prodigal Son went home to his father (Luke 15:14, 20).
9. They found that even famine shall not separate us from the love of Christ (Romans 8:35).

What God's Word Can Do

1. Pierce the heart, convicting us of sin (Hebrews 4:12)
2. Regenerate and transform one's life (1 Peter 1:23)
3. Produce a living faith in God (Romans 10:17)
4. Cleanse and purify one's heart and life (Psalm 119:9-11)
5. Protect from heresy and error (Acts 20:29-32)
6. Bring joy and rejoicing to the heart (Jeremiah 15:16)
7. Speak peace to the troubled soul (Psalm 85:8)
8. Make us wiser than our teachers (Psalm 119:99)
9. Testify about Jesus (John 5:39)
10. Help us by "teaching, rebuking, correcting and training in righteousness" (2 Timothy 3:16)

On the Lamb

The history of the world in 16 ovine acts

1. "Where is the lamb?" asks Isaac (Genesis 22:7).
2. "God himself will provide the lamb," his father replies (Genesis 22:8).
3. The angel of death passes over the houses with the blood of the lamb on the doorposts (Exodus 12).

4. Isaiah sees the Servant being "led like a lamb to the slaughter" and not opening his mouth (Isaiah 53:7).
5. "Look, the Lamb of God!" cries John the Baptist, seeing Jesus (John 1:29).
6. "A lamb without blemish or defect," Peter adds (1 Peter 1:19).
7. "Christ, our Passover lamb, has been sacrificed," Paul confirms (1 Corinthians 5:7).
8. John sees a Lamb on the throne, "looking as if it had been slain" (Revelation 5:6).
9. The elders fall down in worship before this Lamb (Revelation 5:8).
10. "Worthy is the Lamb that was slain," the throngs of angels sing (Revelation 5:12, KJV).
11. A great multitude stands before the Lamb (Revelation 7:9).
12. "Salvation belongs to our God . . . and to the Lamb," they sing (Revelation 7:10).
13. Some have washed their robes in the blood of the Lamb (Revelation 7:14).
14. The Lamb is "Lord of lords and King of kings—and with him will be his called, chosen and faithful followers" (Revelation 17:14).
15. "Let us rejoice and be glad and give him glory!" the multitude shouts. "For the wedding of the Lamb has come" (Revelation 19:7).
16. "Blessed," John writes, "are those who are invited to the wedding supper of the Lamb!" (Revelation 19:9).

Seven Reasons for Coming to the Lord's Supper

1. It is an act of obedience (Matthew 26:26-27; 1 Corinthians 11:24).
2. It is an act of remembrance (Luke 22:19; 1 Corinthians 11:24-25).
3. It is a testimony to his death (1 Corinthians 5:7; 11:26).
4. It is a confession that salvation is through his blood (Matthew 26:28; Revelation 1:5).
5. It is an act of fellowship (1 Corinthians 10:16-17).
6. It is an act of praise and thanksgiving (Luke 22:19; 1 Corinthians 10:16; 11:26).
7. It proclaims his second coming (1 Corinthians 11:26).

Seven Things the Word of God Is Like

1. A hammer (Jeremiah 23:29)
2. Fire (Jeremiah 23:29)
3. A lamp (Psalm 119:105)

4. A sword (Hebrews 4:12)
5. A mirror (2 Corinthians 13:12)
6. Food (1 Peter 2:2)
7. Water (Psalm 1:3)

Ten "No Mores" in the New Jerusalem

1. No more sea (Revelation 21:1)
2. No more mourning or crying (21:4)
3. No more pain (21:4)
4. No more temple (21:22)
5. No more impurity (21:27)
6. No more lamps or sun (21:23; 22:5)
7. No more closed gates (21:25)
8. No more curse (22:3)
9. No more night (22:5)
10. No more death (21:4)

What's New in the New Testament

1. New wine in new wineskins (Matthew 9:17)
2. New life (Acts 5:20; Romans 6:4)
3. A new teaching (Mark 1:27; Acts 17:19)
4. A new covenant in Jesus' blood (Luke 22:20; 1 Corinthians 11:25)
5. A new command: Love (John 13:34; 1 John 2:7-8)
6. We are a new creation (2 Corinthians 5:17; Galatians 6:15)
7. Christ forms one new man out of two, uniting Jews and Gentiles (Ephesians 2:15)
8. We are to put on the new self (Ephesians 4:24).
9. A new heaven and a new earth (2 Peter 3:13; Revelation 21:1)
10. A new Jerusalem (Revelation 21:2)
11. A new song (Revelation 5:9; 14:3)
12. A new birth into a living hope (1 Peter 1:3)

Ten Songs and Poems before David

1. Jacob's blessing (Genesis 49:2-27)
2. Song of Moses and Miriam (Exodus 15:1-18, 21)
3. Song of the poets (Numbers 21:27-30)
4. Song of Balaam (Numbers 23:7-10)
5. Song of Moses (Deuteronomy 32:1-47)
6. Moses' blessing (Deuteronomy 33:1-29)
7. Song of Joshua (Joshua 10:12-14)
8. Song of Deborah and Barak (Judges 5:1-31)
9. Song of Ruth (Ruth 1:16-17)
10. Song of Hannah (1 Samuel 2:1-10)

Ten Marks of the True Christian

(According to James)

1. Perseverance (1:2-4)
2. Slowness to anger (1:19-20)
3. Pure and undefiled religion (1:26-27)
4. Impartiality (2:1-13)
5. Faith acted out in deeds (2:14-26)
6. Controlled speech (3:1-12)
7. Unselfishness (3:13–4:3)
8. Patience (5:7-11)
9. Dependence on God (5:13-18)
10. Concern for the wayward (5:19-20)

Paul's Helpers

1. Silas. Already a church leader, he joined Paul's second journey; later he helped Peter.
2. Barnabas. The encourager, he brought Paul into the apostles' inner circle and joined Paul's first journey.
3. Titus. A Gentile who became a minister on Crete.
4. Timothy. A young man of mixed parentage "adopted" and mentored by Paul; he became a pastor in Ephesus.
5. Mark. A young observer of Jesus' ministry, he joined Paul's first journey but soon bailed out; later he assisted Peter, and Paul called him "helpful."
6. Luke. Gentile doctor who joined Paul's crew in the middle of his second journey.
7. Tychicus. A Christian from the province of Asia who joined Paul's third journey.
8. Trophimus. An Ephesian Christian who joined Paul's third journey, he created a stir when some leaders thought Paul brought him (a Gentile) into the temple.
9. Epaphras. A leader of the Colossian church; it's possible that he's also the Epaphroditus praised in Philippians.
10. Demas. A companion of Paul during his Roman imprisonment, who later deserted him "because he loved this world" (2 Timothy 4:10).

Fifteen "Sons Of"

1. Sons of Aaron: Priests (Leviticus 21:1)
2. Son of Abraham: Any Jew (used of Zacchaeus in Luke 19:9)
3. Sons of Belial: Saul used this term for his enemies (1 Samuel 10:27, KJV). *Belial* was a word for wickedness or the devil.

4. Son of David: Member of the royal dynasty of Judah (used for Jesus in Matthew 21:9 and elsewhere)
5. Son of Encouragement: Barnabas; that's what his name means (Acts 4:36).
6. Son of God: Jesus (Matthew 14:33)
7. Sons of God: Angelic beings? (Genesis 6:1-4; Job 1:6, KJV); peacemakers (Matthew 5:9); and believers (Galatians 3:26)
8. Sons of Israel: Jacob's 12 sons, patriarchs of the 12 tribes (Genesis 45:21)
9. Sons of Levi: The Levites, temple stewards or priests (Deuteronomy 21:5)
10. Sons of light: An option for Jesus' disciples (John 12:36)
11. Son of Man: Jesus' frequent term for himself (Matthew 8:20)
12. Son of perdition: Judas (John 17:12, KJV)
13. Sons of the prophets: A group of young men who supported the prophetic ministry of Elisha; possibly prophets in training (2 King 2:15, KJV); used for Jesus' followers in Acts 3:25
14. Sons of Thunder: James and John, the feisty sons of Zebedee (Mark 3:17)
15. Sons of Zion: Jerusalem's citizens (Lamentations 4:2)

The Real You

If you're a Christian, the book of Ephesians has some choice words for you.

1. You are a saint (1:1).
2. You are God's workmanship (2:10).
3. You are a fellow citizen with God's people (2:19).
4. You are a prisoner of Christ (3:1; 4:1).
5. You are righteous and holy (4:24).
6. You are a citizen of heaven (2:6).
7. You have been marked by the Holy Spirit (1:13).
8. You have been blessed with every spiritual blessing (1:3).
9. You were chosen before the creation of the world (1:4).
10. You were predestined to be adopted by God (1:5).
11. You have been made alive with Christ (2:5).
12. You have received God's saving grace (2:8).
13. You have been raised up, seated with Christ in heaven (2:6).
14. You have direct access to God through the Spirit (2:18).
15. You may approach God with freedom and confidence (3:12).

The Armor of God in Ephesians 6

1. The belt stands for truth.
2. The breastplate stands for righteousness.

3. The sandals stand for the gospel of peace.
4. The shield stands for faith.
5. The helmet stands for salvation.
6. The sword of the Spirit stands for the Word of God.

The Beatitudes (Matthew 5)

Who's blessed, their traits, and what they get.

Who's blessed	Their traits	What they get
The poor in spirit	Humility and dependence on God	Theirs is the kingdom of heaven
Those who mourn	Contriteness and the desire to forgive and and be forgiven	They will be comforted.
The meek	Obedience to God and and a willingness to serve.	They will inherit the earth.
Those who hunger and thirst for righteousness	Moral purity and self-denial	They will be filled.
The merciful	Compassion and forgiveness	They will be shown mercy.
The pure in heart	Integrity and moral sensitivity	They will see God.
The peacemakers	Reconciliation and justice	They will be called sons of God.
Those who are persecuted because of righteousness	Dedication and loyalty	Theirs is the kingdom of heaven.

Twenty Cross-Cultural Encounters in Scripture

1. Lot settled in Sodom.
2. Jacob's clan moved to Egypt to be with Joseph.
3. The spies visited Rahab in Jericho.
4. Samson married a Philistine and dallied with Delilah.
5. Ruth, a Moabite, chose to stay with Naomi.
6. David lived and fought beside the Philistines for a time.
7. The queen of Sheba visited Solomon.
8. Naaman, the Syrian captain, balked at dipping in the Jordan.
9. Nehemiah returned to a Jerusalem overrun by other nations.
10. Daniel assumed power in Babylon.

11. Shadrach, Meshach, and Abednego refused to worship the Babylonian king's image.
12. Esther approached Persian king Xerxes to plead for her people.
13. Jesus asked a Samaritan woman for water.
14. The Good Samaritan helped a Jew.
15. Some Greeks asked to see Jesus.
16. Philip met the Ethiopian official in Gaza.
17. Peter preached the gospel to Cornelius, the Roman centurion.
18. Paul and Silas sang hymns in a Philippian jail and then converted the jailer.
19. Paul preached before the Areopagus in Athens.
20. Paul dazzled the islanders of Malta by not dying from a snakebite.

Mountaintop Experiences

1. Noah's ark came to rest on Mount Ararat.
2. Abraham nearly sacrificed Isaac on Mount Moriah.
3. Moses received God's law on Mount Sinai.
4. Moses died on Mount Nebo.
5. Under Joshua, the Israelites recommitted themselves at the twin mountains of Ebal and Gerizim.
6. The forces of Deborah and Barak defeated their foes near Mount Tabor.
7. David led the procession that brought the ark of the covenant up to Mount Zion.
8. Elijah challenged the prophets of Baal on Mount Carmel.
9. Elijah moped on Mount Horeb.
10. Jesus gave a sermon on a mountainside.

The Best Kings of Judah and Israel

The biblical writers grade their kings more on spiritual issues than on geopolitical status. The key question seems to be: What did this king do about idolatry? Drawing from the books of Kings and Chronicles, here's my selection of the top 10 kings:

1. David, of the united kingdom. Not a perfect king, but a man "after God's own heart." He seemed to unify the nation, keep its enemies at bay, and keep its heart in the right place.
2. Solomon, of the united kingdom. Despite his later apostasy, Solomon achieved much for Israel spiritually as well as economically. He built God a temple, and during Solomon's reign, Israel was as much a world power as it would ever be.
3. Hezekiah, of Judah. It was a tough time. Assyria had gobbled

up the northern kingdom and was threatening the south. Though his father had not followed the Lord, Hezekiah did and led a national revival—even offering refuge to some faithful Jews from the north.

4. Josiah, of Judah. After Manasseh had destroyed everything Hezekiah had built up, it was young Josiah who rediscovered God's Law and led another revival.

5. Jehu, of Israel. The commander who toppled Ahab's regime became king himself and continued a "reign of terror"—at least for Baal worshipers. Among other acts, he turned the Baal temple into a public toilet. One of a very few righteous kings in the north.

6. Joash, of Judah. Here was another young king who made a huge impact, surviving Athaliah's bloodbath and rebuilding the temple.

7. Asa, of Judah. His solid, righteous reign helped stem the tide of apostasy and began to get Judah back to the glory of David and Solomon.

8. Jehoash, of Israel. The last effective king in the north, he increased Israel's territory, though he didn't want to fight with Judah. He seemed to be a man of sense and peace.

9. Uzziah, of Judah. His 52-year reign helped to cement the reforms of Joash, though he didn't totally eradicate Baal worship.

10. Jehoshaphat, of Judah. A capable, though not great, king, he continued the positive trends his father, Asa, had introduced.

The Worst Kings (and Queen) of Judah and Israel

And here are the bottom 10, starting with the worst:

1. Ahab, of Israel. Elijah's nemesis was just awful for Israel. His political marriage to Jezebel opened the gates for an infusion of Baal worshipers from Phoenicia. Pagan practices abounded. God's prophets were hunted down and killed. No wonder Elijah was depressed.

2. Athaliah, of Judah. This grandmother filled a royalty gap with a six-year bloodbath, killing anyone with a claim to the throne. Fortunately she missed little Joash.

3. Manasseh, of Judah. All the good that Hezekiah had accomplished was quickly undone by his son Manasseh, who led the nation back into pagan practices.

4. Ahaz, of Judah. Not only did Ahaz let the nation sink into idolatry, but he played cowardly political games rather than trusting the Lord. Though Isaiah warned him, he invited mighty Assyria into the region to settle a minor border

dispute, a bad idea that resulted in the evaporation of the northern kingdom and nearly the same fate for the south.

5. Jehoahaz, of Israel. Jehu almost had the northern kingdom turned around, but his son Jehoahaz went the wrong way. His army was getting whomped by the Syrians, and Israel was losing territory. In desperation, Jehoahaz "sought the Lord's favor," but it was too little, too late.

6. Jeroboam, of Israel. He may have had good reason to lead the revolt that split the nation in two, but he took the northern kingdom downhill from there. The north plummeted into Baal worship and various pagan practices, and there were very few bright spots. And of course he instantly halved the international power of Solomon's kingdom.

7. Rehoboam, of Judah. The son of Solomon must bear the blame for the conditions that pushed Jeroboam to revolt. He did not follow the Lord, and his policies showed it.

8. Jehoram, of Judah. This son of Jehoshaphat married a daughter of Ahab and tried to make the south just like the idol-worshiping north.

9. Ahaziah, of Judah. He continued the bad ways of his father, Jehoram, and developed the conditions that led to Athaliah's evil reign.

10. Saul, of the united kingdom. As a king, he wasn't terrible, but it's a case of lost potential. One wonders how great he could have been if not for his personal foibles. Why spend your energy hunting down your best warrior (David), who would gladly fight on your side if you asked?

Fifteen Kings of Other Nations

Many monarchs of other lands had substantial impact on the stories of God's people. Here are some of them:

1. Melchizedek, "king of Salem." He received homage from Abraham.

2. Pharaoh, king of Egypt. Joseph became second in command to one unnamed pharaoh.

3. Abimelech. The patriarchs actually dealt with two kings by this name. It is possibly a title (like "Pharaoh"), since it means "my father the king."

4. Pharaoh. A later pharaoh oppressed the Israelites and reluctantly released them after 10 plagues fell on Egypt.

5. Hiram, king of Tyre. He supplied many of the materials for Solomon's temple and was a major trading partner with Israel.

6. Balak, king of Moab. He was one of several kings the Israelites

encountered in their desert wanderings. Balak sought the help of the Israelite prophet Balaam.

7. Ben-Hadad. He was king of neighboring Syria in Elijah's day.
8. Shalmaneser, king of Assyria. His army crushed the northern kingdom of Israel.
9. Sennacherib. The next king of Assyria, he threatened Judah and besieged Jerusalem.
10. Nebuchadnezzar, king of Babylon. He defeated the southern kingdom of Judah and took many captives, including Daniel.
11. Neco, pharaoh of Egypt. He had considerable power in the late 600s B.C., fighting against Judah (killing King Josiah) and toppling the Assyrian forces.
12. Belshazzar, king of Babylon (or at least crown prince). He saw God's writing on the wall before the Medes and Persians conquered him.
13. Darius, king of the Medes. He sent Daniel to the lions' den but rejoiced when Daniel survived.
14. Cyrus, king of Persia. This king authorized the Jews' return from captivity to their own land.
15. Xerxes, king of Persia. Esther was his queen.

How Old Were They?

1. Enoch was 365 years old when God "took him away."
2. Methusaleh was 969 years old when he died.
3. Abraham was 100 years old when Isaac was born.
4. Sarah was 90 when she gave birth to Isaac.
5. Isaac was 40 when he married Rebekah.
6. Joseph was 17 when he was sold by his brothers.
7. When he told Pharaoh, "Let my people go," Moses was 80.
8. Aaron was 83 when the Israelites left Egypt.
9. Caleb was 40 when he spied in Canaan.
10. Moses died at age 120.
11. Eli was 98 when he heard of the death of his sons, then fell and died himself.
12. Both Saul and David were 30 when they became king.
13. When Joash assumed the throne, he was seven.
14. Josiah was eight at his coronation.
15. Jesus was 12 when he visited the temple with his parents.
16. Jesus was about 30 when he began his ministry.
17. Jairus's daughter was 12 when Jesus healed her.

Notable Quotables

These eight Old Testament passages are quoted most often in the New Testament:

1. Psalm 110:1. "The Lord says to my Lord: 'Sit at my right hand until I make your enemies a footstool for your feet.'"
2. Daniel 12:1. "At that time Michael, the great prince who protects your people, will arise. There will be a time of distress such as has not happened from the beginning of nations until then. But at that time your people—everyone whose name is found written in the book—will be delivered."
3. Isaiah 6:1. "In the year that King Uzziah died, I saw the Lord seated on a throne, high and exalted, and the train of his robe filled the temple."
4. Ezekiel 1:26-28. "Above the expanse over their heads was what looked like a throne of sapphire, and high above on the throne was a figure like that of a man. I saw that from what appeared to be his waist up he looked like glowing metal, as if full of fire, and that from there down he looked like fire; and brilliant light surrounded him. Like the appearance of a rainbow in the clouds on a rainy day, so was the radiance around him. This was the appearance of the likeness of the glory of the Lord. When I saw it, I fell facedown, and I heard the voice of one speaking."
5. 2 Chronicles 18:18 (see also 1 Kings 22:19; Psalm 47:8). "Therefore hear the word of the Lord: I saw the Lord sitting on his throne with all the host of heaven standing on his right and on his left."
6. Psalm 2:7. "I will proclaim the decree of the Lord: He said to me, 'You are my Son; today I have become your Father.'"
7. Isaiah 53:7. "He was oppressed and afflicted, yet he did not open his mouth; he was led like a lamb to the slaughter, and as a sheep before her shearers is silent, so he did not open his mouth."
8. Leviticus 19:18. "Do not seek revenge or bear a grudge against one of your people, but love your neighbor as yourself. I am the Lord."

Weddings and Divorces

1. Sarah egged Abraham into sending away Hagar, the handmaid by whom he had fathered Ishmael (Genesis 21:9-14).
2. Laban threw a feast when he gave his firstborn daughter to Jacob in marriage. Unfortunately, Jacob wanted the second born (Genesis 29:22-25).
3. Samson invited many to a seven-day wedding feast, with 30 in the wedding party. But something happened to make him angry. He killed a bunch of people, and his fiancée ended up marrying one of his groomsmen (Judges 14:10-20).

4. After the exile in Babylon, Ezra urged the returning Jews to divorce their foreign wives (Ezra 10).
5. After Queen Vashti refused to come when he called, King Xerxes issued a court order banning Queen Vashti from ever appearing in his presence (Esther 1:19).
6. God said he divorced Israel for infidelity (Jeremiah 3:8).
7. At Cana in Galilee, Jesus was at a wedding reception that ran out of wine. Using stone pots of water, Jesus whipped up some new potables. It was his first miracle (Matthew 22:1-10).
8. Jesus told a parable of a wedding banquet that the invited guests didn't feel like attending. So the host sent his servants "out to the highways and byways" to find other guests (Matthew 22:1-14).
9. In another parable, five young women who attended a wedding missed all the fun because they ran out of oil for their lamps and had to run out for more supplies (Matthew 25:1-13).
10. At the end of time, there will be a wedding feast to end all wedding feasts, as Christ (the Lamb) takes the church as his bride (Revelation 19:7-9).

Love Is Not . . .
(from 1 Corinthians 13)

1. Envious
2. Boastful
3. Proud
4. Rude
5. Self-seeking
6. Easily angered
7. Keeping record of wrongs
8. Delighting in evil

Love Is . . .
(from 1 Corinthians 13)

1. Patient
2. Kind
3. Rejoicing with the truth
4. Always protecting
5. Always trusting
6. Always hoping
7. Always persevering

Judges of Israel

1. Othniel (Judges 3:9-11). Ruled 40 years.
2. Ehud (3:15, 30). Ruled 80 years.

3. Shamgar (3:31). Length of rule unknown.
4. Deborah (4:4; 5:31). Ruled 40 years.
5. Gideon (8:28). Ruled 40 years.
6. Tola (10:1-2). Ruled 23 years.
7. Jair (10:3). Ruled 22 years.
8. Jephthah (11:32; 12:7). Ruled 6 years.
9. Ibzan (12:8-10). Ruled 7 years.
10. Elon (12:11-12). Ruled 10 years.
11. Abdon (12:13-15). Ruled 8 years.
12. Samson (15:20). Ruled 20 years.
13. Eli (1 Samuel 4:18). Ruled 40 years.
14. Samuel (1 Samuel 7:15). Length of rule unknown.
15. Joel and Abijah (1 Samuel 8:1-2). Length of rule unknown.

Dreamers

1. Abram (Genesis 15:1)
2. Abimelech (Genesis 20:3)
3. Jacob (Genesis 28:12)
4. Laban (Genesis 31:24)
5. Joseph, son of Jacob (Genesis 37:5)
6. The cupbearer and baker in prison with Joseph (Genesis 40:5)
7. Pharaoh (Genesis 41:1)
8. A man in Gideon's camp (Judges 7:13)
9. Samuel (1 Samuel 3:15)
10. Solomon (1 Kings 3:5)
11. Job (Job 7:14)
12. Ezekiel (Ezekiel 43:3)
13. Nebuchadnezzar (Daniel 2:1)
14. Daniel (Daniel 7:1)
15. "Your old men" (Joel 2:28)
16. Zechariah, the prophet (Zechariah 1:8)
17. Joseph, husband of Mary (Matthew 1:20)
18. The magi (Matthew 2:12)
19. Pilate's wife (Matthew 27:19)
20. Ananias (Acts 9:10)
21. Cornelius (Acts 10:3)
22. Peter (Acts 10:9-20)
23. Paul (Acts 16:9)

Paul's Prayers

1. For Christians in Rome: "First, I thank my God through Jesus
   Christ for all of you, because your faith is being reported all
   over the world. God, whom I serve with my whole heart in
   preaching the gospel of his Son, is my witness how constantly

I remember you in my prayers at all times; and I pray that now at last by God's will the way may be opened for me to come to you" (Romans 1:8-10).

2. For Israel: "Brothers, my heart's desire and prayer to God for the Israelites is that they may be saved" (Romans 10:1).

3. For Christians in Corinth: "Now we pray to God that you will not do anything wrong. Not that people will see that we have stood the test but that you will do what is right even though we may seem to have failed. . . . Our prayer is for your perfection" (2 Corinthians 13:7, 9).

4. For Christians in Ephesus: "I have not stopped giving thanks for you, remembering you in my prayers. I keep asking that the God of our Lord Jesus Christ, the glorious Father, may give you the Spirit of wisdom and revelation, so that you may know him better. I pray also that the eyes of your heart may be enlightened in order that you may know the hope to which he has called you, the riches of his glorious inheritance in the saints, and his incomparably great power for us who believe. That power is like the working of his mighty strength, which he exerted in Christ when he raised him from the dead and seated him at his right hand in the heavenly realms, far above all rule and authority, power and dominion, and every title that can be given, not only in the present age but also in the one to come" (Ephesians 1:16-21).

5. Again, for Christians in Ephesus: "I pray that out of his glorious riches he may strengthen you with power through his Spirit in your inner being, so that Christ may dwell in your hearts through faith. And I pray that you, being rooted and established in love, may have power, together with all the saints, to grasp how wide and long and high and deep is the love of Christ, and to know this love that surpasses knowledge—that you may be filled to the measure of all the fullness of God" (Ephesians 3:16-19).

6. For Christians in Philippi: "And this is my prayer: that your love may abound more and more in knowledge and depth of insight, so that you may be able to discern what is best and may be pure and blameless until the day of Christ, filled with the fruit of righteousness that comes through Jesus Christ—to the glory and praise of God" (Philippians 1:9-11).

7. For Christians in Colosse: "We have not stopped praying for you and asking God to fill you with the knowledge of his will through all spiritual wisdom and understanding. And we pray this in order that you may live a life worthy of the Lord and may please him in every way: bearing fruit in every good

work, growing in the knowledge of God, being strengthened with all power according to his glorious might so that you may have great endurance and patience, and joyfully giving thanks to the Father, who has qualified you to share in the inheritance of the saints in the kingdom of light" (Colossians 1:9–12).

8. For Christians in Thessalonica: "May God himself, the God of peace, sanctify you through and through. May your whole spirit, soul and body be kept blameless at the coming of our Lord Jesus Christ" (1 Thessalonians 5:23).

9. For Timothy: "I thank God, whom I serve, as my forefathers did, with a clear conscience, as night and day I constantly remember you in my prayers" (2 Timothy 1:3).

10. For Philemon: "I pray that you may be active in sharing your faith, so that you will have a full understanding of every good thing we have in Christ" (Philemon 1:6).

INFORMATION PLEASE

Ten Musical Instruments in Scripture

1. Ram's horn/shophar (Exodus 19:13)
2. Trumpet (Psalm 150:3)
3. Flute/double pipe (Job 21:12; Isaiah 5:12)
4. Lyre (Psalm 33:2)
5. Harp/psaltery (Psalm 43:4)
6. Tambourine/timbrel (Psalm 149:3)
7. Cymbals (Psalm 150:5)
8. Zither/trigon/sackbut (Daniel 3:5)
9. Bells (Exodus 28:33-34)
10. Brass/metal gong (1 Corinthians 13:1)

Ten Tools Used by Biblical Farmers

1. Ax
2. Fans (winnowing)
3. File
4. Goad
5. Harrow
6. Mattock
7. Plough
8. Sickle
9. Sieve
10. Yoke

Eleven Weapons of the Bible

1. Ax
2. Battering ram
3. Bow and arrow
4. Knives/daggers
5. Poison
6. Rocks
7. Slingshot
8. Spear
9. Swords

10. Torches
11. Whip

Occupations of Men in the Bible

1. Astronomer (magus)
2. Carpenter
3. Farmer
4. Fisherman
5. Innkeeper
6. King
7. Magician
8. Merchant
9. Prophet
10. Rabbi
11. Shepherd
12. Silversmith/goldsmith
13. Slave
14. Tax collector
15. Tentmaker
16. Warrior

Occupations of Women in the Bible

1. Cook
2. Dancer
3. Deaconess
4. Helper (Eve)
5. Judge
6. Musician
7. Prophetess
8. Prostitute
9. Queen
10. Seamstress
11. Servant or slave
12. Shepherdess
13. Water bearer
14. Wife and mother

Twenty-one Mountains and Hills of Scripture

1. Ararat (Genesis 8:4)
2. Calvary/Golgotha (Matthew 27:33)
3. Carmel (1 Kings 18:19-20)
4. Ebal (Joshua 8:30)
5. Ephron (Joshua 15:9)

6. Gaash (Joshua 24:30)
7. Gareb (Jeremiah 31:39)
8. Gerizim (Deuteronomy 27:12)
9. Halak (Joshua 11:17)
10. Hor (Numbers 20:22)
11. Horeb/Sinai (Exodus 3:1-10; 19:17-19)
12. Jearim (Joshua 15:10)
13. Moreh (Genesis 12:6)
14. Moriah (2 Chronicles 3:1)
15. Mount of Olives/Olivet (Acts 1:12)
16. Mount of Transfiguration (Matthew 17:1-3)
17. Nebo (Deuteronomy 32:49)
18. Peor (Numbers 23:28)
19. Pisgah (Deuteronomy 3:27)
20. Tabor (Judges 4:6)
21. Zion (Isaiah 24:23)

Ten Islands of Scripture

1. Cauda (Acts 27:16)
2. Cos (Acts 21:1)
3. Crete (Acts 27:7-13)
4. Cyprus (Isaiah 23:1)
5. Kios/Chios (Acts 20:15)
6. Malta/Melita (Acts 28:1)
7. Mitylene on Lesbos (Acts 20:14)
8. Patmos (Revelation 1:9)
9. Rhodes (Ezekiel 27:15)
10. Samos (Acts 20:15)

Eighteen Valleys of Scripture

1. Aijalon (Joshua 10:12)
2. Baca (Psalm 84:6)
3. Beracah (2 Chronicles 20:26)
4. Bithron (2 Samuel 2:29)
5. Craftsmen (Nehemiah 11:35)
6. Elah (1 Samuel 17:2)
7. Eshcol (Numbers 13:23)
8. Hamon Gog (Ezekiel 39:11)
9. Ben Hinnom (Joshua 15:8)
10. Iphtah El (Joshua 19:27)
11. Jehoshaphat (Joel 3:2)
12. Jordan (Genesis 13:10)
13. Kidron (2 Samuel 15:23)
14. Rephaim (2 Samuel 23:13)

15. Salt (2 Samuel 8:13)
16. Siddim (Genesis 14:3)
17. Sorek (Judges 16:4)
18. Zephathah (2 Chronicles 14:10)

Ten Key Rivers of the Bible

1. Abana (2 Kings 5:12)
2. Arnon (Numbers 21:13)
3. Euphrates (Genesis 2:14)
4. Jabbok (Genesis 32:22)
5. Jordan (Numbers 34:12)
6. Kerith/Cherith (1 Kings 17:3)
7. Kishon (Judges 4:7)
8. Nile (Genesis 41:1)
9. Pharpar (2 Kings 5:12)
10. Tigris (Daniel 10:4)

Other Biblical Bodies of Water

1. Ahava Canal
2. Besor Ravine
3. Dead Sea
4. Habor River
5. Kebar River
6. Mediterranean Sea
7. Nimrim Brook
8. Pison River
9. Ravine of the Poplars
10. Red Sea
11. Sea of Galilee
12. Ulai Canal

Cities Visited by Paul

1. Antioch
2. Athens
3. Berea
4. Corinth
5. Damascus
6. Derbe
7. Ephesus
8. Galatia
9. Iconium
10. Jerusalem
11. Lystra

12. Philippi
13. Phrygia
14. Salamis
15. Thessalonica
16. Troas

Means of Transportation in the Bible

1. Camel
2. Caravan (by foot or various animals)
3. Chariot (sometimes of fire)
4. Donkey
5. Foot
6. Horse
7. Ox
8. Swimming
9. Barge
10. Boat
11. Ship
12. Ark

Metals and Minerals in the Bible

1. Brimstone
2. Copper
3. Flint
4. Gold
5. Iron
6. Lead
7. Nitre/Natron
8. Salt
9. Silver
10. Tin

Gems in the Bible

1. Agate
2. Amethyst
3. Beryl
4. Coral
5. Diamond
6. Emerald
7. Jasper
8. Onyx
9. Pearl
10. Ruby

11. Sapphire
12. Topaz

Gems on Aaron's Breastplate

The 12 gems were arranged in this order:

First row: ruby, topaz, beryl
Second row: turquoise, sapphire, emerald
Third row: jacinth, agate, amethyst
Fourth row: chrysolite, onyx, jasper

Birds in the Bible

1. Chicken/fowl
2. Dove/pigeon
3. Eagle
4. Hawk
5. Heron
6. Osprey
7. Ostrich
8. Owl
9. Partridge
10. Peacock
11. Pelican/cormorant
12. Quail
13. Raven
14. Rooster
15. Sparrow
16. Stork
17. Swallow/swift
18. Vulture

Beasts in the Bible

1. Ape
2. Bat
3. Bear
4. Behemoth
5. Camel
6. Cattle
7. Deer
8. Dog
9. Donkey
10. Fish
11. Fox/jackal
12. Goat

13. Horse
14. Hyena
15. Leopard
16. Leviathan
17. Lion
18. Ox
19. Pig
20. Rabbit
21. Rat
22. Sheep
23. Whale
24. Wild donkey
25. Wolf

Insects in the Bible

1. Ants
2. Bees/hornets
3. Caterpillars
4. Crickets/beetles
5. Fleas
6. Gnats
7. Grasshoppers
8. Lice
9. Locusts
10. Moths
11. Spiders

Herbs and Spices in the Bible

1. Bitter herbs
2. Cinnamon
3. Coriander
4. Fitches (poppies)
5. Frankincense
6. Gall
7. Garlic
8. Hyssop
9. Mallow
10. Mint
11. Mustard
12. Myrrh
13. Rue
14. Saffron
15. Spikewood

Grains and Nuts in the Bible

1. Almonds
2. Barley
3. Corn
4. Flax
5. Millet
6. Pistachio nuts
7. Rye
8. Wheat

Fruits and Vegetables in the Bible

1. Apples
2. Beans
3. Cucumbers
4. Figs
5. Grapes
6. Leeks
7. Lentils (pottage)
8. Mandrakes
9. Melons
10. Mulberries
11. Olives
12. Onions
13. Pomegranates
14. Raisins

Flowers in the Bible

1. Lily
2. Myrtle
3. Poppy
4. Rose
5. Saffron
6. Spikenard
7. Wildflowers ("flowers of the field")

Trees in the Bible

1. Acacia
2. Almond
3. Ash
4. Cedar
5. Chestnut
6. Cypress
7. Ebony (Hebrew, *hobinim*)

8. Fig
9. Fir (Hebrew, *berosh*)
10. Gopher wood
11. Laurel
12. Linden (Hebrew, *elan*)
13. Myrtle
14. Oak
15. Olive
16. Palm/date
17. Pine (Hebrew, *tidhar*)
18. Tamarisk
19. Thine
20. Willow

Diseases in the Bible

1. Blindness
2. Boils
3. Canker (gangrene)
4. Consumption
5. Deafness
6. Fever (ague)
7. Lameness
8. Leprosy
9. Paralysis
10. Plagues (epidemics)
11. Worms

Pagan Gods Named in the Bible

1. Adrammelech, worshiped by the Sepharvites (2 Kings 17:31)
2. Anammelech, worshiped by the Sepharvites (2 Kings 17:31)
3. Artemis (Diana), worshiped by all Asia (Acts 19:28)
4. Asherah, worshiped by the Canaanites (2 Chronicles 24:18)
5. Ashima, worshiped by the Hamathites (2 Kings 17:30)
6. Astoreth (Astarte), worshiped by the Sidonians (1 Kings 11:5)
7. Baal, worshiped by the Canaanites (Judges 2:13)
8. Baal-Zebub, worshiped by the Philistines (2 Kings 1:2)
9. Bel, worshiped by the Babylonians (Jeremiah 51:44)
10. Castor and Pollux, worshiped by the Greeks (Acts 28:11)
11. Chemosh, worshiped by the Moabites (1 Kings 11:7)
12. Dagon, worshiped by the Philistines (1 Samuel 5:7)
13. Destiny, worshiped by the Canaanites (Isaiah 65:11)
14. Fortune, worshiped by the Canaanites (Isaiah 65:11)
15. Hermes, worshiped by the Greeks (Acts 14:12)
16. Marduk, worshiped by the Babylonians (Jeremiah 50:2)

17. Molech, worshiped by the Ammonites (1 Kings 11:5)
18. Nebo, worshiped by the Babylonians (Isaiah 46:1)
19. Nergal, worshiped by the Cuthahites (2 Kings 17:30)
20. Nibhaz, worshiped by the Avvites (2 Kings 17:31)
21. Nisroch, worshiped by the Assyrians (Isaiah 37:38)
22. Rephan, worshiped by the Egyptians (Acts 7:43)
23. Rimmon, worshiped by the Assyrians (2 Kings 5:18)
24. Succoth Benoth, worshiped by the Babylonians (2 Kings 17:30)
25. Tammuz, worshiped by the Babylonians (Ezekiel 8:14)
26. Tartak, worshiped by the Avvites (2 Kings 17:31)
27. Zeus, worshiped by the Greeks (Acts 14:12)

SCHOLARSHIP 'N' THINGS

Translations

Twelve Bible Versions Since 1970

1. *New American Bible* (1970)
2. *The New English Bible* (1970)
3. *The Living Bible* (1971)
4. *New American Standard Bible* (1971)
5. New International Version (1973)
6. *Beck's: An American Translation* (1976)
7. *Good News Bible,* Today's English Version (1976)
8. New King James Version (1982)
9. New Century Version (1984)
10. Contemporary English Version (1985)
11. *Revised English Bible* (1989)
12. New Living Translation (1996)

Most-Popular Bible Translations

Over the last four centuries, the King James Version has easily been the most-popular English Bible translation. But what's most popular now? Well, over the last dozen years or so, a handful of new versions has been duking it out with the King James Version for best-seller status.

1983

1. King James Version
2. New International Version
3. *New American Standard Bible*
4. *The Living Bible*
5. *Good News Bible,* Today's English Version

1984

1. King James Version
2. *The Living Bible*
3. New International Version
4. *New American Standard Bible*
5. New King James Version

1989

1. New International Version
2. King James Version
3. *The Living Bible*
4. New King James Version
5. *New American Bible*

1996*

1. New International Version
2. Contemporary English Version
3. King James Version
4. New Living Translation
5. *The Message*

*Based on September 1996 sales in Christian stores. Source: CBA Service Corporation and Spring Arbor Distributors via *Christian Retailing* magazine.

Ten Bible Translations You've Probably Never Heard Of

1. *The Primitive New Testament,* translated by William Whiston (1745)
2. *Young People's Bible,* or *The Scriptures Corrected, Explained and Simplified,* by Harriet Newell Jones (1901)
3. *The Emphasized Bible,* by J. B. Rotherham (1902)
4. *Numeric New Testament,* edited by Ivan Panin (1914)
5. *The Shorter Bible,* by C. F. Kent (1918)
6. *A Plainer Bible for Plain People in Plain America,* by F. S. Ballentine (1922)
7. *The Riverside New Testament,* by W. G. Ballantine (1923)
8. *Revision of Challoner's Edition of the Rheims New Testament,* by J. A. Cary (1935)
9. *The Letchworth Version in Modern English,* by T. F. and R. E. Ford (1948)
10. *The Berkeley Bible,* by Gerrit Verkuyl (1959)

Twelve Key Translators of the Bible

1. Jerome. Produced the Latin Vulgate, which the church used for centuries.
2. John Wycliffe. One of the first to put the Bible in English.
3. Martin Luther. Led the Reformation that finally trusted common people with the Scriptures, but he also translated a groundbreaking German Bible.
4. William Tyndale. Two centuries after Wycliffe, Tyndale fought persecution to produce an English translation.

5. Miles Coverdale. An assistant of Tyndale, Coverdale produced the *Great Bible* that heavily influenced the King James Version.

6. William Whittingham. A major translator of the *Geneva Bible,* another forerunner of the King James Version.

7. Brooke Foss Westcott. British bishop/scholar who helped pull together a more reliable Greek text of the New Testament and served on the committee for the English Revised Version.

8. Phillips. Another British church leader, Phillips began the spate of modern translations with his neat paraphrase.

9. Kenneth N. Taylor. His *Living Bible* started as a gift to his kids. This paraphrase has been a gift to the world.

10. Edwin Palmer. Headed up the committee that produced the New International Version, which is quickly becoming a modern standard.

11. Eugene Nida. A force behind the *Good News Bible,* Nida developed the "dynamic equivalence" theory that has revolutionized modern translation work around the world.

12. Missionary translators. Even as you read this, there are missionaries interviewing tribespeople or hunched over laptop computers, giving their lives to get the Scriptures into new languages.

Ten Translations of Philippians 4:19

1. "My God shall supply all your need according to his riches in glory by Christ Jesus" (King James Version).

2. "My God will gloriously supply all your needs with his wealth, through your union with Christ Jesus" (Goodspeed).

3. "And my God will give you all you have need of from the wealth of his glory in Christ Jesus" (Basic English).

4. "And with all his abundant wealth through Christ Jesus, my God will supply all your needs" (Today's English Version).

5. "You can be sure that God will take care of everything you need, his generosity exceeding even yours in the glory that pours from Jesus" *(The Message).*

6. "And it is he who will supply all your needs from his riches in glory, because of what Christ Jesus has done for us" *(The Living Bible).*

7. "My God will supply all that you need from his glorious resources in Christ Jesus" (Phillips).

8. "And this same God who takes care of me will supply all your needs from his glorious riches, which have been given to us in Christ Jesus" (New Living Translation).

9. "But my God—so great is His wealth of glory in Christ Jesus—will fully supply every need of yours" (Weymouth).

10. "My God, who is very rich in Christ Jesus, will use his riches
to give you everything you need" (New Century Version).

Archaeology and the Ancient World

Ten Things in the Bible That Archaeologists Have Never Found

1. The Garden of Eden
2. Noah's ark
3. Joseph's coat
4. Aaron's rod that budded
5. Rahab's scarlet cord
6. Gideon's broken pitchers
7. David's harp
8. Ezekiel's wheel in a wheel
9. John the Baptist's camel-hair garment
10. Moldy bread left over from Jesus' feeding of the 5,000

Ten Things in the Bible That Archaeologists Have Found

1. The Moabite stone, which tells of the Moabites' revolt against
Israel (see 2 Kings 3)
2. The Black Obelisk, which tells of King Jehu submitting to
Shalmaneser III
3. Sennacherib's Prism, which tells of King Hezekiah being
"shut up like a bird in a cage" (see 2 Chronicles 32)
4. The clay seal of Baruch, Jeremiah's scribe
5. Hezekiah's Tunnel, running through 1,700 feet of solid rock
6. The Lachish Letters, describing the attack on that city in Jeremiah's time
7. Inscription in Corinth naming Erastus (see Romans 16:23)
8. The theater at Ephesus (see Acts 19:29)
9. The Pool of Siloam (see John 9:7)
10. A first-century fishing boat from the Sea of Galilee

Ten Tells and What They Have Told

A *tell* is an archaeological excavation site. Deep down, these remnants
of ancient societies have a lot to say. Dig?

1. Ur, Abraham's hometown, revealed an advanced civilization in
the patriarch's time and evidence of an earlier flood.
2. Babylon revealed the greatness of Nebuchadnezzar's kingdom.
Tablets were found bearing the names of Jehoiachin, a king of
Judah, and his sons.
3. Nimrud, located 20 miles south of Nineveh, revealed the
Black Obelisk of Shalmaneser III, depicting Jehu, king of
Israel, kissing the feet of Shalmaneser.

4. Ugarit in Syria revealed the Ras Shamra tablets, containing valuable information on the social, religious, and political life in Old Testament times.

5. More recently, Ebla has revealed a vast library of more than 20,000 tablets. Names similar to the Old Testament patriarchs are noted. Because the language bears similarities to both Hebrew and Ugaritic, new insights into the Old Testament will be derived as scholars delve deeper.

6. Ashdod has revealed new understanding of the Philistine people who lived there.

7. Beersheba, a key city in Israel from the days of Abraham, has revealed information on the time of the kings of Judah and its southern fortification.

8. Caesarea Maritima has revealed an inscription regarding Pilate and an amazing seaport developed by Herod.

9. Jericho is revealing information on a city that may be the oldest in the world, perhaps going back to 7000 B.C.

10. Lachish, captured by Nebuchadnezzar along with Jerusalem in the sixth century B.C., is revealing much corroborative insight on the prophet Jeremiah and the last days of Judah.

What the Dead Sea Scrolls Contain

A treasure trove of ancient scrolls, the library of a scribal community at Qumran, near the Dead Sea, has provided archaeologists with great information about the first century A.D. Here's just some of what the collection includes:

1. Lengthy sections of Isaiah

2. An almost complete scroll of Psalms

3. Several versions of the apocryphal book of Tobit

4. Sections of the apocryphal books of Judith, Ecclesiasticus, Baruch, 1 and 2 Maccabees, and the Wisdom of Solomon

5. Multiple fragments of the ancient book of Enoch

6. Fragments or mentions of several other pseudepigraphal books: Jubilees, the Book of Noah, the Testament of Levi, the Testament of Naphtali, the Sayings of Moses, and others

7. A lengthy commentary on Habakkuk

8. Commentaries on Genesis, 2 Samuel, Isaiah, Hosea, Micah, Nahum, and Zephaniah

9. Many sectarian documents regarding life in this Essene community

10. Collections of biblical passages and commentary regarding the Messiah

Ten Ancient Civilizations That Believed in the Great Flood

1. Egypt. The Egyptians believed the gods purified the earth.
2. England. The Druids believed that a patriarch was saved in a big ship.
3. Greece. The Greeks believed Deucalion built an ark, sent on doves.
4. China. The founder of Chinese civilization is said to have survived the flood along with his wife, his three sons, and their wives.
5. India. In Hindu tradition, Manu built a ship and alone survived the deluge.
6. Polynesia. Tradition says that eight escaped.
7. Mexico. Mexicans believed that one man, his wife, and his children were saved in a ship.
8. Peru. One man and one woman are said to have been saved in a box.
9. America. Different Native American tribes tell differing stories about a man who survived by building a ship that landed on a high mountain.
10. Greenland. The earth tilted over; everyone drowned except one man and one woman.

Twelve World Events between David's Time and Ezra's

1. Mayan civilization thrives in Central America.
2. Phoenicians establish Carthage (810 B.C.).
3. *Iliad* and *Odyssey* written, perhaps by Homer.
4. First Olympic Games (776).
5. According to legend, Romulus founds Rome (753).
6. Nubians rule Egypt 750–661.
7. The Acropolis is established in Athens.
8. Assyrians rule Mideast, then fall to Egypt and Babylon at Carchemish (616)
9. Lao-Tse (born 604) develops Taoism.
10. Buddha (563–483) starts Buddhism in India.
11. Confucius (551–479) starts saying witty things.
12. Aeschylus writes *Oedipus Rex*.

Ten Important Things That Happened between Malachi and Matthew

1. Alexander the Great of Macedonia conquers the Persian Empire (336–323 B.C.); dies in Babylon in 323.
2. Alexander's generals divide up the empire. The Ptolemies win out in Palestine (321–198). Ptolemy I settles in Alexandria,

rules Palestine kindly; many Jews come to live in Alexandria. Greek culture is spread throughout the region.

3. Under Ptolemy II, translation of the Old Testament into Greek (the Septuagint) begins.

4. Antiochus III overpowers Palestine, expelling the Ptolemies (198). Palestine is annexed to the Seleucid empire.

5. Antiochus IV Epiphanes prohibits Judaism, sacks Jerusalem, profanes temple, and offers sacrifices to Zeus on the altar of burnt offerings.

6. The Maccabean revolt, led by Mattathias and his five sons, is successful. In 166, under Judas the Maccabee, the Syrian armies are defeated and the temple is cleansed and rededicated.

7. The Hasmonean period extends from 166 to 63, the Septuagint is completed, and many of the apocryphal books of the Old Testament are written.

8. Khirbet Qumran, headquarters of the Dead Sea Essenes, was founded about 110. Many of the Dead Sea Scrolls date from about that time.

9. In 63, Pompey brings the land of Palestine under Roman control and (along with Julius Caesar and Crassus) forms the First Triumvirate.

10. Under a Roman grant, Herod the Great is made king of Judea in 37.

Bible Study

How to Study the Bible

1. With a regenerate mind (1 Corinthians 2:14)
2. With a willing mind (John 7:17)
3. With an obedient mind (James 1:21-22)
4. With a teachable mind (Matthew 11:25)
5. With open eyes (Psalm 119:18)
6. In awe of God's holiness (Exodus 3:5)
7. Remembering it is God's Word (1 Thessalonians 2:13)

Principles of Inductive Bible Study

1. Observe the whole.
2. Observe each part.
3. Summarize the whole.
4. Ask: What does it say?
5. Ask: What does it mean?
6. Ask: What does it mean to me?

Types of Bible Study Resources

1. Assorted versions: It often helps to use a paraphrase alongside a translation.
2. Study Bible: Bible text with notes on the meaning.
3. Topical or Reference Bible: Sorts Scripture by topic or includes cross-referencing on certain topics.
4. Concordance: Index of words in Scripture. If you want to find the location of a verse you sort of know.
5. Bible Dictionary: Gives background on various Bible-related topics.
6. Bible Handbook: Gives some background; often goes book by book through the Bible with introductions and outlines.
7. Commentary: Either on the whole Bible or on individual books or sections, it is some scholar's idea of what the text means.
8. Atlas: Maps that give you an idea of the historical and geographical sweep of Scripture.
9. Bible Survey/Introduction: Overview of Scripture. Often a good resource for beginning students.
10. Bible Study Guide: Step-by-step instruction in certain texts, with lots of questions and sometimes blanks to fill in. For individuals or groups.

Shapers of Bible Study

Many Bible study groups are meeting regularly, all around the world. But it wasn't always this way. Who has blazed the trail for us to get here? (Apologies to Catholic readers. Volumes could be written—have been written, I'm sure—about the development of group Bible study in the Roman tradition: monks, Jesuits, universities, Vatican II, basic Christian communities around the world, etc. But you'll have to look elsewhere. That's outside my ken.)

1. Origen. This third-century scholar took the Bible seriously, even publishing a "parallel" text of Hebrew and Greek translations.
2. Augustine. He wrenched Bible interpretation away from its dependence on wild allegorizing and began to look for the plain meaning of a text.
3. Andrew of St. Victor's and Stephen Langton. In the 1100s, these scholars were on the cutting edge of Bible study, pushing Augustine's fourfold approach: history; etiology (the "why?" questions); analogy; and allegory.
4. Thomas Aquinas. Allegory didn't die easily; Aquinas promoted a rational understanding of the Scriptures.
5. Martin Luther and John Calvin. Luther put the Scriptures in the language of the (German) people, with a "dynamic equiva-

lence" translation that was way ahead of its time; Calvin pushed a French translation. Both encouraged the common folk to study Scripture.

6. The Puritans and Moravians. These groups and others developed communal Bible study, gathering regularly to discuss the meaning of Scripture and to pray.

7. John Wesley. Heavily influenced by the Moravians, John Wesley's "method" included regular meetings with a "class"—basically a Bible study group.

8. Karl Barth. Love him or hate him, but this German pastor moderated the deconstruction of liberal Bible scholarship and urged people to look for the personal, practical meaning of a text.

9. InterVarsity and the Inductive Movement. In the twentieth century, several organizations have promoted group Bible study that pointedly lets the Bible speak for itself, including the Navigators and Neighborhood Bible Studies.

10. Lyman Coleman and Serendipity. The 1960s were about breaking the rules, and Coleman was one of the first to concentrate on making Bible study fun. Since then, Serendipity has developed solid group-dynamics theory along with their wacky questions.

Ten Tips for Leading Group Bible Studies

1. Don't prepare too much. Put your prep time into developing good questions.

2. Have everyone sit in a circle. You need to see them all, and they need to see each other.

3. Appreciate the value of a good icebreaker, preferably one that fits the theme of the study.

4. Go for the child in people. Icebreakers (and other questions) often work best if they refer to some childhood memory or emotion—that was a key learning time for all of us.

5. Make sure everyone has a translation he or she can understand.

6. Read the text. Really read it. See what it says. Don't jump to interpretation before you catch its simple meaning.

7. Let the Bible teach. You ask questions.

8. Stand up to preachers. I'm talking about group members who pronounce the meaning of the text for everyone else. Keep the door open for discussion, even if that means shushing a loudmouth.

9. Be gentle but persistent with wallflowers. Some people learn by listening and don't have much to say. Others are waiting to be asked.

10. Ask: "So what?" Press for an application of the truths you've been learning.

Six Characters in Search of a Bible Study

Like a bad sitcom, most Bible studies have certain stock characters you should be aware of.

1. The Watchdog. She keeps tabs on the group theologically. If you veer anywhere close to heresy, the Watchdog will lay down the law.
2. The Greek Geek. Even if this guy just took one semester of Greek in a correspondence course, he feels compelled to end every argument by appealing to "what it really means in the original."
3. The Tangent Waiting to Happen. Who knows how this person's mind works? But any verse can lead to another subject far, far away.
4. The Grump. Doesn't want to be there; doesn't want to talk.
5. The Life of the Party. Always ready with a joke, even when the group wants to get serious.
6. The Needer. The whole Bible study is suddenly about this person's problems—and the needer has lots of problems. Some experts call these people EGR—Extra Grace Required.

Three Characters You Need in a Bible Study

Yet to function well, a Bible study group needs three other characters. These roles need not be official positions, and often one person plays more than one role, but good groups have these things happening.

1. The Leader. Directing traffic, sensing needs, providing expertise, asking great questions, and synthesizing answers—strong leadership is crucial in a small group.
2. The Lookout. Often an assistant leader, this person watches other people in the group when the leader is focusing on the one person speaking. The Lookout reads reactions and draws people into the discussion.
3. The Mom. Whether male or female, this person cares for the basic comforts of the group members. Seats, temperature, refreshments, etc. In a home Bible study, this person is usually the host.

Ten Classic Resources for Personal or Group Bible Study

Thanks to Larry Sibley, the book-section editor of the now-defunct *Bible Newsletter,* where this list first appeared.

1. *Methodical Bible Study,* by Robert Traina (1952)
2. *Independent Bible Study,* by Irving Jensen (Moody, 1972)

3. *Enjoy Your Bible,* by Irving Jensen (Moody, 1969)
4. The Bible Self-Study Guide Series, written and edited by Irving Jensen (Moody)
5. *Leading Bible Discussions,* by James Nyquist and Jack Kuhatschek (InterVarsity, 1966)
6. *Discovering the Gospel of Mark,* by Jane Hollingsworth (Inter-Varsity, 1943/1966)
7. *Basic Christianity,* by Margaret Erb (InterVarsity, 1952)
8. *Teaching the Bible from the Inside Out, an Inductive Guide,* by Linda Walvoord Girard (Cook, 1978)
9. *How to Start a Bible Study,* by Marilyn Kunz and Catharine Schell (Neighborhood Bible Studies/Tyndale House, 1966)
10. *How-to Handbook for Bible Study Leaders,* by Gladys Hunt (Shaw, 1971)

Ten Principles of Bible Interpretation

1. Look for the plain meaning of the text. Don't go for elaborate schemes when the simple point is staring you in the face.
2. Understand the situational context of the text. Every biblical passage was written within a particular situation. Thus every interpretation has to adapt the meaning in some way from that situation to your own.
3. Take the literary genre of the text into account. Parable? Command? Narrative? Poem? Each genre has a particular sense to it.
4. Look for biblical consistency, but allow for creativity. If your interpretation of Romans totally disagrees with what Matthew says, you're doing something wrong. But allow for the fact that God reveals himself through different writers in different ways.
5. Give the New Testament priority over the Old. This is basic to the Christian faith. Old Testament law is good in that it shows us God's character, but the New Testament makes it clear that Christians are free from the law of Moses.
6. Treat biblical examples with care. Just because Abraham, Moses, or David did something doesn't mean you should do it.
7. Keep an open mind. Don't just use the Bible to prove what you already think. Let God surprise you.
8. Avoid legalism. Don't look for a command in every text.
9. Beware of "private interpretations." When someone says, "God showed me that this verse really means . . . ," watch out! You still need to weigh that interpretation against the rest of Scripture and rational thought.
10. Use reference books; don't worship them. The people who

write Bible study books are human, too. (Hey, even I wrote notes for a study Bible once.)

How to Deal with Bible Difficulties

Matthew says *tomayto,* Mark says *tomahto.* Should you call the whole thing off?

1. Know that an explanation exists, though you haven't found it yet.
2. Don't give up your trust in Scripture just because you can't solve a problem.
3. Study the context to see what the verses mean in their setting.
4. Do your homework—including word study.
5. Harmonize multiple accounts, understanding that different perspectives may yield different reports (especially in the Gospels).
6. Consult good commentaries.
7. Understand that there are some scribal errors.
8. Don't let the archaeologists bamboozle you. Some are quick to show how the latest digs disagree with biblical accounts. But remember that the Bible itself is an excellent historical document. If archaeologists don't take it seriously, they're violating the rules of their own trade.

Adapted from *An Encyclopedia of Bible Difficulties,* by Gleason L. Archer (Zondervan, 1982).

Eight Reasons to Trust the Gospels

The rage in liberal Bible scholarship lately has been to pick through the Gospels, questioning what Jesus really said and how much the writers made up. In a *Christianity Today* article ("Who Do Scholars Say That I Am?", March 4, 1996), scholar James R. Edwards gives eight reasons to believe the Gospels are accurate accounts of Jesus' ministry.

1. When the Gospels were written, many eyewitnesses of Jesus' ministry were still alive—and therefore could verify or debunk these reports.
2. The rabbinic tradition valued accuracy. Any attempt to teach the young church with false reports would have been doomed from the start.
3. Problematic, embarrassing material: The Gospels are not shy about showing the foibles of the apostles.
4. There are no parables in Acts or the Epistles. If (as liberal scholars suggest) the early church just invented the Gospels, which include many parables, why don't they use any parables in these other writings?

5. Paul's ideas are absent from the Gospels. Again, if the church invented the stories of Jesus, you would expect a backwash of Paul's theology into the Gospels, but it's not there.

6. In his epistles, Paul is careful to distinguish between his own teaching and that of Jesus (1 Corinthians 7:10, 12, 25).

7. Matthew and Luke use Mark faithfully. Though they expand on Mark's bare-bones reporting, they don't change it. If these were invented stories, wouldn't the Gospel writers invent widely different accounts?

8. The absence of the Gentile question. This was the dominant issue of the early church, but it's hard to find much about it in the Gospels.

Random Theological Terms (A to J)

I was going to go through the whole alphabet, but I nodded off after 10 letters. (Loosely adapted from *The Concise Dictionary of Christian Theology,* by Millard J. Erickson [Baker, 1986].)

1. *Antinomianism.* An opposition to law, specifically a rejection of the idea that the Christian's life must be governed by laws.

2. *Bibliolatry.* Worshiping the Bible (rather than God).

3. *Covenant theology.* A system that sees the relationship between God and humanity as a kind of agreement or contract. (Big among Presbyterians.)

4. *Demythologization.* A theological method that explains away the supernatural elements ("myths") of Scripture. Developed by Rudolf Bultmann.

5. *Existentialism.* A philosophy emphasizing existence over essence. Don't ask, "What is it?" Ask, "Does it exist?" (And wear a beret.)

6. *Functionalism.* A pragmatist philosophy that defines something by the effects it has. Functionalists like verbs rather than nouns or adjectives.

7. *Gnosticism.* A first-century movement that emphasized a "higher" knowledge (Greek, *gnosis*) that some special people received from God. Gnostics taught that physical matter was evil (or irrelevant) and denied the humanity of Jesus. First John was probably written to counter Gnostic theology.

8. *Heilsgeschichte. (Gesundheit!)* German for "salvation history"—the ongoing story of God's redemptive activity.

9. *Incarnational theology.* When theologians use the term, it's the Christian belief that the second person of the Trinity became human in the form of Jesus Christ. When ordinary folks use it, it means we Christians carry on Christ's work in the world.

10. *Justification.* God's restoration of a sinner to a state of righteousness ("just as if I'd never sinned").

QUOTES

Ten Quotes about the Bible from Famous People

1. Charles Dickens: "The New Testament is the best book the world has ever known or will know."
2. Samuel Taylor Coleridge: "For more than a thousand years the Bible, collectively taken, has gone hand in hand with civilization, science, law—in short, with the moral and intellectual cultivation of the species, always supporting and often leading the way."
3. Horace Greeley: "It is impossible to mentally or socially enslave a Bible-reading people."
4. Ulysses S. Grant: "Hold fast to the Bible as the sheet-anchor of your liberties; write its precepts in your hearts and practice them in your lives. To the influence of this book we are indebted for all the progress made in true civilization, and to this we must look as our guide for the future."
5. Thomas Jefferson: "I have always said . . . that the studious perusal of the sacred volume will make better citizens, better fathers, and better husbands."
6. Abraham Lincoln: "This great book is the best gift God has given to man. . . . But for it we could not know right from wrong."
7. Patrick Henry: "The Bible is worth all other books that have ever been printed."
8. Cecil B. DeMille: "The greatest source of material for motion pictures is the Bible, and almost any chapter in the Bible would serve as a basic idea for a motion picture."
9. Mark Twain: "Most people are bothered by those passages in Scripture which they cannot understand; but as for me, I always noticed that the passages in Scripture which trouble me most are those which I do understand."
10. Willye White, 1956 Olympic silver medalist, women's long jump: "I was nervous, so I read the New Testament. I read the verse about *have no fear,* and I felt relaxed. Then I jumped farther than I have ever jumped in my life."

Favorite Bible Verses of 10 Noted Christians

1. Francis of Assisi: "God forbid that I should glory, save in the cross of our Lord Jesus Christ" (Galatians 6:14, KJV).
2. William Penn: "This is the victory that overcometh the world, even our faith" (1 John 5:4, KJV).
3. Catherine Booth (Salvation Army): "My grace is sufficient for thee" (2 Corinthians 12:9, KJV).
4. Michael Faraday (famous physicist): "I . . . am persuaded that he is able to keep that which I have committed unto him against that day" (2 Timothy 1:12, KJV).
5. William Tyndale (Bible translator): "We love him, because he first loved us" (1 John 4:19, KJV).
6. John Newton: "Thou shalt remember that . . . the Lord thy God redeemed thee" (Deuteronomy 15:15, KJV).
7. William Wilberforce (leader in Britain's antislavery movement): "God be merciful to me a sinner" (Luke 18:13, KJV).
8. William Carey (founder of modern missions): "Lengthen thy cords, and strengthen thy stakes" (Isaiah 54:2, KJV).
9. Charles Haddon Spurgeon (London Baptist pastor and writer): "Look unto me, and be ye saved, all the ends of the earth" (Isaiah 45:22, KJV).
10. Martin Luther: "The just shall live by faith" (Romans 1:17, KJV).

Five Quotes about the Bible from Famous Christians

1. A. W. Tozer: "I did not go through the Book. The Book went through me."
2. F. F. Bruce: "The Bible was never intended to be a book for scholars and specialists only. From the very beginning it was intended to be everybody's book, and that is what it continues to be."
3. Thomas Merton: "By reading the Scriptures I am so renewed that all nature seems renewed around me and with me. The sky seems to be a pure, a cooler blue, the trees a deeper green. . . . The whole world is charged with the glory of God and I feel fire and music . . . under my feet."
4. Charles Haddon Spurgeon: "Nobody ever outgrows Scripture; the book widens and deepens with our years."
5. John Chrysostom: "It is not possible ever to exhaust the mind of the Scriptures. It is a well that has no bottom."

Ten Shakespearean Quotations That Sound As If They Come from the Bible but Don't

1. "The devil can cite Scripture for his purpose." From *The Merchant of Venice*

2. "In time we hate that which we often fear." From *The Tragedy of Antony and Cleopatra*

3. "O, how bitter a thing it is to look into happiness through another man's eyes!" From *As You Like It*

4. "Neither a borrower nor a lender be. / . . . This above all—to thine own self be true, / And it must follow, as the night the day, / Thou canst not then be false to any man." From *Hamlet*

5. "Virtue is bold, and goodness never fearful." From *Measure for Measure*

6. "If I could pray to move, prayers would move me; / But I am constant as the northern star." From *The Tragedy of Julius Caesar*

7. "Do not as some ungracious pastors do, / Show me the steep and thorny way to heaven." From *Hamlet*

8. "The evil that men do lives after them, / The good is oft interred with their bones." From *The Tragedy of Julius Caesar*

9. "I am that way going to temptation / Where prayers cross." From *Measure for Measure*

10. "And death once dead, there's no more dying then." From Sonnet 146

PART 10

USING OUR IMAGINATIONS

The Bible tells us an awful lot, but what about the things it *doesn't* tell us? If we could interview some of the great characters of Scripture, what would they say about their likes and dislikes?

John the Baptist's Favorite Restaurants

Of course, John spent most of his time baptizing people. But a man's got to eat, even if his taste in food is a bit on the entomological side. If his world were like ours, where might he go after a long day in the river?

1. The Walls (at Jericho). Went there once with a Pharisee friend. Swanky spot. Great food—I had the "brood of vipers" appetizer—but they established a dress code after I left. "No Shirt, No Sandals, No Service." Can't go there anymore.
2. Camel Quik. Fast, easy food, if you don't mind a few camel hairs in your milk shake.
3. The Jordan Joint. Your basic diner, but it's close by. Some of my followers have started to go there since they began offering their Repenter Rates on Tuesdays and Thursdays.
4. Bartholomew's Bar-B-Q. Bart built a business by putting strange spices in a sauce and smearing it on meat. But I'm not sure what'll happen to the place now that Bart has left it all to follow Jesus.
5. The Honey Haven. Sweet stuff, simply made. They have a honey muffin to die for.
6. Locust Pocus. These folks work magic with the little critters.
7. Insect Express. Another fast-food place I can visit on the fly.
8. Capernaum Fried Crickets. They say it's the "centurion's secret recipe" that makes this food so good.
9. Grubs 'n' Stuff. When you don't need a big meal, but just a bite.
10. Bugger King. They say Herod has an interest in this franchise. But I still think the food here is the best I've ever had— though my friends say I'm losing my head.

Jacob's Greatest Practical Jokes

Jacob was a trickster, no doubt about it. His wit easily overmatched his brother Esau's, but crafty Uncle Laban was another story. We asked the patriarch to recall his best tricks.

1. Slipping some leek juice into Esau's venison stew. Funny thing was, the guy never noticed.
2. Greasing the camel's hump while teaching Reuben to ride. The poor kid slid halfway to Hebron.
3. Going down to the Haran bazaar and yelling, "Midianites!" At the thought of a nomadic invasion, those merchants went flying.
4. Shaving "Kick me" into Esau's back. He was awfully hairy, and he was fast asleep, so . . .
5. Sawing a few inches off of Dad's walking staff. Isaac never did see very well, so for a few moments he actually thought he had grown taller!
6. Putting Esau's porridge in a dribble bowl. Again, he never noticed. He kind of dribbled anyway.
7. Sliding some cactus onto Leah's chair. You should have seen her jump!
8. Drugging Laban's prize camel on race day. And Laban was betting big on a victory.
9. Putting itching powder in Mom's sandals. And she told me she couldn't dance!
10. Putting that "boomerang bend" in Esau's hunting arrows. He noticed. Did he ever!

Paul's Best Tents

The apostle, of course, worked as a tentmaker to fund his missionary outreach. We asked him to name his favorite models.

1. The "Home Away from Home" model. This features extra flaps to give a multiroom feeling. But my single stitching keeps the price affordable.
2. The Extralarge Family Shelter. The greater mobility of the Roman Empire is great for business, but it's tearing families apart. But what if merchants could bring their families along on their business trips?
3. Lydia's Purple Pup. Custom-made for a friend in Philippi who traveled a lot and slept alone—at least after her conversion. She even provided the material, making a major fashion statement on the campground.
4. "Future Tents" by Priscilla and Aquila. The best line of canvas quarters I have ever seen. From Rome to Ephesus, these state-

of-the-art products have drawn raves. Once they hired Apollos as a spokesman, sales went through the roof, so to speak.

5. Ichthus Express. Sleek, cheap, with quick assembly—for the missionary on the run. Why name a tent for a fish? You figure it out.

Martha's Winning Recipes

Martha, who lived in Bethany with sister, Mary, and brother, Lazarus, was the quintessential homemaker of her day, always able to whip up a feast on short notice.

1. Lentil-and-Cucumber Pottage. When a friend shows up unexpectedly with 12 hungry friends, just throw a bunch of lentils and cucumbers in a pot of olive oil and simmer until your sister decides to help out.

2. Baked Barley. A staple in our home. Soak in olive oil overnight. Bake over hot coals for two hours. Sprinkle some coriander on top.

3. Mock-Fig Surprise. The surprise is, there are no figs in it. Just some citron peel, olive oil, and matzo crackers.

4. Martha's Miracle. Five barley loaves. Two small fishes. Make sandwiches. Spread with olive oil. Pray. Serves 5,000.

5. Apricot Cobbler. Slice the apricots. Slather with olive oil. Stir in a healthy pinch of cassia. Garnish with walnuts. Lazarus just dies for this dessert. And, well, he did. The first time.

Moses' Other Commandments

A dubious document was recently uncovered by archaeologists in the basement of a Cairo pawn shop. It seems to be a copy of a second-century B.C. newspaper—*Sid's Sinai Sun-Times.* According to this report, Moses was asked to make suggestions about what should be included in the Ten Commandments, but obviously, none of his ideas passed muster. Here are the supposed suggestions:

1. No turn on Red.

2. Thou shalt not even talk about scratching fingernails on chalkboards.

3. Yod before Koph, except after Aleph.

4. Remember to chew your food eight times before swallowing.

5. Thou shalt not talk with thy mouth open.

6. Thou shalt not belch in public, and a belching competition is an abomination.

7. When you shall enter the land you have been promised, be sure to wipe your feet on the mat.

8. Do not think about elephants.

9. You see, you're thinking about elephants now, aren't you?
10. Don't drink and herd sheep.

Things Peter Wishes He Had Never Done

You could probably quickly name a handful—denying Christ, urging him not to go to Jerusalem, wanting to build three tents at the Mount of Transfiguration, slicing off Malchus's ear. But this is just the tip of the canoe. What *other* things did Peter regret?

1. Asking Jesus to heal my mother-in-law. (Just kidding!)
2. Throwing back that huge sturgeon that had the coin in its mouth.
3. Calling James and John "Sons of Blunder."
4. The next day, I tried walking on water again. Oops.
5. When I swam back to shore to have breakfast with Jesus, I left my clothes in the boat.
6. After Malchus became a Christian, I kept teasing him about getting his "ear pierced."
7. After that vision on the rooftop, I ate pork chops for a week.
8. When the angel released me from prison, before I left I chained the two guards together.
9. Jesus scolded the others for keeping children away from him. In private he chastised me for threatening to send monsters to eat the kids if they wouldn't run away.
10. I sold my book rights to Mark.

Seven Animals That Missed the Last Call for Noah's Ark

Our world is packed with the critters that were saved from the Flood, but what about those that didn't make it? We can only guess.

1. The Wild Kazoo. A turkeylike bird that made an odd humming noise.
2. The Leaping Cow. Specially fortified in its lower joints. Paleontologists theorize it could leap straight up as high as 10 feet.
3. The Zaftig. A round ball of fur that really didn't do anything.
4. The Himalayan Squirrel. Seems to have moved by sliding down snow-covered mountains on its broad, flat tail.
5. The Orange Velma. Little is known about this creature except for its hideous color.
6. The Siberian Ice Lizard. Disguised itself as an icicle, which it just sort of *became*.
7. The Hairy Onion-Eater. Survived by . . . well, would *you* want to get close to it?

PART 11

SCRIPTURES TO CONSULT . . .

. . . When You Get a Raise, or When You Don't

1. Psalm 62:10
2. Proverbs 3:9
3. Proverbs 11:4
4. Proverbs 15:16
5. Proverbs 16:16
6. Proverbs 22:1
7. Matthew 6:24, 33
8. Matthew 25:15-29
9. 2 Corinthians 9:7-8
10. 1 Timothy 6:17

. . . When Your Kids Are Driving You Crazy

1. 1 Samuel 1:27-28
2. 2 Samuel 18:33
3. Proverbs 3:3
4. Proverbs 16:21
5. Proverbs 22:15
6. Proverbs 29:17
7. Matthew 17:14-20
8. Matthew 23:37
9. Luke 15:11-32
10. Colossians 3:21

. . . When You've Maxed Out Your Credit Cards

1. Psalm 119:37
2. Proverbs 6:5
3. Proverbs 22:7
4. Proverbs 22:26-27
5. Proverbs 23:4-5
6. Ecclesiastes 5:10
7. Matthew 18:23-35
8. Luke 14:28-30
9. Philippians 4:12-13
10. 2 Thessalonians 3:7-8

. . . When You're Tempted Sexually

1. Psalm 24:3-4
2. Proverbs 5:3-10
3. Proverbs 7–8
4. Romans 8:9-16
5. Ephesians 4:17-24
6. Colossians 3:1-5
7. 2 Timothy 2:22
8. 1 Peter 2:11-12
9. 2 Peter 2:18-19
10. 1 John 2:17

. . . When You're Depressed

1. 1 Kings 19
2. Psalm 6:8-10
3. Psalm 31:12-14
4. Psalm 56:8
5. Psalm 94:17-19
6. Psalm 126:5-6
7. John 11:35
8. Romans 8:16
9. 2 Corinthians 1:3-5
10. Philippians 4:4

. . . On Election Day

1. 1 Samuel 8
2. Psalm 9:20
3. Psalm 20:7
4. Psalm 89:15
5. Proverbs 20:28
6. Proverbs 21:1
7. Proverbs 29:4, 14
8. John 18:36
9. Romans 13:1-7
10. 1 Peter 2:13-14

. . . When You Don't Feel Like Going to Church

1. Psalm 26:8
2. Psalm 73:13-17
3. Psalm 84:1-3
4. Psalm 84:10
5. Psalm 91:1
6. Psalm 95:6

7. Psalm 118:24
8. Psalm 122:1
9. Matthew 18:20
10. Hebrews 10:24-25

. . . When Disaster Strikes

1. Job
2. Psalm 29:10
3. Psalm 50:15
4. Psalm 43:2-3
5. Psalm 107:27-31
6. Psalm 112:1-8
7. Psalm 118:6
8. Psalm 119:71
9. Mark 4:39
10. Luke 13:1-5

. . . When You're Feeling Inferior

1. Psalm 18:35
2. Psalm 34:5
3. Psalm 45:10-11
4. Psalm 68:6
5. Psalm 127:1
6. Isaiah 40:28-31
7. Matthew 5:3
8. Romans 8:31-39
9. 1 Corinthians 1:27
10. Philippians 4:13

. . . Before a Church Potluck Supper

1. Psalm 22:26
2. Psalm 63:4-5
3. Psalm 111:5
4. Psalm 136:23-26
5. Psalm 145:15
6. Proverbs 13:25
7. Ecclesiastes 2:25
8. Isaiah 55:1
9. Luke 12:23, 29
10. 1 Corinthians 10:31

SECTION
TWO

The Church

CHURCH LIFE

What to Say to a Pastor after an Especially Bad Sermon

You want to be truthful, but it just wasn't that good. And of course you can't slip out without shaking the pastor's hand. What do you say?

1. Nice tie.
2. It just occurred to me as you were preaching—you deserve a vacation.
3. It must be difficult to come up with an interesting topic every week.
4. You did that sermon even better than Schuller did it on TV last week.
5. I hear they're offering some great communications courses at the county college.
6. I believe the Lord is calling you to the mission field.
7. Well, you didn't talk as long as you did last week.
8. Praise the Lord! I think you've cured my insomnia.
9. It's just a shame the people who needed to hear that message weren't here.
10. Thanks so much for your message on 1 Peter. It helped me understand suffering in a whole new way.

Excuses for Not Going to Church

You roll out of bed Sunday morning and . . . you roll back in. Days later, the pastor calls with that sweet-but-probing "We missed you in church Sunday." Of course you don't want to *lie*, but what can you say?

1. I was up all night praying for world missions, and I must have overslept.
2. With all the snow, I thought we canceled church. . . . Oh, it wasn't snowing where you were?
3. In order to witness more effectively to my neighbors, I felt I needed to understand their Sunday-morning experience.
4. Still trying to get the hang of that daylight saving time.
5. But in my dream, I *did* go to church.
6. I had to study up for the youth-group meeting I was leading Sunday night.

7. But don't you think the Sabbath ought to be observed on Saturday, as originally intended? And, by the way, I missed you in church on Saturday.
8. I dreamt that the Rapture occurred, so I just assumed no one would be in church.
9. I gave all my clothes to Goodwill, and I didn't have a thing to wear.
10. But don't we consider Sunday a day of rest?

Politically Correct Terms for Christians

Let's face it. So much of what we talk about in church is just plain offensive. Why not try these new phrases?

Out	In
Sinful	Morally impaired
Dishonest	Reality deficient
Boastful	Self-appreciative
Envious	Acquisitionally aware
Lustful	Hormonally active
Gossip	Information
Evil	Goodness deprivatioin
Adultery	Multiparamourism
Repentance	Personal choice
Sacrifice	[No translation available]

Seasons of the Christian Year

1. Advent. The four Sundays before Christmas, a season of expectancy, looking forward to the Lord's coming.
2. Christmastide. December 25 and the next two Sundays (up to Epiphany), celebrating our Lord's birth.
3. Epiphany. January 6 and the next four to nine Sundays, depending upon the date of Easter. The season of the gospel, celebrating the magi's worship of the Christ child and, by extension, the Lord's outreach to all Gentiles. Culminates in the Festival of the Transfiguration.
4. Lent. Ash Wednesday to Easter. A season of penitence and renewal, symbolized by Jesus' 40 days in the wilderness.
5. Eastertide. The season of the Resurrection, beginning with Easter and continuing for 40 days, ending on Ascension Day.
6. Ascensiontide. Includes Ascension Day and the Sunday after the Ascension. Commemorates the Lord's return to heaven.

7. Pentecost (or Whitsuntide). Fifty days after Easter, including Whitsunday, which closes out the first half of the Christian year and serves as a sort of pivot point. Up to now the focus has been on the objective events in Jesus' life. Now the Christian focuses on his or her subjective response to those events.

Celebrations in the Christian Year
1. Advent. Four Sundays before Christmas
2. Christmas
3. Easter. The first Sunday after the first full moon that happens on or after March 21
4. Ash Wednesday. The beginning of Lent, 46 days before Easter
5. Palm Sunday. The Sunday before Easter
6. Whitsunday. Fifty days after Easter
7. Trinity Sunday. The Sunday after Whitsunday
8. Pentecost Season. The Sundays from Pentecost to the first Sunday in Advent

Unofficial Church Calendar
1. Youth-Retreat Sunday. Things are quiet in the service, and the back pew is empty. Precedes the season of the youth leader's vacation.
2. Return-from-Convention Season. For about a month the newly returned pastor is full of new ideas. The church board usually outlasts him, and the ideas are soon forgotten.
3. Aunt-Sadie's-New-Hat Sunday. Also known as Easter.
4. Choir-Cantata Sunday. Preceded by the Season of Frantic Activity.
5. Missions-Conference Week. Features the annual Appearance of the Slide Projector and the Veneration of the World Map. Another highlight: The Banquet of Odd Food.
6. Softballtide. Lasting from just after daylight saving time to the time when the church can no longer field nine uninjured players.
7. Youth Sunday. A day when the church tries to make young people feel as if they're really important. The following Sunday, normal patterns return.
8. Betty's-Turn-to-Sing-Again Sunday. She's not very good, but she's an institution, so people try their best not to cringe when she warbles "The Old Rugged Cross."
9. Something-Else-Is-Going-On Sunday. Every year or so there's some bit of gossip that everyone's talking about but no one is saying anything about. So the whole service has a surreal subtext, but no one's really paying attention.

10. The Season of Burnout. Starts about six months after people start to do things and continues as long as they keep doing them.

Ten Church Supplies Beginning with the Letter A

1. Advent calendars
2. Advertising gimmicks
3. Altar cloths
4. Angels
5. Anointing oil
6. Art supplies
7. Atlases
8. Attendance-record books
9. Audiovisual equipment
10. Awards

Church Supplies from A to Z

A. (See above)
B. Bulletins
C. Candles
D. Devotional books
E. Erasable-marker boards
F. Flannelgraphs
G. Games
H. Hymnals
I. Instruments
J. Jesus, pictures of
K. Key rings
L. Lecterns
M. Maps
N. Nativity scenes
O. Offering plates
P. Pews
Q. Quizzes
R. Robes
S. Stained glass
T. Tracts
U. Undertaker, fans from
V. VBS snacks
W. Wireless microphones
X. Xylophones
Y. Youth curriculum
Z. Zip-code directory

Ten Delicacies of Church Suppers

1. Baked beans
2. Deviled eggs
3. Fried chicken
4. Lemonade
5. Meat loaf
6. Potato salad
7. Scalloped potatoes and ham
8. Spanish rice
9. Tuna casserole
10. Red Jell-O with fruit and marshmallows

Adapted from *Growing Up Born Again,* by Klein, Bence, Campbell, Pearson, and Wimbish (Revell, 1987).

What a Tactful Choir Director Can Say to a Choir Member Who Can't Sing

Music schools teach choir directors how to select music and keep a beat, but you may need this crash course on directorial tact.

1. You have excellent posture.
2. Did you know there's a Bible study starting up on the same night as choir rehearsal? I think you'd get a lot out of it.
3. You have such a unique range. You hit both of those notes very well.
4. It's a shame composers don't write more songs to fit your style.
5. Here's a book on finding your spiritual gift. Perhaps you could find some effective place of ministry in the church.
6. We're still looking for good people to join the handbell choir.
7. Singing can really aggravate chronic sinus trouble.
8. I wouldn't want you to strain your voice by singing too loudly.
9. We need strong singers out in the congregation to help them sing the hymns.
10. I'm sorry, but we ran out of choir robes.

Ten No-Nos for Pastors and Church Leaders

1. Don't say, "If this isn't true, may lightning strike me"—especially if you're at the church picnic and the sky is beginning to cloud up.
2. Don't ask everyone to stand and hold hands—especially if you're at the church picnic and everyone's just had fried chicken.
3. Don't stop singing "A Mighty Fortress Is Our God" after the first verse. Then it sounds like the devil wins.

4. But don't use more than four verses of any hymn. Then people stop caring whether the devil wins.

5. If you must sing "Just As I Am," don't do it more than once. Just once. One verse. Done.

6. On Stewardship Sunday, don't say, "We'll stay here all night in order to meet our budget." Maybe *you'll* stay there all night.

7. Don't refer to the singles group as "Unclaimed Freight."

8. Don't ask the young people to move to the front pew. They will find a way to move farther back.

9. Please stop saying, "And everybody said . . . ?" when you want an *Amen*. If we're not sayin' it, we don't wanna.

10. Don't use the closing prayer to preach the last point of your sermon. God already knows what you planned to say, and he made sure you ran out of time.

PART 2

DENOMINATIONS

Baptist Denominations in the U.S.

1. American Baptist Association
2. American Baptist Churches in the U.S.A.
3. Baptist Bible Fellowship International
4. Baptist General Conference
5. Baptist Missionary Association of America
6. Conservative Baptist Association of America
7. General Association of General Baptists
8. General Association of Regular Baptist Churches
9. Liberty Baptist Fellowship
10. National Association of Free Will Baptists
11. National Baptist Convention of America, Inc.
12. National Baptist Convention, U.S.A., Inc.
13. National Missionary Baptist Convention of America
14. National Primitive Baptist Convention, Inc.
15. North American Baptist Conference
16. Primitive Baptists
17. Progressive National Baptist Convention, Inc.
18. Separate Baptists in Christ
19. Seventh Day Baptist General Conference, U.S.A. and Canada
20. Southern Baptist Convention
21. Sovereign Grace Baptists

Presbyterian Denominations in the U.S.

1. Associate Reformed Presbyterian Church (General Synod)
2. Cumberland Presbyterian Church
3. Cumberland Presbyterian Church in America
4. Evangelical Presbyterian Church
5. General Assembly of the Korean Presbyterian Church in America
6. Orthodox Presbyterian Church
7. Presbyterian Church in America
8. Presbyterian Church (U.S.A.)
9. Reformed Presbyterian Church of North America

Lutheran Denominations in the U.S.

1. American Association of Lutheran Churches
2. Apostolic Lutheran Church of America
3. Association of Free Lutheran Congregations
4. Church of the Lutheran Brethren of America
5. Church of the Lutheran Confession
6. Conservative Lutheran Association
7. The Estonian Evangelical Lutheran Church
8. Evangelical Lutheran Church in America
9. Evangelical Lutheran Synod
10. Latvian Evangelical Lutheran Church in America
11. Lutheran Church–Missouri Synod
12. Wisconsin Evangelical Lutheran Synod

Methodist Denominations in the U.S.

1. African Methodist Episcopal Church
2. African Methodist Episcopal Zion Church
3. Allegheny Wesleyan Methodist Connection
4. Bible Holiness Church
5. Christian Methodist Episcopal Church
6. Evangelical Methodist Church
7. Free Methodist Church of North America
8. Fundamental Methodist Church, Inc.
9. Primitive Methodist Church in the U.S.A.
10. Reformed Methodist Union Episcopal Church
11. Reformed Zion Union Apostolic Church
12. Southern Methodist Church
13. United Methodist Church
14. Wesleyan Church

Pentecostal Denominations in the U.S.

1. Apostolic Faith Mission Church of God
2. Apostolic Faith Mission of Portland, Oregon
3. Apostolic Overcoming Holy Church of God, Inc.
4. Assemblies of God
5. Assemblies of God International Fellowship
6. Bible Church of Christ, Inc.
7. Bible Way Church of Our Lord Jesus Christ Worldwide, Inc.
8. Christian Church of North America, General Council
9. Church of God
10. Church of God (Cleveland, Tennessee)
11. Church of God in Christ
12. Church of God in Christ, International

13. Church of God, Mountain Assembly, Inc.
14. Church of God of Prophecy
15. Church of Our Lord Jesus Christ of the Apostolic Faith, Inc.
16. Congregational Holiness Church
17. Elim Fellowship
18. Full Gospel Assemblies International
19. Full Gospel Fellowship of Churches and Ministers International
20. International Church of the Foursquare Gospel
21. International Pentecostal Church of Christ
22. International Pentecostal Holiness Church
23. Open Bible Standard Churches, Inc.
24. Pentecostal Assemblies of the World, Inc.
25. Pentecostal Church of God
26. Pentecostal Fire-Baptized Holiness Church
27. Pentecostal Free Will Baptist Church, Inc.
28. United Holy Church of America, Inc.
29. United Pentecostal Church International

Church of God Denominations in the U.S.

With all the Church of God names in the list above, you might think that all Church of God denominations are Pentecostal. Not so. There are also a few distinctly non-Pentecostal Church of God groups.

1. Church of God (Anderson, Indiana)
2. Church of God by Faith, Inc.
3. Church of God (Seventh Day), Denver, Colorado
4. Church of God, General Conference

Now You Try It!

Want to start your own denomination? Can't think of a name? Just follow these simple steps, and you'll have your group up and running in no time.

A. What general denomination group do you want to be? Baptist? Methodist? Other?
B. Choose one grouping term:
   Association
   Churches
   Convention
   Conference
   Fellowship
   Synod
   (or make up your own)
C. (optional) Is there a particular doctrinal stance your denomi-

nation will take? Predestinarian? Supralapsarian? Chorus singing? Pastor bashing? You might throw in something about what you believe.

D. (optional) Just how patriotic are you? You may want to identify with this great land of ours—or not. Choose one:
National
in the U.S. (or U.S.A.)
of the U.S. (or U.S.A.)
American
North American
International
(other)

E. (optional) Do you want to add a regional description? If you're feeling nostalgic about Civil War days, a "Southern" or "Northern" would be nice. Or you could name it for your hometown.

F. Adding "Inc." gives you a neat corporate feeling. Want to try it?

G. Extra credit for any of the following terms:
Missionary
Evangelical
Bible
Gospel
United

H. Now put all these terms together, in no particular order, and enjoy your newly named denomination.

The 10 Major Religions of the U.S.

1. Christianity 146.6 million (84.1%)
2. Mormonism 4.6 million (2.6%)
3. Judaism 3.1 million (1.8%)
4. Islam 527,000
5. Unitarian/Universalist 502,000
6. Buddhism 401,000
7. Hinduism 227,000
8. Native American faiths 47,000
9. Scientology 45,000
10. Baha'i 28,000

Top 10 Christian Denominations in the U.S., 1996

1. Roman Catholics, 60.2 million
2. Southern Baptists, 15.6 million
3. United Methodists, 8.6 million
4. National Baptists (U.S.A.), 8.2 million

5. Church of God in Christ, 5.5 million
6. Evangelical Lutherans (ELCA), 5.2 million
7. Presbyterian Church (U.S.A.), 3.7 million
8. National Baptists (of America), 3.5 million
9. African Methodist Episcopal, 3.5 million
10. Lutherans (Missouri Synod), 2.6 million

Top 10 Christian Denominations in the U.S., 1976

1. Roman Catholics, 48.7 million
2. Southern Baptists, 12.5 million
3. United Methodists, 10.1 million
4. National Baptists (U.S.A.), 5.5 million
5. Lutheran Church in America, 3.0 million
6. Episcopal Church, 2.9 million
7. Lutherans (Missouri Synod), 2.8 million
8. National Baptists (of America), 2.7 million
9. United Presbyterians (U.S.A.), 2.7 million
10. American Lutheran Church, 2.4 million

Top 10 Christian Denominations in the U.S., 1956

1. Roman Catholics, 32.4 million
2. Methodists, 9.2 million
3. Southern Baptists, 8.1 million
4. National Baptists (U.S.A.), 4.5 million
5. Episcopal Church, 2.7 million
6. National Baptists (of America), 2.6 million
7. United Presbyterians (U.S.A.), 2.5 million
8. United Lutherans, 2.1 million
9. Disciples of Christ, 1.9 million
10. Lutherans (Missouri Synod), 1.9 million

Most of the information above was gathered from the *Yearbook of American Churches* for the years 1996, 1976, and 1956 (National Council of Churches).

Tracking the Top 12 Denominations over the Past 50 Years

Denomination	1940	1970	1995	Trend
Roman Catholic Church	1	1	1	Unchanged
Southern Baptist Convention	3	2	2	Up some
United Methodist Church★	2	3	3	Down some
National Baptist Convention	4	4	4	Unchanged
Evangelical Lutheran Church★	5	6	5	Unchanged
Presbyterian Church U.S.A.★	6	5	6	Unchanged
Lutheran Church (Missouri Synod)	10	8	7	Up
The Episcopal Church	7	7	8	Down some
Assemblies of God	+	12	9	Up
United Church of Christ★	9	9	10	Down some
Disciples of Christ	8	11	11	Down
American Baptist Convention	11	10	12	Down some

★ In denominations that have merged since 1940, membership totals of both merging denominations were included in earlier statistics.
+ Not among the top 12 denominations in membership.

Ten Denominations with the Best Per Capita Giving Records

1. Seventh-day Adventists
2. Evangelical Methodist Church
3. Mennonite Church
4. Mennonite General Conference
5. Presbyterian Church in America (PCA)
6. Reformed Episcopal Church
7. Christian & Missionary Alliance
8. Brethren in Christ
9. Orthodox Presbyterian Church
10. Free Methodist Church

Who Pays Their Pastors the Most?

1. Methodists
2. Reformed
3. Episcopalians
4. Lutherans
5. United Church of Christ

6. Evangelical Free
7. Baptists
8. Presbyterians
9. Church of God
10. Nondenominational

Ranking is based on average base salary, as compiled by the 1992 Church Compensation Report (Christianity Today, Inc., 1991). The same source is used for the following two lists.

Who Pays Their Youth Pastors the Most?

1. Lutherans
2. Baptists
3. Christian Church/Disciples of Christ/Church of Christ
4. Presbyterians

Full-time positions. Methodists, Catholics, and UCC had too few in the sample to get a valid average.

Who Pays Their Music Directors the Most?

1. Methodists
2. Baptists
3. Presbyterians
4. Nondenominational

Full-time positions. Catholics, Christian Church/Disciples of Christ/Church of Christ, Episcopalians, and Lutherans had too few in the sample to get a valid average.

Ten Subjects to Avoid in Conversation with Christians of Other Denominations

1. Predestination. Did God choose us or do we choose him?
2. Eternal security. Once saved, always saved? Or can a person lose it?
3. Modes of baptism. Dunking? Sprinkling? As children? As adults?
4. The meaning of the Lord's Supper. Is this really the Lord's body? In what way? (Denominations have split over this. You won't solve it in 15 minutes.)
5. The Baptism of the Holy Spirit. Does the Spirit come at salvation or in a later event?
6. Speaking in tongues. Is this a spiritual gift for modern times? (Related issues: healing, miracles, prophecy, "word of knowledge." Are these for today?)
7. Choruses vs. hymns. Are the good old hymns of the faith good, or just old? Do the modern choruses say anything?

Have we lost a sense of awe? (Related issue: style of worship. Seeker-church style? Liturgical? Formal? "Creative"?)

8. The best Bible version. KJV? NIV? TEV? TLB? NASB? NKJV? NLT? (When someone starts quoting Greek phrases, leave the room.)

9. Tithing. Do we still need to give 10% of our income to the Lord's work? Does that standard apply today, or was it just for Old Testament Israel? (When people start asking for your bank statements, leave the state.)

10. TV evangelists. Are any of them doing good? Which ones? What image of Christianity do they present? Are they reaching anyone?

Five Things about the Holy Spirit That Charismatics and Non-Charismatics Can Agree On

From *Paul, the Spirit, and the People of God,* by Gordon Fee (Hendrickson).

1. The coming of the Spirit is God's promise fulfilled: his presence returned to his people.

2. Through the Spirit, God empowers his people in both ordinary and extraordinary ways.

3. The Spirit makes the many, one.

4. The Spirit's ministry includes both "fruit" and "gifts."

5. The Spirit, if invited, transforms worship.

PART 3

MISSIONS

Where the Christians Are

Continents, by the percentage of total Christians living there. For the purposes of this study, Russia (with the former republics of the U.S.S.R.) is considered a separate continent, East Asia and South Asia are divided, and Latin America includes both Central and South America.

1900

1. Europe 49.9%
2. Russia 18.8%
3. North America 14.1%
4. Latin America 11.1%
5. South Asia 3.0%

1970

1. Europe 33.3%
2. Latin America 22.0%
3. North America 17.0%
4. Africa 11.8%
5. Russia 7.1%

1985

1. Europe 27.2%
2. Latin America 25.3%
3. Africa 15.3%
4. North America 14.7%
5. South Asia 8.1%

Note that more than two-fifths of all Christians now live in Africa and Latin America. At the turn of the century, that figure was one-eighth.

Countries with the Greatest Number of Christians

1. United States
2. Brazil
3. Former U.S.S.R.

4. Mexico
5. Germany
6. China
7. Philippines
8. Italy
9. France
10. United Kingdom

Source: *Mission Handbook 1993–95,* by John A. Kenyon and John Siewert (Mission Advanced Research and Communication Center, 1993).

Countries with the Most Non-Christians

1. China
2. India
3. Former U.S.S.R.
4. Indonesia
5. Japan
6. Bangladesh
7. Pakistan
8. Nigeria
9. Turkey
10. Iran

Source: *Mission Handbook 1993–95,* by John A. Kenyon and John Siewert (Mission Advanced Research and Communication Center, 1993).

Ten (of 50) Ways You Can Reach the World

1. Stretch the comfort zones.
2. Zero in on a country.
3. Question your categories.
4. Vacation with a purpose.
5. Organize an action committee.
6. Budget priorities.
7. Explore community.
8. Be a pioneer.
9. Consider urban ministry.
10. Teach missions.

Now, to figure out what these things *mean,* and to get the other 40 ways, you'll have to see the book *Fifty Ways You Can Reach the World,* by Tony Campolo and Gordon Aeschliman (InterVarsity, 1993).

How to Be a World-Class Christian

1. Gather global information.
2. Pray world-class prayers—manageably, practically, strategically.

3. Simplify your lifestyle.
4. Give generously and wisely.
5. Befriend international people in your world.
6. Consider gradual involvement (short-term missions?).

Adapted from *How to Be a World-Class Christian* by Paul Borthwick
(Victor, 1991).

Ten Steps to Start Global Praying

1. Start where you are and build from there. Don't set impossible
    standards.
2. Practice prayer arrows—those momentary thought-prayers
    throughout the day.
3. Fuel prayer with information. Learn about those you're pray-
    ing for.
4. Pray as part of your correspondence. Participate in the team
    effort of prayer.
5. Gather others with you, perhaps at church.
6. Find a personal plan. Get a prayer schedule that fits your life.
7. Choose appropriate tools. Prayer cards, maps, etc.
8. Remember to intercede. Prayer for missions is spiritual
    warfare.
9. Pray by faith (not by results). God sometimes works slowly,
    quietly.
10. Learn to say no. The need is so great it can overwhelm you.
    Set limits.

Adapted from *How to Be a World-Class Christian* by Paul Borthwick
(Victor, 1991).

Nine Worlds to Win

These "worlds" loom as the major challenges for modern missions.

1. The world of the poor and needy
2. The Hindu world
3. The Buddhist world
4. The Muslim world
5. The Communist and post-Communist world
6. The tribal world
7. The urban world
8. The world of youth and children
9. The so-called Christian world

Adapted from *Nine Worlds to Win,* by Floyd McClung and Kalafi
Moala (Youth With A Mission, 1988).

Seven Key Questions for Global Missions Today

1. What is missions?
2. Why do missions?
3. Who are the missionaries?
4. Who are the missionized?
5. Where do we mission?
6. How do we mission?
7. What is the nature of the competition?

From *Ministry and Theology in Global Perspective: Contemporary Challenges for the Church,* edited by Don A. Pittman, Ruben L. F. Habito, and Terry C. Muck (Eerdmans, 1996).

Twenty Little Countries of the World Where Missionaries Serve

There's only one major American mission group working in each of these countries.

1. Tonga: Assemblies of God
2. Bophuthatswana: Southern Baptists
3. Turks and Caicos Islands: Episcopal Church
4. North Yemen: Southern Baptists
5. Vanuatu: Presbyterian Church, U.S.A.
6. Togo: Association of Baptists for World Evangelization
7. Seychelles: Africa Inland Mission
8. Djibouti: Red Sea Mission
9. Guinea-Bissau: New Tribes Mission
10. Oman: Reformed Church of America
11. Monaco: Trans World Radio
12. Malta: Baptist Bible Fellowship
13. Mariana Islands: Pioneers
14. Iceland: Greater Europe Mission
15. Grenada: Baptist International
16. Belize: Assemblies of God
17. Antigua: Churches of Christ
18. Azores: Church of the Nazarene
19. Benin: SIM International
20. Burkina Faso: Christian and Missionary Alliance

The 10 Leading Missionary-Sending Countries in the Third World

The U.S. isn't the only country that sends missionaries. Besides Canadians and Europeans, there are many missionaries from Third World countries who leave their homelands to share the gospel—and the number is rapidly increasing.

1. India (8,905)
2. Nigeria (2,959)
3. Zaire (2,731)
4. Myanmar/Burma (2,560)
5. Kenya (2,242)
6. Brazil (2,040)
7. Philippines (1,814)
8. Ghana (1,545)
9. Zimbabwe (1,540)
10. Korea (1,183)

Source: *Mission Handbook 1993–95,* by John A. Kenyon and John Siewert (Mission Advanced Research and Communication Center, 1993).

Countries Expected to Be Sending the Most Missionaries in A.D. 2000

1. United States
2. Spain
3. Italy
4. France
5. Germany
6. Canada
7. Netherlands
8. Great Britain
9. Belgium
10. Brazil

Source: *Mission Handbook 1993–95,* by John A. Kenyon and John Siewert (Mission Advanced Research and Communication Center, 1993).

Greatest Per Capita Missionary-Sending Countries

Sure, the U.S. sends a lot of missionaries, but we've got a lot of people to begin with. When you figure in the population of these countries, which countries send the greatest percentage of their population out as missionaries?

1. Ireland
2. Belgium
3. Spain
4. Netherlands
5. Portugal

6. Canada
7. Italy
8. Switzerland
9. France
10. New Zealand
11. United States

Source: *Mission Handbook 1993–95,* by John A. Kenyon and John Siewert (Mission Advanced Research and Communication Center, 1993).

The 20 Top U.S. Missions Agencies for Long-Term Missionaries

By number of missionaries sent for four years or more.

1. Southern Baptist Foreign Mission Board (3,660)
2. Wycliffe Bible Translators (2,338)
3. New Tribes Mission (1,837)
4. Assemblies of God Foreign Missions (1,485)
5. Christian Churches/Churches of Christ (1,118)
6. Churches of Christ (916)
7. Youth With A Mission (885)
8. Baptist Bible Fellowship International (711)
9. The Evangelical Alliance Mission (TEAM) (701)
10. Seventh-day Adventists (676)
11. Christian and Missionary Alliance (654)
12. Baptist Mid-Missions (644)
13. Association of Baptists for World Evangelism (639)
14. Baptist International Missions (544)
15. Conservative Baptist Foreign Mission Society (531)
16. Church of the Nazarene, World Mission (506)
17. Society for International Ministries (SIM) (464)
18. Mission to the World/Presbyterian Church in America (444)
19. United Methodist Board of Global Ministries (435)
20. Brethren Assemblies (435)

Source: *Mission Handbook 1993–95,* by John A. Kenyon and John Siewert (Mission Advanced Research and Communication Center, 1993).

The 20 Leading Missions Agencies for Short-Term Missionaries

By number of missionaries serving four years or less.

1. Southern Baptist Foreign Mission Board (10,209)
2. Youth With A Mission (6,600)

3. Church of the Nazarene, World Mission (5,500)
4. Youth for Christ/U.S.A., World Outreach (1,801)
5. Assemblies of God Foreign Missions (1,485)
6. Teen Missions International (1,413)
7. Mission to the World/Presbyterian Church in America (1,392)
8. Campus Crusade for Christ International (731)
9. Foursquare Missions International (721)
10. Free Methodist World Missions (578)
11. Wycliffe Associates (500)
12. Church of God World Missions (484)
13. World Gospel Missions (480)
14. Operation Mobilization (415)
15. InterVarsity Missions (395)
16. OMS International (365)
17. Teen World Outreach (348)
18. Wycliffe Bible Translators (296)
19. Pentecostal Holiness Church World Missions (286)
20. New Tribes Mission (261)

Source: *Mission Handbook 1993–95,* by John A. Kenyon and John Siewert (Mission Advanced Research and Communication Center, 1993).

The 20 Leading U.S. Missions Agencies in Income for Overseas Ministries

In millions of dollars

1. ★World Vision (176)
2. Southern Baptist Foreign Mission Board (165.7)
3. Assemblies of God Foreign Missions (96.3)
4. Seventh-day Adventists (72.2)
5. Wycliffe Bible Translators (57.2)
6. Churches of Christ (52)
7. ★MAP International (50.1)
8. ★Church World Service and Witness Unit of the National Council of Churches (47.8)
9. Campus Crusade for Christ International (45.5)
10. ★Compassion International (44)
11. ★Larry Jones International Ministries (39.8)
12. ★Children International (34.1)
13. The Gideons International (34)
14. ★Food for the Hungry (32.7)
15. ★Mennonite Central Committee (30.3)
16. Church of the Nazarene, World Mission (30)
17. United Methodist Board of Global Ministries (27.9)

18. *Lutheran World Relief (27.7)
19. Presbyterian Church (U.S.A.) Global Mission (25.2)
20. Christian Churches/Churches of Christ (24)

*Primarily involved in hunger relief and development

Source: *Mission Handbook 1993–95,* by John A. Kenyon and John Siewert (Mission Advanced Research and Communication Center, 1993).

Where Most of the Overseas Missionaries from the U.S. Are Working

1. Brazil (2,229)
2. Philippines (1,961)
3. Mexico (1,691)
4. Japan (1,636)
5. Kenya (1,337)
6. Papua New Guinea (1,186)
7. Indonesia (957)
8. France (756)
9. Germany (756)
10. Ecuador (755)

Source: *Mission Handbook 1993–95,* by John A. Kenyon and John Siewert (Mission Advanced Research and Communication Center, 1993).

PART 4

COUNSELING AND CHRISTIAN EDUCATION

Principles of Counseling

Yes, counseling is a profession involving years of training. But it's also something that wise Christians do in a variety of church and personal situations. Here are some pointers:

1. Be willing to give all the time it may take.
2. Be principled as you handle confidences.
3. Be patient.
4. Be professional.
5. Know your own limitations.
6. Nurture the relationship.
7. Rely totally upon the Lord.

Resources for Christian Counseling

Thanks to Thomas A. Whiteman and Douglas R. Flather.

1. *The Resource Guide for Christian Counselors,* Douglas R. Flather (Baker)
2. *Christian Counseling: A Comprehensive Guide,* Gary Collins (Word, 1988)
3. *The Handbook of Christian Counseling,* Timothy Foster (Nelson, 1995)
4. *The Biblical Basis of Christian Counseling for People Helpers,* Gary Collins (NavPress, 1993)
5. *Psychology, Theology, and Spirituality in Christian Counseling,* Mark McMinn (Tyndale, 1996)
6. *Strategic Pastoral Counseling: A Short-Term Structured Model,* David Benner (Baker, 1992)
7. *Understanding People,* Larry Crabb (Zondervan)
8. *The Complete Life Encyclopedia,* Minirth, Meier, Arterburn (Nelson, 1995)
9. *Why Do Christians Shoot Their Wounded?,* Dwight Carlson (InterVarsity, 1994)
10. *Marriage Counseling,* H. Norman Wright (Regal, 1995)

Ten Stress Generators for Christians

1. The desperate need to conform to everyone else in our church or community
2. The fear that God is out to get us
3. The avoidance of creative thinking
4. Our possession by our possessions
5. Our busy lives
6. Neglect of relationships
7. False ideals about where our lives should go
8. Pretending to be more spiritually minded than we are
9. Guilt
10. Neglect of our bodies

Adapted from *Regaining Control of Your Life,* by Judson Edwards (Bethany House, 1989).

Nine Steps toward a Balanced Self-Esteem

Self-esteem has gotten a bad name from counselors who have pushed it to the point of absurdity. Christians know that self-centeredness is neither righteous nor healthy. The Christian ideal is a balanced self-esteem, in which we love our neighbors as ourselves, humbly appreciating our own position as children of God.

1. Make an honest personal inventory of your good points and bad points.
2. Give yourself some mild compliments in the presence of others.
3. Isolate a problem in your life, and work at conquering it.
4. Identify the villains that have stolen your self-esteem.
5. Find unconditional love in a vibrant relationship with God.
6. Learn to recognize the self-defeating messages society sends your way, and defy them.
7. Discover something you can do well—and do it.
8. See how you can enrich someone else's life.
9. Try to make your balanced self-esteem a central part of a whole new lifestyle.

Adapted from *Becoming Your Own Best Friend,* by Thomas A. Whiteman and Randy Petersen (Nelson, 1994).

Twelve Marks of a Healthy Family

1. Communication/listening
2. Affirmation/support
3. Respect for others
4. Trust
5. Humor/play

6. Spending time together
7. Shared responsibility
8. An awareness of right and wrong
9. A sense of family/rituals/traditions
10. Shared faith
11. Respect for privacy
12. Willingness to get help and give it

Adapted from *Traits of a Healthy Family,* by Dolores Curran (Ballantine, 1983).

Marriage/Family Resources for Churches

Fresh Start
63 Chestnut Rd.
Paoli, PA 19301

Marriage Savers Resource Collection
Quadrus Media
721 E. State St.
Rockford, IL 61104

MOPS International
(Mothers of Pre-Schoolers)
1311 S. Clarkson
Denver, CO 80210

PRAISE
P.O. Box 29472
Washington, DC 20017

PREPARE
P.O. Box 190
Minneapolis, MN 55440

Systematic Training for Effective Parenting
American Guidance Services
Circle Pines, MN 55014-1796

Worldwide Marriage Encounter
1908 E. Highland #A
San Bernardino, CA 92404

Seven Men Who "Love Too Little"

Everyone's suddenly interested in men—how we think, act, relate, what makes us do the things we do. And why are we so bad at relationships? A recent Christian book identified seven types of men who frustrate the women who love them

1. The Angry Man. Flips out at the least provocation.
2. The Passive Man. No response at all.

3. The Passive-Aggressive Man. Stores up his gripes, then explodes.
4. The Compulsive Man. Prone to addictions of all sorts.
5. The Supervisor. Controls the lives of others.
6. The Sponge. Self-absorbed, proud of himself.
7. The Stranger. Emotionally distant, afraid of commitment.

Adapted from *Men Who Love Too Little,* by Thomas A. Whiteman and Randy Petersen (Nelson, 1995).

A New Approach for Men's Groups

Researchers are finally admitting something people have known all along—men are different from women. So why do we still run men's groups in the same way we run women's groups? What would a men's group look like if it truly took the distinctives of men into account?

1. **Distinctive:** Men have the ability to compartmentalize their thinking.
   Group strategy: Stress application of biblical teaching, and push for lifestyle decisions. If the group doesn't push to combine them, the average man will keep truth and life in two different compartments.
2. **Distinctive:** Men are less verbal than women.
   Group strategy: Allow for "cave time." Women process things in conversation with others; men often process alone. Build personal time into each small-group session. "Go off by yourself for the next 15 minutes and work on this; then let's get together and compare notes."
3. **Distinctive:** Men are less relational than women.
   Group strategy: Develop *small* small groups. Coleman's "fearsome foursome."
4. **Distinctive:** Men are doers and are goal oriented.
   Group strategy: Include project-based options. Make your softball team a fellowship group. Get the church trustees to pray together. Let men *grow* as they *do.*
5. **Distinctive:** Men like to be in control.
   Group strategy: Work at sharing control of the group. Men need to share responsibility for the group, perhaps taking turns leading the whole session or some aspect of the session.
6. **Distinctive:** Men like to feel independent.
   Group strategy: Assure privacy. Assume that most men have personal issues they're dealing with. Offer help, but in veiled terms. Use the old "unspoken request."
7. **Distinctive:** Men tend to have a stronger self-focus.
   Group strategy: Market toward men's self-interest. It won't

work to say, "You *should* be involved in this group." (Men don't have the guilt sensitivity of women.) Show them how it will make their lives better.

What Small Groups Contribute to American Religion

Small groups have revolutionized the church in the last generation. One of the best observers of this phenomenon is Robert Wuthnow, who has written several fine books on the subject. Here are 12 gifts that he sees small groups giving to churches:

1. Small groups make faith available to everyone.
2. Small groups get back to the basics.
3. Small groups are diverse, meeting diverse needs.
4. Small groups extend the church's ministry to the crevices of society.
5. Small groups encourage a greater individual responsibility for the nurturing of one's faith.
6. Small groups help people adapt a childlike faith to adulthood.
7. Small groups help people consider what the Bible means.
8. Small groups help individuals put their faith into practice.
9. Small groups undergird the plausibility of faith.
10. Small groups provide time for prayer.
11. Small groups help people learn to pray by allowing them to hear others pray.
12. Small groups give people the opportunity to show care for each other.

Adapted from "The Small Group Movement in the Context of American Religion," by Robert Wuthnow, a chapter in *I Come Away Stronger: How Small Groups Are Shaping American Religion,* edited by Wuthnow (Eerdmans, 1994).

Small-Group Principles

1. People join groups to satisfy some personal need and will continue with the group as long as that need is being met.
2. People like to join groups that include others who are like them in age, attitude, class, etc. But homogeneity does not always make the best groups.
3. The larger the group, the less individual participation.
4. The smaller the group, the more shared leadership.
5. The physical environment affects the success of the group. (Pay attention to room size, temperature, comfy chairs, etc.)
6. Groups function well when they're clear about what the purpose is.

7. Good groups regularly reassess how well they're achieving their goals.
8. Each group member has the potential to enhance the way the group functions or to destroy it.
9. The best group members are those who want to learn, rather than those who want to show what they know.
10. A strong leader can derail the group process if he or she takes too much control.

Five Jobs of a Small-Group Leader

1. Facilitation: Weave the group together, spurring expression.
2. Environment: Promote security, acceptance within the group.
3. Vision: Set an example; inspire the group; show the way to where you're going.
4. Encouragement: Find the good in what people say and leverage it.
5. Resource: Do your homework to know some answers, and know where to find what you don't know.

Ten Resources for Small-Group Ministry

1. *Getting Together: A Guide for Good Groups,* by Em Griffin (Inter-Varsity, 1982).
2. *Group Talk!,* by Ed Stewart and Nina Fishwick (Regal, 1986).
3. *Growing Christians in Small Groups,* by John Mallison (Anzea, 1989).
4. *How to Lead Small Groups,* by Neal F. McBride (NavPress, 1990).
5. *Joining Together: Group Theory and Group Skills,* by Frank Johnson (Prentice-Hall, 1987).
6. *Serendipity Bible for Groups,* edited by Lyman Coleman (Serendipity, 1988).
7. *Sharing the Journey,* by Robert Wuthnow (Macmillan, 1994).
8. *Small Group Leaders' Handbook,* by Ron Nicholas (InterVarsity, 1982).
9. *Twelve Dynamic Bible Study Methods for Individuals or Groups,* by Richard Warren (Victor, 1981).
10. *Using the Bible in Groups,* by Roberta Hestenes (Westminster, 1983).

Ten Great Vacation Bible School Snacks

1. Animal crackers
2. Red Kool-Aid
3. Chocolate-chip cookies

4. Reese's Pieces
5. Orange Kool-Aid
6. Ritz crackers
7. Pretzels
8. Yellow Kool-Aid
9. Saltines
10. Blue Kool-Aid

Five Concerns of Sunday School Teachers, 1947

1. Will the child bring a Bible to Sunday school?
2. Will the child bring any visitors?
3. Will the child have a daily quiet time at home?
4. Will the child pay attention for the full hour?
5. Will the child do well in the "Sworddrill"?

Five Concerns of Sunday School Teachers, 1997

1. Will the child know what a Bible is?
2. Will the child have any friends?
3. Will the child ever turn off the TV at home?
4. Will the child pay attention for the complete three-and-a-half-minute video I'm showing?
5. Will anyone pull a gun?

If you ever cite the information above, please include the fact that it is *not* based on any survey, just hatched in my odd little brain.

Six Basic Needs of Young People

1. The need to believe that life is meaningful and has a purpose
2. The need for a sense of community and deeper relationships
3. The need to be appreciated and loved
4. The need to be listened to—to be heard
5. The need to feel that they're growing in their faith
6. The need for practical help in developing a mature faith

From *The Religious Life of Young Americans,* by George H. Gallup Jr. and Robert Bezilla (The George H. Gallup International Institute, 1992).

Nine Marks of Successful Church Youth Programs

1. They teach the basics of the faith.
2. They teach kids to serve.
3. The leaders understand the kids.
4. Young people are mentored by those who remember what it was like to be young.
5. The young people are accepted as they are.
6. Kids are taught to develop their gifts.

7. Young people are given responsibility and leadership.
8. Kids are taught to live righteously.
9. Love.

Adapted from *The Religious Life of Young Americans,* by George H. Gallup Jr. and Robert Bezilla (The George H. Gallup International Institute, 1992).

Ten Myths and Realities about Young People Today

1. **Myth:** They don't believe in God.
   Reality: Nearly all believe in God or a universal spirit.
2. **Myth:** If they believe in God, they probably think of him as some abstract force.
   Reality: The great majority believe in a personal God, one who observes them and punishes or rewards them.
3. **Myth:** They don't think much about life after death.
   Reality: They are more likely than their elders to believe in heaven or hell.
4. **Myth:** They only pray or read the Bible when they have to—in church.
   Reality: Most pray and read the Bible when they're alone.
5. **Myth:** They think church youth groups are hokey and boring.
   Reality: They give high marks to youth groups, religious instruction, and youth ministers.
6. **Myth:** They go to church youth groups only to meet members of the opposite sex or because they're forced to.
   Reality: Some do, but more go because it helps them deal with their problems or get a better understanding of their faith.
7. **Myth:** Only older folks tune in to programs on Christian radio or TV.
   Reality: One out of three teens responds favorably to Christian broadcasting.
8. **Myth:** They're greedy and narcissistic.
   Reality: They often volunteer and give to charity and would do so more often if they were asked.
9. **Myth:** Soon after entering college, they become atheists or agnostics.
   Reality: Many stop attending church at that time, but most do not lose their faith.
10. **Myth:** They think religion is too old-fashioned to answer complex modern problems.
    Reality: Most reject the notion that religion is not relevant in the modern world.

Adapted from *The Religious Life of Young Americans,* by George H. Gallup Jr. and Robert Bezilla (The George H. Gallup International Institute, 1992).

Tips for Reaching Generation X

1. Don't call them Generation X.
2. Use all the programs you'd use with high schoolers, but understand that young adulthood has a host of new life issues.
3. Tell stories. For this group, truth is narrative, not propositional.
4. Talk about your experiences, not your knowledge. For this group, life proves more than logic.
5. Ask good questions.
6. You don't have to be coy about raising spiritual issues. In general, this group is very interested in spiritual things.
7. Don't assume they know the Bible.
8. Use examples from old sitcoms.
9. Try meeting somewhere besides the church.
10. Don't waste a lot of effort defending the institutional church. Talk about Jesus.
11. Don't expect steady attendance, and don't give them grief if they miss a meeting.
12. Serve coffee.

How to Tell When Your Youth Leader Is Getting Too Old

1. She begins every time of singing with "Pass It On."
2. He thinks MTV means Missionary Travel Vehicle.
3. The first time she saw a kid with a nose ring, she called an ambulance.
4. After the five-minute opening icebreaker, he needs 10 more minutes to catch his breath.
5. She hasn't gotten the hang of video curriculum—still prefers flannelgraph.
6. His idea of "contemporary Christian music" is anything by John W. Peterson.
7. She asked her son what he wanted for his birthday. The son said, "Nine Inch Nails." She went to a hardware store.
8. He worries that Twila Paris music is a bit too wild.
9. She went to a sleep over with the girls in the youth group and she actually slept.
10. The other youth leaders call him mister.

PART 5

CHRISTIAN LIVING

Ten Things That Once Were Taboo for Christians
(At least in some quarters)

1. Drinking
2. Smoking
3. Chewing tobacco
4. Dancing
5. Jazz/Rock/New Age music
6. Going to movies
7. Playing cards (except Rook)
8. Shopping on Sundays
9. Having a television
10. Saying "Gosh."

Notes for a New Believer

1. Pray all the time. It's as natural as breathing. Let God be a part of your daily life.
2. Set aside a special time for special prayer. Take time to stop and listen to God.
3. Learn the Bible. Find some sort of survey course that will give you the gridwork of Scripture so you can start putting in the pieces.
4. But read the Bible, too. It's not always an academic exercise. This is how God speaks to you.
5. Share your faith naturally. Don't let anyone guilt you into "evangelizing." Just share what you're learning.
6. Let God's Spirit shape your lifestyle. There may be some hard decisions to make, some major changes in your behavior. Look out for the legalists who will restrict, but pay close attention to God's guidance.
7. Go to a good church. You need a community of believers who will nurture your faith, not stomp on it. Find a Christ-centered church where you feel joy.
8. Get involved with a small group of believers. Even the best church can't give you the personalized attention you need. A small group can.

9. Form a plan for dealing with doubt. Times will come when you start to doubt everything—God, yourself, your faith. Memorize Scripture, find good counselors, etc.
10. Rejoice. Your natural radiance is a gift to the church. Don't let anyone diminish it.

Questioning Our Consumption

As a Christian in our consumer culture, how can you tell if you're spending, buying, and consuming too much? Here's a list of questions to ask:

1. Does this purchase hurt the environment?
2. Does it deplete the earth's resources, thus depriving future generations?
3. Could I rent, borrow, or co-own this thing instead of buying it?
4. Would a Christian from a Third World nation understand why I need this item?
5. Is this the most efficient, most durable model I can buy?
6. Instead of buying this, could I repair or modify something I already have?
7. Will this purchase make me less likely to serve Jesus in the next five years?

Adapted from "Responsible Living Means Living for People, Not Things," by Gary Gunderson and Tom Peterson, *SEEDS Magazine,* June 1985.

Six Ways to Fight the Love of Money

1. Realize you are rich. Stop comparing your income to the few people who have more. Get a worldwide perspective.
2. Decide as a family what to do. Economic planning has to involve the whole household. Get everyone on board.
3. List what you really need. Get to the bottom line. What would your life be like without that new CD player, TV, or RV?
4. Decide to do one thing this month to rebel against the tyranny of money. Try another thing next month.
5. Give your excess money wisely. How about church, missions, hunger relief, education, investment in developing nations?
6. Don't be discouraged. It's not easy to loosen money's grip on us, but keep at it.

Adapted from "The Love of Money," by Randy Petersen, *Bible Newsletter,* October 1982.

Nine Political Principles from Scripture

From the brochure *Evangelicals for Social Action.*

1. The family is a divinely willed institution (Genesis 2:23-24; Matthew 19:3-9).
2. Every human life is sacred (Genesis 1:27; 1 Timothy 2:3-6).
3. Religious and political freedom are God-given, inalienable rights (Matthew 5:45; 13:36-43).
4. God and his obedient people have a very special concern for the poor (Psalms 35:10; 103:6; Jeremiah 22:1-5; 1 John 3:17).
5. God requires just economic patterns in society (Isaiah 10:1-4; Jeremiah 5:26-29; James 5:1-5).
6. God requires Christians to be peacemakers (Micah 4:3; Matthew 5:9).
7. The Creator requires stewardship of the earth's resources (Genesis 1:28; Psalm 24:1).
8. Sin is both personal and social (Amos 4:1-2; Isaiah 5:8-11; Ezekiel 22:6-11).
9. Personal integrity is vital.

Seven More Biblical Political Principles

1. We should obey the government . . .
2. . . . except when we're asked to do something that violates God's commands.
3. We should not engage in private violence.
4. When governments fight, we should align ourselves with the one that stands closest to what's right and good.
5. We should seek freedom for all but understand that freedom has fences.
6. We should seek justice for all.
7. We are citizens of two kingdoms, with responsibilities in both.

Adapted from "A Creed for Christian Citizens," by Kenneth Kantzer, *Christianity Today,* September 11, 1995.

Seven Promises of a Promise Keeper

Few organizations have ever hit the ground running like Promise Keepers, a Christian organization calling men to be better husbands, fathers, citizens, churchmen. Here are the seven promises on which PK is based:

1. A Promise Keeper is committed to honoring Jesus Christ through worship, prayer, and obedience to God's Word through the power of the Holy Spirit.
2. A Promise Keeper is committed to pursuing vital relation-

ships with a few other men, understanding that he needs
brothers to help him keep his promises.

3. A Promise Keeper is committed to practicing spiritual, moral,
ethical, and sexual purity.

4. A Promise Keeper is committed to building a strong marriage
and family through love, protection, and biblical values.

5. A Promise Keeper is committed to supporting the mission of
his church by honoring and praying for his pastor and by
actively giving his time and resources.

6. A Promise Keeper is committed to reaching beyond any racial
and denominational barriers to demonstrate the power of biblical unity.

7. A Promise Keeper is committed to influencing his world,
being obedient to the great commandment (Mark 12:30) and
the great commission (Matthew 28:19-20).

Five Interesting Facts from the Pollsters

The pollster in question is George Barna, as he reports in his 1991
book, *What Americans Believe* (Regal).

1. Not surprisingly, 93% of "born-again Christians" find it "very
desirable" to have a closer relationship with God. But so do
60% of those who are *not* born-again Christians.

2. About one-third (34%) of Americans claim to be born-again
Christians, but 62% say they've made a personal commitment
to Jesus Christ that is still important in their lives today.

3. More than two-thirds (71%) of all Americans agree that the
Bible "is the written Word of God and is totally accurate in all
it teaches."

4. But only 45% of the 71% listed above had read the Bible in
the previous week. (And only 58% of self-described "Christians" had done so.)

5. Regularly, about 45% of Americans attend church in a given
week. (But that number jumped to 49% in the year of the
Gulf War.)

Ten Examples of Christianese

1. Just ("I just want to thank you, Lord. . . .")

2. Lord, Lord ("Lord, I just . . . Lord, I want to thank you . . .
Lord, Lord . . .")

3. Special music (as opposed to all the other ordinary music we
do?)

4. Quiet time (like sleep?)

5. Burden ("I've been very burdened for you.")

6. Bless/Blessed/Blessing ("I feel *so* blessed.")
7. Fellowship (See *food*.)
8. Led (". . . as you are led.")
9. Share ("I feel led to share this with you.")
10. Witness ("I've been witnessing to people all week.")

I'm not saying these are bad words. But they are unique to our Christian culture, leaving an outsider to say, "Huh? What? You just feel led to share a burden about the blessing of witnessing?"

PART 6

MORE QUOTES

What 10 Famous People Had to Say about Prayer

1. Ralph Waldo Emerson: "Prayer as a means to a private end is meanness and theft."
2. Oscar Wilde: "When the gods choose to punish us, they merely answer our prayers."
3. Samuel Taylor Coleridge: "He prayeth well who loveth well / Both man and bird and beast."
4. Victor Hugo: "Certain thoughts are prayers. There are moments when, whatever be the attitude of the body, the soul is on its knees."
5. Margaret Mead: "Prayer does not use up artificial energy, doesn't burn up fossil fuel, doesn't pollute."
6. Voltaire: "I have never made but one prayer to God, a very short one: 'O Lord, make my enemies ridiculous.' And God granted it."
7. Abraham Lincoln: "We, on our side, are praying to Him to give us victory, because we believe we are right; but those on the other side pray to Him, too, for victory, believing they are right. What must He think of us?"
8. Benjamin Franklin: "Serving God is doing good to man, but praying is thought an easier service and therefore more generally chosen."
9. Mark Twain: "It is best to read the weather forecasts before we pray for rain."
10. William Shakespeare, *Hamlet:* "My words fly up, my thoughts remain below. / Words without thoughts never to heaven go."

What 10 Famous People Had to Say about Christians

1. Roman writer Lucian: "The Christians are unhappy people who are persuaded that they will survive death and live forever; as a result, they despise death and are willing to sacrifice their lives to their faith."
2. William Penn: "To be like Christ is to be a Christian."
3. Lord Byron: "Some Christians have a comfortable creed."
4. Blaise Pascal: "Let it not be imagined that the life of a good

Christian must be a life of melancholy and gloominess: for he only resigns some pleasures to enjoy others infinitely better."

5. William Shakespeare, *Twelfth Night:* "Methinks sometimes I have no more wit than a Christian."

6. George Bernard Shaw: "This man [Jesus] has not been a failure yet, for nobody has ever been sane enough to try his way."

7. Alfred, Lord Tennyson: "The churches have killed their Christ."

8. Albert Camus: "What the world expects of Christians is that they should speak out, loud and clear, and that they should voice their condemnation in such a way that never a doubt, never the slightest doubt, could arise in the heart of the simplest man. They must get away from abstractions and confront the blood-stained face that history has taken on today."

9. Tammy Faye Bakker: "You don't have to be dowdy to be a Christian."

10. Historian Will Durant, in *The Story of Civilization:* "There is no greater drama in human record than the sight of a few Christians, scorned or oppressed by a succession of emperors, bearing all trials with a fierce tenacity, multiplying quietly, building order while their enemies generated chaos, fighting the sword with the word, brutality with hope, and at last defeating the strongest state that history has known. Caesar and Christ had met in the arena, and Christ had won."

What 10 Famous People Had to Say about God

1. Elizabeth Barrett Browning: "God himself is the best poet / And the real is his song."

2. Robert Browning: "But God has a few of us / whom he whispers in the ear; / The rest may reason and welcome; / 'tis we musicians know.

3. Albert Einstein: "God is a scientist, not a magician."

4. Napoleon Bonaparte: "God is always on the side of the big battalions."

5. Benjamin Franklin, suggesting that the Constitutional Convention begin with prayer: "The longer I live, the more convincing proofs I see of this truth—that God governs in the affairs of men. And if a sparrow cannot fall to the ground without his notice, is it probable that an empire can rise without his aid?"

6. Tori Amos, modern rock singer: "God, sometimes you just don't come through."

7. Winston Churchill: "I am ready to meet my Maker. Whether my Maker is prepared for the ordeal of meeting me is another matter."

8. Buckminster Fuller: "God is a verb."
9. George H. Gallup: "I could prove God statistically. Take the human body alone—the chances that all the functions of an individual would just happen is a statistical monstrosity."
10. Woody Allen, in the movie *Manhattan:*
    Yale: You're so self-righteous. I mean, we're just people, we're just human beings. You think you're God!
    Ike: I gotta model myself after someone!

Assorted Quotes from Great Christians

1. Blaise Pascal: "Human beings must be known to be loved; but the Divine must be loved to be known."
2. Harry Emerson Fosdick: "True prayer is putting oneself under God's influence."
3. Archbishop Trench: "We must not conceive of prayer as an overcoming of God's reluctance, but as a laying hold of his highest willingness."
4. Thomas à Kempis: "It is a great art to commune with God."
5. Charles Haddon Spurgeon: "If we look for mercy in that day, we must show mercy in this day."
6. Dwight L. Moody: "The Christian on his knees sees more than the philosopher on tiptoe."
7. Donald Grey Barnhouse: "I am not so sure I believe in 'the power of prayer,' but I believe in the power of the Lord who answers prayer."
8. John Bunyan: "Prayer is a shield to the soul, a sacrifice to God, and a scourge to Satan."
9. C. S. Lewis: "The hardness of God is kinder than the softness of men, and his compulsion is our liberation."
10. George Macdonald: "I find doing the will of God leaves me no time for disputing about his plans."

PART 7

MUSIC

Hymns and Choruses

Hymns Written by Saints

1. "All Creatures of Our God and King," Francis of Assisi
2. "Of the Father's Love Begotten," Aurelius Prudentius
3. "Splendor of God's Glory Bright," Ambrose
4. "Christian, Dost Thou See Them on the Holy Ground," Andrew of Crete
5. "Jesus the Very Thought of Thee," Bernard of Clairvaux
6. "Jerusalem the Golden," Bernard of Cluny
7. "The Day of Resurrection," John of Damascus
8. "All Glory, Laud, and Honor," Theodulph of Orleans
9. "Shepherd of Eager Youth," Clement of Alexandria
10. "O Christ, Our King, Creator Lord," Gregory the Great

Hymns and Responses by Classical Composers

1. "O Sacred Head, Now Wounded," arranged by J. S. Bach
2. "Sing with All the Sons of Glory," Ludwig van Beethoven
3. "The Strife Is O'er," Giovanni Palestrina
4. "Saviour, Hear Us, We Pray," Johannes Brahms
5. "Joy to the World!" George Frideric Handel
6. "Glorious Things of Thee Are Spoken," Franz Joseph Haydn
7. "Now Thank We All Our God," Felix Mendelssohn
8. "Jesus, I My Cross Have Taken," Wolfgang Amadeus Mozart
9. "Be Still, My Soul," Jean Sibelius
10. "Onward, Christian Soldiers," Arthur S. Sullivan (of Gilbert & Sullivan)

Ten Songs That Are Difficult to Sing While Seated

1. "The Hallelujah Chorus"
2. "Stand Up for Jesus"
3. "Rise Up, O Men of God!"
4. "Standing on the Promises"
5. "Wonderful Grace of Jesus"
6. "Stand Up and Bless the Lord"

7. "Be Exalted, O God"
8. "Christ the Lord Is Risen Today"
9. "Onward, Christian Soldiers"
10. "Victory in Jesus"

Ten Favorite Choruses, 1940 to 1955

1. "Rolled Away"
2. "For God So Loved the World"
3. "Every Day with Jesus" (sometimes combined with "The Hash Chorus")
4. "Cheer Up Ye Saints of God"
5. "I'm So Happy and Here's the Reason Why"
6. "Some Golden Daybreak"
7. "Safe Am I"
8. "Thank You Lord for Saving My Soul"
9. "Hallelu"
10. "V Is for Victory"

Ten Favorite Choruses, 1955 to 1970

1. "He's Able"
2. "He Owns the Cattle"
3. "Give Me Oil"
4. "God Can Do Anything"
5. "Isn't He Wonderful"
6. "My Lord Knows the Way through the Wilderness"
7. "Life Is a Symphony"
8. "A Mansion over the Hilltop"
9. "Happiness Is the Lord"
10. "Do, Lord"

Ten Favorite Choruses, 1970 to 1985

1. "Worthy Is the Lamb"
2. "Oh, How He Loves You and Me"
3. "He Is Lord"
4. "Alleluia"
5. "Pass It On"
6. "God Is So Good"
7. "I've Got Peace like a River"
8. "Because He Lives"
9. "His Name Is Wonderful"
10. "Seek Ye First the Kingdom of God"

Ten Favorite Choruses after 1985

1. "How Majestic Is Your Name"
2. "He Has Made Me Glad"

3. "Jesus, Name above All Names"
4. "Let There Be Glory and Honor and Praises"
5. "This Is the Day That the Lord Has Made"
6. "Majesty"
7. "Our God Reigns"
8. "Sing Hallelujah to the Lord"
9. "Thou Art Worthy"
10. "Be Exalted, O God"

Worship Songs Written by Twila Paris That Are Commonly Used in Churches

1. "Faithful Men"
2. "He Is Exalted"
3. "How Beautiful"
4. "Lamb of God"
5. "The Warrior Is a Child"
6. "We Bow Down"
7. "We Will Glorify"
8. "You Have Been Good"

Ten Tunes to Which You Can Sing "Amazing Grace" (or Vice Versa)

1. "Joy to the World!"
2. "Am I a Soldier of the Cross?"
3. "O for a Thousand Tongues"
4. "The Lord's My Shepherd, I'll Not Want"
5. "Must Jesus Bear the Cross Alone?"
6. "According to Thy Gracious Word"
7. "Alas! and Did My Saviour Bleed?"
8. "Jesus, the Very Thought of Thee"
9. "O God, Our Help in Ages Past"
10. "All Hail the Power of Jesus' Name"

Ten Hymns in Which the Last Stanza Refers to Death and Dying

1. "Guide Me, O Thou Great Jehovah"
2. "O God, Our Help in Ages Past"
3. "O Could I Speak the Matchless Worth"
4. "What Wondrous Love Is This"
5. "Nearer, Still Nearer"
6. "There Is a Fountain"
7. "Rock of Ages"
8. "Because He Lives"
9. "More Love to Thee"
10. "I Am Thine, O Lord"

Ten Hymns That Include the Word Wave or Waves

1. "Jesus Saves!"
2. "Send the Light!"
3. "The Cleansing Wave"
4. "Let the Lower Lights Be Burning"
5. "I've Anchored in Jesus"
6. "Master, the Tempest Is Raging"
7. "Hark, Hark, My Soul"
8. "Love Lifted Me"
9. "Grace Greater than Our Sin"
10. "Throw out the Lifeline"

Ten Hymns from 10 Different Denominations

1. "He Leadeth Me," by Rev. Henry Gilmore, First Baptist Church, Philadelphia
2. "This Is My Father's World," by Rev. Maltbie Babcock, Presbyterian church in Lockport, New York
3. "O Little Town of Bethlehem," by Rev. Phillips Brooks, Holy Trinity Episcopal Church, Philadelphia
4. "A Mighty Fortress Is Our God," by Dr. Martin Luther, Wittenburg, Germany
5. "What a Friend We Have in Jesus," by Joseph Scriven, Brethren preacher, Port Hope, Ontario
6. "The Way of the Cross Leads Home," by Mrs. Jessie Brown Pounds, wife of a minister in the Christian church, Indianapolis, Indiana
7. "My Faith Looks Up to Thee," by Rev. Ray Palmer, Congregational church in Albany, New York
8. "The Old Rugged Cross," by George Bennard, Salvation Army evangelist, near Battle Creek, Michigan
9. "And Can It Be" (and many, many others), by Charles Wesley of the Methodist church
10. "Jesus, Thy Blood and Righteousness," by Nicholas Ludwig von Zinzendorf of the Moravian Church

Ten Women Hymn Writers and the Hymns They Wrote

1. Katharina von Schlegel (1697–?): "Be Still, My Soul"
2. Charlotte Elliott (1789–1871): "Just As I Am"
3. Cecil Frances Alexander (1818–1895): "There Is a Green Hill Far Away"
4. Anna Bartlett Warner (1820–1915): "Jesus Loves Me"
5. Elizabeth C. Clephane (1830–1869): "Beneath the Cross of Jesus"

6. Frances Ridley Havergal (1836–1879): "Take My Life, and Let It Be"
7. Anne Ross Cousin (1824–1906): "The Sands of Time"
8. Frances Jane Van Alstyne, a.k.a. Fanny Crosby (1820–1915): "All the Way My Savior Leads Me" and many others
9. Lina Sandell Berg (1832–1903): "Day by Day"
10. Helen Howarth Lemmel (1864–1961): "Turn Your Eyes upon Jesus"

Ten Hymn Stanzas That Make You Say "Huh?" after You Have Sung Them

1. The fell disease on every side
   Walks forth with tainted breath
   And pestilence, with rapid stride,
   Bestrews the land with death.
   ("IN GRIEF AND FEAR TO THEE, O LORD")

2. Bacchus long has held his reign
   Causing want, and woe and pain
   Broken hearts and ruined homes once bright and fair
   Heeding not the mother's fear, nor the wives' and children's tears
   From their heart's blood, snatching jewels rich and rare.
   ("WE'RE AN ARMY BRAVE AND TRUE")

3. Soil not thy plumage, gentle dove
   With sublunary things,
   Till in the fount of light and love,
   Thou shalt have bathed thy wings.
   ("THE CHRISTIAN TO HIS SOUL")

4. Then with my waking tho'ts
   Bright with Thy praise
   Out of my stony griefs
   Bethel I'll raise;
   So by my woes to be
   Nearer, my God, to Thee!
   Nearer, my God, to Thee,
   Nearer to Thee!
   ("NEARER, MY GOD, TO THEE")

5. Sweet hour of prayer, sweet hour of prayer,
   May I thy consolation share.
   Till, from Mount Pisgah's lofty height,
   I view my home, and take my flight.
   This robe of flesh, I'll drop, and rise

To seize the everlasting prize,
And shout, while passing through the air,
Farewell, farewell, sweet hour of prayer.
("SWEET HOUR OF PRAYER")

6. Here I raise mine Ebenezer
Hither by Thy help I'm come;
And I hope by Thy good pleasure
Safely to arrive at home.
("COME, THOU FOUNT")

7. I'd sing the characters he bears
And all the forms of love he wears
("OH, COULD I SPEAK THE MATCHLESS WORTH")

8. Ah me, Ah me, that I
In Kedar's tents here stay.
("JERUSALEM ON HIGH")

9. Onward, bark! the cape I'm rounding;
See the blessed wave their hands.
("SAFE WITHIN THE VALE")

10. Fly me, riches! fly me, cares!
While I that coast explore;
Flattering world! with all thy snares,
Solicit me no more.
("RISE, MY SOUL, AND STRETCH THY WINGS")

Ten Appropriate Hymns to Sing When the Sermon Is on Philippians 2:9-11

1. "All Hail the Power of Jesus' Name"
2. "At the Name of Jesus"
3. "Blessed Be the Name"
4. "Jesus Shall Reign"
5. "Majestic Sweetness"
6. "O for a Thousand Tongues"
7. "Praise Him, Praise Him"
8. "Rejoice, the Lord Is King"
9. "To God Be the Glory"
10. "Majesty"

Ten Appropriate Hymns to Sing When the Sermon Is on the Armor of God in Ephesians 6:10-17

1. "Am I a Soldier of the Cross?"
2. "Faith Is the Victory"
3. "Fight the Good Fight"

4. "He Who Would Valiant Be"
5. "Lead On, O King Eternal"
6. "Onward, Christian Soldiers"
7. "Soldiers of Christ Arise"
8. "Stand Up, Stand Up for Jesus"
9. "The Son of God Goes Forth to War"
10. "Who Is on the Lord's Side?"

Ten Appropriate Hymns to Sing When the Sermon Is on "Come unto Me" in Matthew 11:28, KJV

1. "Come, Ye Sinners, Poor and Needy"
2. "Softly and Tenderly Jesus Is Calling"
3. "Jesus Is Tenderly Calling"
4. "I Heard the Voice of Jesus Say"
5. "I Lay My Sins on Jesus"
6. "I Must Tell Jesus"
7. "Just When I Need Him"
8. "Moment by Moment"
9. "Near to the Heart of God"
10. "Whosoever Will"

Ten Appropriate Hymns to Sing When the Sermon Is on Psalm 23

1. "All the Way My Savior Leads Me"
2. "Day by Day"
3. "Guide Me, O Thou Great Jehovah"
4. "He Leadeth Me"
5. "Savior, Like a Shepherd Lead Us"
6. "Shepherd of Love"
7. "Shepherd of Tender Youth"
8. "Surely Goodness and Mercy"
9. "The King of Love My Shepherd Is"
10. "The Lord's My Shepherd"

Ten Great Third Stanzas That Should Never Be Treated like Third Stanzas

1. You fearful saints, fresh courage take;
   The clouds you so much dread
   Are big with mercy and shall break
   In blessings on your head.
   ("GOD MOVES IN A MYSTERIOUS WAY")

2. And when I think that God, His Son not
       sparing,
   Sent Him to die, I scarce can take it in,
   That on the cross, my burden gladly bearing,

He bled and died to take away my sin.
("HOW GREAT THOU ART")

3. Well might the sun in darkness hide,
   And shut its glories in,
   When Christ, the mighty Maker, died
   For His own creature's sin.
   ("ALAS! AND DID MY SAVIOR BLEED?")

4. That He should leave His place on high,
   And come for sinful man to die,
   You count it strange? So once did I
   Before I knew my Savior.
   ("MY SAVIOR")

5. My sin—O the bliss of this glorious thought—
   My sin, not in part, but the whole,
   Is nailed to the cross, and I bear it no more;
   Praise the Lord, praise the Lord, O my soul.
   ("IT IS WELL WITH MY SOUL")

6. What a wonderful redemption!
   Never can a mortal know
   How my sin, though red like crimson,
   Can be whiter than the snow.
   ("ALL THAT THRILLS MY SOUL")

7. He pointed to the nailprints
   For me His blood was shed;
   A mocking crown, so thorny,
   Was placed upon His head.
   I wonder what He saw in me
   To suffer such deep agony.
   ("IN TENDERNESS HE SOUGHT ME")

8. When through the deep waters I call thee to go,
   The rivers of sorrow shall not overflow,
   For I will be with thee thy troubles to bless
   And sanctify to thee thy deepest distress.
   ("HOW FIRM A FOUNDATION")

9. The dearest idol I have known,
   Whate'er that idol be,
   Help me to tear it from Thy throne
   And worship only Thee.
   ("O FOR A CLOSER WALK WITH GOD")

10. For the love of God is broader
    Than the measure of man's mind.

And the heart of the Eternal
Is most wonderfully kind.
("THERE'S A WIDENESS IN GOD'S MERCY")

Great Hymns from Psalms

1. "The King of Love My Shepherd Is" (Psalm 23)
2. "Lift Up Your Heads, Ye Mighty Gates" (24)
3. "A Mighty Fortress Is Our God" (46)
4. "Jesus Shall Reign Where'er the Sun" (72)
5. "O God, Our Help in Ages Past" (90)
6. "Joy to the World!" (98)
7. "All People That on Earth Do Dwell" (100)
8. "Praise My Soul the King of Heaven" (103)
9. "Worship the King" (104)
10. "Praise to the Lord, the Almighty" (150)

Ten Hymns That Use the Word Sleep or Asleep

So avoid using them in your watch-night service.

1. "O Little Town of Bethlehem"
2. "Anywhere with Jesus"
3. "Silent Night"
4. "Sun of My Soul"
5. "I Lift My Heart to Thee"
6. "Away in a Manger"
7. "Asleep in Jesus"
8. "We're Going Home, No More to Roam"
9. "Rise My Soul to Watch and Pray"
10. "With the Morn in Radiance Breaking"

Ten Hymns That Use the Word Wake or Awake

1. "Crown Him with Many Crowns"
2. "Awake My Soul to Joyful Days"
3. "I Want a Principle Within"
4. "Awake My Soul and with the Sun"
5. "Far, Far Away in Heathen Darkness Dwelling"
6. "Wake the Song"
7. "I Am Thinking Today of That Beautiful Land"
8. "Wonderful Story of Love"
9. "Holy Spirit, Truth Divine"
10. "Away in a Manger"

Christmas Songs with Angels Mentioned in the First Verse

1. "Angels from the Realms of Glory"
2. "Hark, the Herald Angels Sing"
3. "Angels We Have Heard on High"
4. "The First Noel"

5. "In a Cave, a Lowly Stable"
6. "It Came upon the Midnight Clear"
7. "What Child Is This?"
8. "While Shepherds Watched Their Flocks by Night"
9. "O Come, All Ye Faithful"
10. "Infant Holy, Infant Lowly"

Ten Renaissance Christmas Carols

1. "King Jesus Hath a Garden"
2. "Ding Dong Merrily on High"
3. "Jesus Christ the Apple Tree"
4. "There Stood in Heaven a Linden Tree"
5. "Tomorrow Shall Be My Dancing Day"
6. "Up! Good Christian Folk and Listen"
7. "Blessed Be That Maid Mary"
8. "Joseph Dearest, Joseph Mine"
9. "Ding, Dong, Virgin Mary"
10. "Past Three a Clock"

Classical Music

Eight Classical Composers Who Were Devout Christians

1. Johann Sebastian Bach (1685–1750)
2. Dietrich Buxtehude (1637–1707)
3. Erdmann Neumeister (1671–1756)
4. Georg Philipp Telemann (1681–1767)
5. Franz Joseph Haydn (1732–1809)
6. Felix Mendelssohn (1809–1847)
7. Anton Bruckner (1824–1896)
8. Antonín Dvořák (1841–1904)

Top 10 Oratorios

"Top 10" is, of course, a matter of opinion. But I consulted my favorite music scholar for her knowledgeable opinions, which you'll find throughout this section.

1. *Messiah,* George Frideric Handel
2. *Elijah,* Felix Mendelssohn
3. *Christ on the Mount of Olives,* Ludwig van Beethoven
4. *Christus,* Franz Liszt
5. *Blessed Is the Man,* Antonio Vivaldi
6. *Paradise and the Peri,* Robert Schumann
7. *The Childhood of Christ,* Hector Berlioz
8. *The Creation,* Franz Joseph Haydn

9. *St. Matthew's Passion,* Johann Sebastian Bach
10. *The Dream of Gerontius,* Sir Edward Elgar

Top 10 Requiems

1. Mozart *Requiem*
2. Victoria *Requiem*
3. Brahms *A German Requiem*
4. Bruckner *Requiem*
5. Verdi *Requiem*
6. Berlioz *Grande Messe des Morts*
7. Fauré *Requiem*
8. Duruflé *Requiem*
9. John Rutter *Requiem*
10. Andrew Lloyd Webber *Requiem*

Bach's Top 10

1. "Jesu, Joy of Man's Desiring"
2. *Mass in B Minor*
3. *Magnificat*
4. *"Ein Feste Burg"* ("A Mighty Fortress")
5. *St. John Passion*
6. *St. Matthew Passion*
7. *Christmas Oratorio*
8. *Jesu, Meine Freunde (Jesus, My Joy)*—Motet
9. *Christ Lag in Todesbanden (Christ Lay in Death's Dark Prison)*—Cantata no. 4
10. *Gott Ist Mein König (God Is My King)*—Cantata no. 71

The 20th Century's 14 Best Works of Sacred Music

1. *Symphony of Psalms,* Igor Stravinsky
2. *Sacred Service,* Ernest Bloch
3. *War Requiem,* Benjamin Britten
4. *Ceremony of Carols,* Benjamin Britten
5. *Saint Nicholas,* Benjamin Britten
6. *Hodie,* Ralph Vaughan Williams
7. *The Peaceable Kingdom,* Randall Thompson
8. *Mass,* Leonard Bernstein
9. *Mass in G Major,* Francis Poulenc
10. *Missa Brevis,* Zoltán Kodály
11. *Lamentations of Job,* Daniel Pinkham
12. *King David,* Arthur Honegger
13. *Dies Irae,* Krzysztof Penderecki
14. *Psalm 90,* Charles Ives

Composers of Musical Settings of St. John Passion

1. Anotonio Scandello (1517–1580)
2. Christoph Demantius (1567–1643)
3. Heinrich Schütz (1585–1672)
4. Johann Sebastian Bach (1685–1750)
5. George Frideric Handel (1685–1759)

Best Choirs Singing Classical Christian Music

1. Vienna Boys' Choir
2. The Waverly Consort
3. Choir of Westminster Abbey
4. Robert Shaw Festival Singers
5. Choir of King's College, Cambridge
6. The King's Singers
7. Philharmonia Chorus
8. The Benedictine Monks of Santo Domingo de Silos
9. St. Petersburg Chamber Choir
10. The Monteverdi Choir

Contemporary Christian Music

My Favorite Christian Musicians in the '70s

I'm just one guy, but I was a college student in the '70s, and I knew what I liked.

1. Larry Norman
2. Phil Keaggy
3. Second Chapter of Acts
4. Love Song
5. Ken Medema
6. Lamb
7. The Archers
8. Randy Stonehill
9. Children of the Day
10. Rebirth (a local band from the Lancaster, Pennsylvania, area, I believe)

My Favorite Christian Musicians in the '80s

I was getting a job, setting up an apartment, and what was playing on my stereo?

1. Leslie Phillips
2. DeGarmo and Key
3. The Seventy Sevens
4. Petra
5. Daniel Amos

6. Steve Taylor
7. Michael Omartian
8. Glad
9. Mark Heard
10. Paul Smith

My Favorite Christian Musicians in the '90s

Mellowing out? Hardly. Probably just desperately grabbing for a few last measures of youth.

1. Hoi Polloi
2. Rachel Rachel
3. Margaret Becker
4. Charlie Peacock
5. Susan Ashton
6. Jars of Clay
7. Glenn Kaiser
8. Out of the Grey
9. Kim Hill
10. Point of Grace

Some Christian Artists in Mainstream Pop Music

1. Amy Grant
2. Michael W. Smith
3. Kathy Troccoli
4. Take 6
5. DC Talk
6. Jars of Clay
7. Bebe and Cece Winans

Ten Artists/Groups on the Cover of CCM Magazine

Between December 1995 and October 1996, the following musicians graced the cover of *CCM Magazine* (formerly *Contemporary Christian Music*):

1. DC Talk
2. Wayne Watson
3. Newsboys
4. Gary Chapman
5. Audio Adrenaline
6. Mark Lowry
7. Twila Paris
8. Peter King (Dakoda Motor Company)
9. Kirk Franklin
10. Steven Curtis Chapman

Top Christian Albums, October 1996

1. *Jars of Clay,* Jars of Clay
2. *Whatcha Lookin' 4,* Kirk Franklin & The Family
3. *Jesus Freak,* DC Talk
4. *I Love to Tell the Story,* Andy Griffith
5. *Them,* PFR
6. *The Message,* 4HIM
7. *God,* Rebecca St. James
8. *Take Me to Your Leader,* Newsboys
9. *I'll Lead You Home,* Michael W. Smith
10. *Bloom,* Audio Adrenaline
    Extra Credit: Which of these things is not like the others?

Top Christian Albums in 1986

Best-selling albums of April 1986, as reported by *CCM Magazine* (June 1986):

1. *Morning like This,* Sandi Patty
2. *Unguarded,* Amy Grant
3. *Hymns Just for You,* Sandi Patty
4. *Captured in Time and Space,* Petra
5. *The Champion,* Carman
6. *Instrument of Praise,* Phil Driscoll
7. *Songs from the Heart,* Sandi Patty
8. *Black and White in a Grey World,* Leslie Phillips
9. *Age to Age,* Amy Grant
10. *Straight Ahead,* Amy Grant

Twelve Albums by Twila Paris

Paris is one of those people who give Christian music a good name. Her personal integrity and heart for Christian service are apparent. Here's a brief discography of her notable career:

1. *Knowin' You're Around* (1981)
2. *Keepin' My Eyes on You* (1982)
3. *The Warrior Is a Child* (1984)
4. *Kingdom Seekers* (1986)
5. *Same Girl* (1987)
6. *For Every Heart* (1988)
7. *It's the Thought* (1989)
8. *Cry for the Desert* (1990)
9. *Sanctuary* (1991)
10. *A Heart That Knows You* (1992)
11. *Beyond a Dream* (1994)
12. *Where I Stand* (1996)

Dove Awards, 1996

Annually, the Dove Awards recognize the best in Christian music.

+ Artist of the Year: DC Talk
+ Group of the Year: Point of Grace
+ Song of the Year: "Jesus Freak" (written by Mark Heimermann, Toby McKeehan)
+ Male Vocalist of the Year: Gary Chapman
+ Female Vocalist of the Year: Cece Winans
+ New Artist of the Year: Jars of Clay
+ Songwriter of the Year: Michael W. Smith

Also honored:

+ Church of Rhythm (rap)
+ Charlie Peacock (alternative song)
+ Sixpence None the Richer (alternative album)
+ Petra (rock album)
+ Holy Soldier (metal album)
+ Point of Grace (pop album)
+ Larnelle Harris (inspirational album)
+ MidSouth (country song)
+ Michael James (country album)
+ Anointed (urban and contemporary gospel)
+ Angelo & Veronica (urban album)
+ Shirley Caesar (traditional Gospel album)
+ Audio Adrenaline (video)

Dove Awards, 1991

+ Artist of the Year: Steven Curtis Chapman
+ Group of the Year: Petra
+ Song of the Year: "Another Time, Another Place" (written by Gary Driskel)
+ Male Vocalist of the Year: Steven Curtis Chapman
+ Female Vocalist of the Year: Sandi Patty
+ New Artist of the Year: 4HIM
+ Songwriter of the Year: Steven Curtis Chapman

Also honored:

+ The Winans (rap song)
+ DC Talk (rap album)
+ Holy Soldier (metal album)
+ Bruce Carroll (inspirational song)
+ Take 6 (contemporary black Gospel)
+ Carman (video)

Pop Music

Eight Popular Songs with Heaven in the Title

1. "Knocking on Heaven's Door"
2. "Stairway to Heaven"
3. "Heaven Help the Man"
4. "Pennies from Heaven"
5. "Thank Heaven for Little Girls"
6. "Heaven Must Be Missing an Angel"
7. "My Blue Heaven"
8. "Heaven beside You"

Five Popular Songs with Angel in the Title

1. "I'm Living Right Next Door to an Angel"
2. "Teen Angel"
3. "Johnny Angel"
4. "Angel of the Morning"
5. "Angel from Montgomery"

Ten Popular Songs That Refer to God or Jesus

1. "American Pie," recorded by Don McLean: "The Father, Son, and Holy Ghost . . ."
2. "Rocky Mountain High," John Denver: "You can talk to God and listen to the casual reply."
3. "Fire and Rain," James Taylor: "Won't you look down upon me, Jesus?"
4. "Grow Old with Me," John Lennon: "God bless our love."
5. "Mrs. Robinson," Simon and Garfunkel: "Jesus loves you more than you will know."
6. "Jesus Is Just Alright with Me," Doobie Brothers
7. "From a Distance," Bette Midler: "God is watching us from a distance."
8. "The River," Garth Brooks: "With the good Lord as my captain . . ."
9. "One of Us," Joan Osborne: "What if God was one of us?"
10. "God Shuffled His Feet," Crash Test Dummies

Pop Singers Who Have Recorded Spiritual Lyrics

I'm not saying all these folks are Christians, but in their music they have expressed some aspect of faith and spirituality.

1. Van Morrison
2. Al Green
3. Bob Dylan
4. Bono (U2)

5. Sting
6. Prince
7. Whitney Houston
8. Tori Amos
9. Wynonna
10. Sarah McLachlan

Thanks to *CCM Magazine,* July 1996.

Nine Groups/Artists with Religious-Sounding Names

1. Genesis
2. Abba
3. Billy Joel
4. Tori Amos
5. Jesus and Mary Chain
6. God Lives Underwater
7. Collective Soul
8. Soul Asylum
9. Stone Temple Pilots

CHURCH HISTORY

The Religious and Social Groups of First-Century Israel

1. Hassideans. An old religious-reform group that was dying out by Jesus' time. Influenced the Pharisees.
2. Pharisees. A religious and political party, the group tried to make religion not a temple-only thing but an everyday family thing. This may explain their comprehensive legal code.
3. Sadducees. An aristocratic, priest-centered group that exercised considerable control under the Roman authorities. Denied bodily resurrection and angels.
4. Zealots. Fanatics for the Jewish faith, they refused any compromise with Rome and would not pay taxes.
5. Sicarii. An extreme splinter group of Zealots between A.D. 50 and 70. Conducted terrorist activities against those who collaborated with Rome.
6. Herodians. Not a religious group at all, they supported the Herods and accepted Greek culture.
7. Essenes. An ascetic, legalistic, monastic-type group throughout Judea. From the Dead Sea Scrolls, we know there was a community of them at Qumran, and we know something of their strict behavioral code.

Prophets and "Messiahs" in Jesus' Time and After

As the New Testament tells us, there were others who surfaced in Israel claiming to be specially chosen by God to deliver his people. Here are some of them:

1. Judas, son of Hezekiah (c. 4 B.C.)
2. Simon (c. 4 B.C.)
3. Athronges (c. 4–2 B.C.)
4. "The Samaritan" (c. A.D. 26–36)
5. Theudas (c. A.D. 45)
6. "The Egyptian" (c. A.D. 56)
7. Jesus, son of Hananiah (A.D. 62–69)
8. Menahem, son of Judas the Galilean (c. A.D. 66)

9. Simon bar Giora (A.D. 68–70)
10. Bar Kochba (A.D. 132–135)

Basics of the Gospel

What were the apostles teaching in the early years of the church? The book of Acts presents several sermons that have similar outlines. From these, we can identify the essential *kerygma,* or germ, of the gospel.

1. Jesus fulfills Old Testament promises.
2. Jesus did mighty works, empowered by God.
3. He was crucified, according to God's plan.
4. He was raised from the dead, and the apostles were witnesses of this.
5. God has exalted Jesus as "Lord."
6. The Holy Spirit has come to Jesus' followers.
7. Jesus will come again to judge the world and restore all things.
8. Everyone who hears this should repent and be baptized.

What Happened to the Apostles?

Except for Peter and John, we lose track of Jesus' disciples after the Gospels. Where did they go? For this, we have to rely on ancient church traditions since we have little hard evidence.

1. Peter. Possibly visited Britain and Gaul (France). Crucified upside down during Nero's persecution.
2. Andrew. Preached in Scythia, Asia Minor, Greece. Crucified in Achaia.
3. James, son of Zebedee. Scripture tells us he was killed by Herod Agrippa and was the first apostle martyred.
4. John. The elder of the Ephesian church. Exiled to Patmos. Returned to Ephesus, where he died a natural death, the only apostle not martyred.
5. Philip. Ministered in Asia Minor and was crucified there.
6. Matthew. Could have gone to Ethiopia, Parthia, Persia, or Macedonia. Pick one.
7. Thomas. Preached in Babylon and went on to India, where he was martyred.
8. Bartholomew. Went with Philip to Hierapolis in Asia Minor, then to Armenia, where he was martyred.
9. James, son of Alphaeus. May have preached in Syria.
10. Thaddaeus/the other Judas. May have gone to Edessa.
11. Simon the Zealot. Possibly went to Persia, Egypt, Carthage, or Britain.
12. Judas Iscariot. Betrayed Jesus, then hanged himself.

Ten Reasons the Romans Didn't Like Christians

1. Fear of a growing movement.
2. Christians met in secret, fostering suspicion.
3. Christians talked about "love" between "brothers and sisters"—moral Romans misunderstood this as incest.
4. Christians ate the "body and blood" of the "Son"—this was misunderstood as cannibalism.
5. Christians followed a "criminal," Jesus, who received capital punishment for his "crimes."
6. Christians didn't have the normal altars, temples, or images you'd expect from a "real" religion.
7. Christians welcomed the poor and lower class, earning sneers from Roman social climbers.
8. Christians tended to avoid the Roman festivals (which honored their gods) and thus were considered antisocial.
9. Christians tended to be pacifists and avoided military service and thus were considered unpatriotic.
10. Christians refused to honor the emperor as a deity, and their refusal was taken as treason.

Fourteen Caesars
And how they affected Christianity

1. Augustus (27 B.C.–A.D. 14). His census got Mary and Joseph to Bethlehem. His *Pax Romana* made travel safe for later missionaries.
2. Tiberius (A.D. 14–37). He appointed Pontius Pilate and was the "Render to Caesar" Caesar.
3. Claudius (41–54). He expelled Jews from Rome (including Aquila and Priscilla). He considered Christianity a form of Judaism, which gave it legal protection but unofficial skepticism.
4. Nero (54–68). Nero was the Caesar to whom Paul appealed and who eventually had him killed (Peter, too). In 64, he launched a fierce persecution against Christians, blaming them for a fire in Rome.
5. Vespasian (69–79). He and his son Titus quashed the Jewish Revolt, destroying the temple in 70. This was a watershed event separating Jews from Christians. Christianity was now a world religion; it had no Judean base to call home.
6. Domitian (81–96). He liked to be called "Lord and God." He resumed persecution against Christians, especially among the nobility, and was probably the one who exiled John to Patmos.
7. Trajan (98–117). Trajan had a "don't ask, don't tell" policy regarding Christians, as we know from his correspondence

with Governor Pliny. He was the first of a series of "good" emperors of Rome, but these emperors continued to support the arrest and execution of Christians by local authorities.

8. Septimius Severus (193–211). He launched several severe but sporadic sweeps of Christians, especially in North Africa.

9. Alexander Severus (222–235). He oversaw a period of calm for Christians. He had some highly placed Christians in his household and may have been a secret believer himself. During this time, some churches actually had their own church buildings!

10. Decius (249–251). He demanded that Christians show their loyalty by offering incense to the emperor-deity. Most Christians refused and suffered persecution.

11. Valerian (253–260). The empire was crumbling, and Valerian blamed the Christians. Persecution continued.

12. Diocletian (284–305). He began the Great Persecution in 301, destroying Christian books and buildings and arresting bishops and then common believers.

13. Galerius (305–311). Galerius continued the Great Persecution savagely until a week before his death. He issued the Edict of Toleration that called for a stop to the persecution (though a few local incidents were still reported).

14. Constantine (312–337). Through a miraculous conversion or political opportunism, he became a Christian in 312 and, as co-emperor, issued the Edict of Milan in 313, officially granting Christianity freedom of religion. In 324, as sole emperor, he made Christianity the official faith of the realm.

Ten Early-Church Fathers

1. Clement
2. Ignatius
3. Polycarp
4. Justin Martyr
5. Irenaeus
6. Clement of Alexandria
7. Hippolytus
8. Origen
9. Tertullian
10. Cyprian

Ten Early-Church Mothers

1. Anthusa, mother and teacher of John Chrysostom
2. Cecelia, a second-century martyr from a noble family

3. Helena, mother of Constantine and funder of rebuilding projects in Palestine
4. Macrina, fourth-century church leader, sister of and counselor to Basil the Great and Gregory of Nyssa; founded perhaps the first convent
5. Marcella, fourth-century noblewoman who led Bible classes and financially supported Jerome's translation of the Bible
6. Marcellina, fourth-century churchwoman known for her prayer, her teaching, and her support of her brother, Bishop Ambrose; he sent her three important letters on theology
7. Olympias, correspondent and friend of John Chrysostom; this fourth-century noblewoman gave freely to the poor.
8. Paula, associate and close friend of the translator Jerome, a noblewoman who gave of her money and intellect to build the church
9. Perpetua, a martyr in North Africa at the start of the third century; the story of her courageous death has inspired many
10. Thecla, a legendary associate of Paul. A fanciful story emerged about such a woman in the third century, with dubious details, but it was probably based on a real person. The historical Thecla probably carried on a teaching and healing ministry near Seleucia, even starting a hospital.

Heresies of the Early Church

1. Docetism. The belief that Jesus was God but only appeared to be human.
2. Gnosticism. Similar to Docetism but held that God reserved special knowledge for special people. Jesus was one of several angelic beings on the ladder to the full knowledge of God.
3. Modalism/Monarchianism/Sabellianism. Held that God had three modes—Father, Son, and Spirit—but only one at a time.
4. Arianism. Believed that Jesus was a godlike being but not "of the same substance" as the Father.
5. The Ebionites' teaching. Like the Judaizers of Paul's day, these felt it was necessary for Christians to keep the Jewish law.
6. Montanism. Adventist and charismatic, Montanists also observed a strict moral code. Perhaps it's a bit too unpredictable for the orthodox believers.
7. Novatianism. The question: How do you treat traitors, those who compromised their faith to avoid persecution? Novationists took a hard line; the mainstream church offered forgiveness.
8. Donatism. Same question, different century. Donatists essen-

tially set up their own separatist church primarily in North Africa in the 400s.

How Many Christians?

The estimated percentage of world population that was at least nominally Christian in selected years.

A.D. 100—0.6%
500—22.4%
1000—18.7%
1500—19.0%
1800—23.1%
1900—34.4%
1985—32.4%
2000—32.3% (projected)

. . . In Africa

The estimated percentage of African population that was at least nominally Christian, in selected years.

A.D. 100—2.3% (Ethiopian treasurer, Matthew, city of Alexandria)
500—40.0% (Strong Christian community in North Africa)
1000—15.2% (The Muslim movement takes hold)
1500—2.8% (Crusades saved Europe but lost Africa)
1800—1.4% (North is Muslim, south is unreached)
1900—9.2% (Missions begin in south, David Livingstone)
1985—45.4% (Church in south grows like crazy)

. . . In Russia

The estimated percentage of the total population in Russia and the territory of the former U.S.S.R. that was at least nominally Christian

A.D. 100—0.0% (No significant outreach yet)
500—3.0% (Early missionaries)
1000—5.4% (Cyril, Methodius, not much else)
1500—50.0% (Orthodox church grows)
1800—80.0% (Christianity woven . . .
1900—83.6% . . . into Russian culture)
1985—36.3% (Communism rules, church goes underground)

Ten Prominent Missionaries before the Dawn of Modern Missions

1. Ulfilas (311–381): Apostle to the Goths on the lower Danube
2. Patrick (389–461): Missionary to Ireland
3. Columba (521–597): Missionary to Scotland

4. Augustine, archbishop of Canterbury (d. c. 604): Missionary to England
5. Willibrod (658–739): Missionary to Holland and Denmark
6. Boniface (680–755): Missionary to the Germans
7. Cyril (826–869): Missionary to the Slavs
8. Methodius (d. 885): Missionary to Moravia
9. Raymond Lull (1235–1315): Missionary to the Muslims
10. Christian Frederick Schwartz (1726–1798): Missionary to India

Five Non-Christian Religions
Who started them and when and where they are dominant

1. Islam. Founded by Muhammad in Arabia in A.D. 622, it is dominant in the Mideast and northern Africa and is prevalent in parts of Asia.
2. Hinduism. Developed gradually since about 1200 B.C., it has become the dominant religion in India.
3. Buddhism. About 525 B.C., Siddhartha Gautama Buddha of India developed his Four Truths of Enlightenment, and Buddhism is now the dominant religion of the Far East.
4. Shintoism. The written record of Shintoism can be traced only to the sixth and seventh centuries A.D., but it undoubtedly goes back further than that. It is the dominant religion of Japan.
5. Animism. Primitive peoples around the world have developed various forms of spirit worship, believing in worship of the dead, fetishism, totemism, and nature.

Martin Luther's 10 Best Theses
These are taken from the 95 he posted on the door of the church in Wittenberg, sparking the Protestant Reformation.

1. (#1) When our Lord and Master Jesus Christ says repent, He means that the whole life of believers upon earth should be a constant and perpetual repentance.
2. (#32) Those who fancy themselves sure of salvation by indulgences will go to perdition along with those who teach them so.
3. (#35) They are teachers of anti-Christian doctrines who pretend that to deliver a soul from purgatory, or to buy an indulgence, there is no need of either sorrow or repentance.
4. (#36) Every Christian who truly repents of his sins, enjoys an entire remission both of the penalty and of the guilt, without any need of indulgences.

5. (#37) Every true Christian, whether dead or alive, participate in all the blessings of Christ or of the Church, by God's gift, and without a letter of indulgence.
6. (#42) We should teach Christians that he who gives to the poor, or lends to the needy, does better than he who purchase an indulgence.
7. (#62) The true and precious treasure of the Church is the holy gospel of the glory and grace of God.
8. (#76) The indulgence of the pope cannot take away the small est daily sin, as far as regards the guilt or the offense.
9. (#86) Why, say they, does not the pope, who is richer than the richest Croesus, build the mother-church of St. Peter with his own money, rather than that of poor Christians?
10. (#95) For it is far better to enter into the kingdom of heaven through much tribulation than to acquire a carnal security by the consolation of a false peace.

The Beginnings of 10 Protestant Denominations
Who started them and when

1. Lutheran church: Martin Luther in 1530, when the Augsburg Confession was formulated.
2. Presbyterian church: John Calvin in 1541, when he organized the church in Geneva, Switzerland. And/or John Knox in 1560, when he returned to Scotland from Europe and Protestantism was made the official religion of Scotland.
3. Moravian church: John Hus in 1415, when he was burned at the stake (but the roots of the Moravian church go back to a still earlier date).
4. Episcopal church: Thomas Cranmer in 1533. Henry VIII revolted against the pope, but it was Cranmer, archbishop of Canterbury, who had the Bible translated into the vernacular and formulated the Thirty-Nine Articles of the Church.
5. Mennonite church: Menno Simons in 1536, when he renounced the Roman Catholic church and joined the Anabaptist movement.
6. Baptist church: John Smyth in 1608, shortly after he and his Separatist church had left England and fled to Holland, where he came in contact with Anabaptists.
7. Friends (Quakers): George Fox in about 1652, when he experienced the "inner light" and direct communication with God
8. Methodist church: John Wesley in 1739, a year after his Aldersgate Street conversion.
9. Christian Churches (Disciples of Christ): Thomas and Alexan

der Campbell in 1827, shortly after their Restoration Movement was launched and they drifted apart from the Baptists.
10. Salvation Army: William and Catherine Booth in 1878, when they formed their society into an organization with military form.

Ten Groups Whose Views Diverge from Historic Christian Beliefs
Who started them and when

1. Jehovah's Witnesses: Charles Taze Russell in 1879, when the *Watchtower* magazine was begun
2. The Church of Jesus Christ of Latter-Day Saints (Mormons): Joseph Smith in 1830
3. Theosophy: Helena Blavatsky in 1875
4. Christian Science: Mary Baker Eddy in 1879
5. The Unity School: Charles Fillmore in 1889
6. Church of Scientology: L. Ron Hubbard in 1950
7. Unification Church: Sun Myung Moon in 1954
8. Transcendental Meditation: Maharishi Mahesh Yogi in 1958
9. The Church Universal and Triumphant: Mark Prophet, succeeded by his widow, Elizabeth Clare Prophet, in 1958
10. Children of God: David Berg in 1970

Nine Respected Colleges That Started in Colonial Days as Religious Schools

1. Harvard (1636)
2. William & Mary (1693)
3. Yale (1701)
4. Penn (1740)
5. Princeton (1746)
6. Columbia (1754)
7. Brown (1764)
8. Rutgers (1766)
9. Dartmouth (1769)

Famous Evangelists in America before 1900

1. Francis Asbury
2. Peter Cartwright
3. Dwight L. Moody
4. Jonathan Edwards
5. Charles G. Finney
6. George Whiteford
7. James McGready

8. Gilbert Tennent
9. Miguel Serra
10. Phoebe Palmer

Ten Shapers of American Church Music

1. *The Bay Psalm Book* of 1661
2. Singing schools, 1720–1775
3. Development by Moravians of group singing and instrumental accompaniment
4. Camp meetings, c. 1800
5. Lowell Mason, composer, director, instructor
6. Singin' Billy Walker's *Southern Harmony* songbook (1835)
7. Shaped notes (to teach people to read music)
8. The Fisk University Singers and the popularity of Negro spirituals
9. The Sunday school movement
10. Ira Sankey, Moody's musical sidekick

Twenty-three Famous Christian Williams

Thanks to my researcher and father, William J. Petersen, former editor of *Eternity Magazine*.

1. William Blaikie, Scottish Presbyterian theologian, author of *The Personal Life of David Livingstone* and other books
2. William Booth, founder of the Salvation Army
3. William Bradford, second governor of Plymouth Colony, author of *History of the Plymouth Colony*
4. William Bramwell, Methodist preacher and revivalist under Wesley
5. Billy Bray, fiery Cornish evangelist
6. Bill Bright, founder of Campus Crusade for Christ
7. William Jennings Bryan, American political leader, lawyer, and biblical apologist
8. William Carey, missionary to India, called the father of modern missions
9. William Cowper, poet, writer of "There Is a Fountain Filled with Blood," and "O for a Closer Walk with God"
10. William Doane, businessman, inventor and composer; wrote music for "Jesus, Keep Me Near the Cross," "I Am Thine, O Lord," and many others
11. Bill Gaither, popular gospel musician and songwriter in the 1970s; wrote "There's Just Something about That Name" and many others
12. Bill Gothard, director of the Basic Youth Conflicts seminars

13. Billy Graham, 20th-century evangelist
14. William Holman Hunt, British painter of religious subjects, including "The Light of the World"
15. William Law, British scholar, best known for his *Serious Call to a Devout and Holy Life*
16. William McGuffey, Presbyterian minister and educator, best known for the McGuffey readers, which sold more than 20 million copies
17. William of Ockham, 14th-century scholastic philosopher who taught that the Bible was the only infallible source of authority in matters of faith and life
18. William Penn, Quaker preacher, author of *No Cross, No Crown,* and founder of Pennsylvania as a "holy experiment"
19. William Ramsey, Scottish archaeologist and church historian, noted for his writings on the apostolic church
20. Billy Sunday, professional baseball player and American evangelist in early part of 20th century
21. William Tennent, Presbyterian clergyman and educator, established a "log college" that eventually became the parent of Presbyterian educational institutions, including Princeton College and Seminary
22. William Tyndale, Bible translator, reformer, and martyr
23. William Wilberforce, English statesman, philanthropist, and abolitionist who led the fight against slavery in England

Eight Strange Places Where People Met Christ

1. Out in the woods by some fallen trees in upstate New York (Charles G. Finney)
2. On his way to a cricket match in England (C. T. Studd)
3. In a cell at Sing Sing penitentiary (Jerry McAuley)
4. In a Boston shoe store (D. L. Moody)
5. In a Civil War hospital bed in Marietta, Georgia (Russell Conwell)
6. Under a eucalyptus tree in Hollywood, California (Charles E. Fuller)
7. While strategizing a gang rumble in New York City (Tom Skinner)
8. After awaking with a Sunday-morning hangover in a Florida motel (D. James Kennedy)

Ten Famous Christians Who Spent Time in Prison

1. Dietrich Bonhoeffer
2. John Bunyan
3. Charles Colson

  4. Miles Coverdale
  5. George Fox
  6. Madame Guyon
  7. Ignatius of Antioch
  8. John Knox
  9. Raymond Lull
  10. Samuel Rutherford

Ten Forgotten Wives of Famous Preachers

  1. Emma Moody, wife of D. L.
  2. Polly Newton, wife of John
  3. Susie Spurgeon, wife of Charles Haddon
  4. Katie Luther, wife of Martin
  5. Idelette Calvin, wife of John
  6. Anna Zwingli, wife of Huldrych
  7. Anne Smith, wife of Rodney (Gypsy)
  8. Nancy Morgan, wife of G. Campbell
  9. Bethany Lloyd-Jones, wife of Martyn
  10. Nell Sunday, wife of Billy

Ten Times in Church History When Christians Have Had End-Times Fever

  1. The church at Thessalonica in approximately A.D. 52 (see 2 Thessalonians).
  2. The Montanists in Phrygia in 156.
  3. The Doomsday Explosion of 1000; earlier in the century, a Catholic ecumenical council had predicted the return of Christ at the end of the millennium.
  4. At the time of the Third Crusade in 1186, a "Letter of Toledo" was circulated throughout Europe predicting the end in the near future.
  5. Brother Arnold, Friend of the Poor, in 1260 predicted "the end" in his writings from Swabia.
  6. Outside of Prague in 1420, Martinek Hauska predicted that God would destroy the earth with fire on February 20.
  7. Early Anabaptists predicted that the Millennium would begin in 1533 and that Strassburg had been chosen by God to be the new Jerusalem.
  8. In upstate New York, William Miller predicted that Christ would return between March 21, 1943, and March 21, 1944, and thousands of followers gathered on hilltops to await his coming.
  9. The Jehovah's Witness cult has set numerous dates, including 1914, 1915, 1918, 1923, 1925, and 1975.

10. As we approach the end of another millennium, many more predictions have emerged. A best-selling book was entitled *Christ Returns by 1988: 101 Reasons Why.* The president of a prominent Christian radio network publicly aired his prediction of Christ's return in 1995. Others are saying 2000.

Ten American Martyrdoms Since 1900

The *World Mission Digest* has estimated that 119 million Christians have been martyred during this century.

1. 1900: Mary Huston and Hattie Rice of the China Inland Mission were attacked by a mob in Shangsi Province. All told, 188 missionaries and their children were murdered in the Boxer Rebellion that year.
2. 1934: John and Betty Stam of the China Inland Mission were slain by Communist guerrillas in Anhwei Province.
3. 1936: In Ethiopia, Tom Devers and Cliff Mitchell of the Sudan Interior Mission were slain and mutilated by tribesmen.
4. 1952: Paul and Priscilla Johnson of the Christian and Missionary Alliance were martyred by terrorists after serving in Thailand for five years.
5. 1952: Walter Erickson and Edward Tritt of The Evangelical Alliance Mission were slain and mutilated by tribesmen in western New Guinea.
6. 1956: Five missionaries from three different missions boards were slain as they attempted to bring the gospel to Auca Indians in Ecuador. The missionaries were Jim Elliot, Nate Saint, Roger Youderian, Ed McCully, and Pete Fleming.
7. 1962: Elwood Jacobsen of Wycliffe Bible Translators was shot in the head by the Viet Cong 60 miles out of Saigon, Vietnam.
8. 1964: Dr. Paul Carlson of the Evangelical Covenant Church was captured and taken hostage by Simba rebels and later killed, along with others.
9. 1977: In Ethiopia, veteran missionaries Don and Lyda McClure of the United Presbyterian Church were slain by bandits.
10. 1978: In Cameroon, Ernest and Miriam Erickson of the Lutheran Brethren Church were killed after 33 years of missionary service. Some speculated they may have been victims of spirit worshipers.

Eight Shapers of Mainstream Protestant Churches

In a thoughtful book, *Vital Signs: The Promise of Mainstream Protestantism,* by Milton J. Carter, John M. Mulder, and Louis B. Weeks (Eerdmans, 1996), the authors present "eight of the most important developments that have shaped American mainstream Protestant history in the 20th century."

1. The third disestablishment. The first was the legal division between church and state (1780s). The second was the popular acceptance of Catholicism, Judaism, and other faiths (early 1900s). Now Christianity is losing its cultural support, with our culture becoming "post-Christian."
2. Politicized religion. For a time, churches stayed on the sidelines of political contests. But with revolutions in the 1960s and 1980s, churches are now very political.
3. Christianity as a world religion. Parts of Africa, Asia, and Latin America are now more thoroughly Christian than the U.S.A
4. Ecumenism. This reappraises the differences between denominations.
5. The Fundamentalist schism. The growth in fundamentalism has torn some mainstream denominations apart.
6. Pluralism. Influence is exerted from both genders and many races. But there is also the creeping assumption that everyone values are equally valid, and that all points of view should be accepted.
7. Choice. Freedom of religion now includes freedom from religion. Our society has exalted personal choice as a supreme valu
8. The declining significance of denominationalism. Who cares whether you're Presbyterian or Lutheran? Where do you stan on certain modern issues?

Top Religion Stories of 1995

Chosen by *The Christian Century*

1. The assassination of Yitzhak Rabin, prime minister of Israel
2. The Million Man March on Washington, D.C.
3. The Christian Coalition
4. Church-state debates
5. Financial scandals (Episcopal, Methodist, New Era)
6. John Paul II's agenda
7. Promise Keepers
8. Ethno-religious war in Bosnia
9. Beijing women's conference
10. Southern Baptists' apology for racism

Top Religion Stories of 1985

Again, chosen by *The Christian Century*

1. The Sanctuary movement (churches housing Central American refugees)

2. The troubles in South Africa
3. Mideast terrorism
4. Rumblings in the Roman Catholic church
5. The Bitburg furor (Reagan's visit to a German war cemetery)
6. Famine in Africa
7. The AIDS crisis
8. Encroachments on church-state separation
9. The Roth case (Lutheran minister defrocked because of activism on behalf of the unemployed)
10. Southern Baptist feuding

Top Religion Stories of 1975

According to *The Christian Century*

1. Ethical dilemmas—Karen Quinlan and others
2. The fight over women's ordination in the Episcopal Church
3. The anti-Zionism resolution passed by the U.N.
4. Christians in repressive societies (Chile, South Korea, Philippines, South Africa)
5. Church response to refugees from Saigon
6. The charismatic movement and the tension it causes in various denominations
7. Political/theological civil war in the Lutheran church—Missouri Synod
8. World Council of Churches' Fifth Assembly in Nairobi
9. Trend toward conservatism in several mainline denominations
10. Liberation and civil-rights struggles around the world

Great Journeys of Christians

1. Paul's second missionary journey, when he enters Europe.
2. Constantine marches on Rome.
3. Francis leaves Assisi for itinerant ministry.
4. Luther makes a pilgrimage to Rome.
5. John Knox flees to Geneva and returns to Scotland.
6. The Pilgrims sail to the New World on the *Mayflower*.
7. John Wesley travels to America and meets some Moravians on the way.
8. William Carey, the father of modern missions, goes to India.
9. The Judsons travel as missionaries from America to Burma.
10. Martin Luther King Jr. leads a march on Washington, D.C.

Six Things That Happened on April Fool's Day

1. 1548: British Parliament ordered first printing of *The Book of Common Prayer*.

2. 1745: American David Brainerd began his missionary work with Indians at Kaunaumeek, Massachusetts.
3. 1925: Hebrew University was inaugurated in Jerusalem by Lord Balfour.
4. 1927: The Eastern European Mission was founded in Chicago
5. 1932: Gerhard Kittel put out the first partial volume of his *Theological Dictionary of the New Testament,* a classic work of biblical scholarship.
6. 1956: William R. Newell died. This Congregationalist pastor wrote the song "At Calvary."

Nine Shared Birthdays (or "Deathdays") of Famous Christians

1. January 31
   1892: Death of Charles Haddon Spurgeon, great British preacher/author
   1955: Death of John R. Mott, founder of the Student Christian movement

2. February 21
   1109: Death of Anselm of Canterbury, the church's greatest thinker since Augustine
   1142: Death of Peter Abelard, French scholar/teacher linked romantically with Heloise
   1945: Death of Eric Liddell, Olympic champion and missionary to China (His story is told in the movie *Chariots of Fire*

3. April 25
   1599: Birth of Oliver Cromwell, British Protestant leader
   1792: Birth of John Keble, founder of the Oxford Movement to restore Anglicanism
   1887: Birth of Charles E. Fuller, evangelist, cofounder of Fuller Seminary

4. May 27
   1819: Birth of Julia Ward Howe, social reformer, author of "The Battle Hymn of the Republic"
   1902: Birth of Peter Marshall, chaplain of the U.S. Senate, husband of author Catherine Marshall
   1927: Birth of Ralph Carmichael, composer, who was contemporary Christian music before CCM was cool
   735: Death of the Venerable Bede, monk and scholar
   1564: Death of John Calvin, reformer

5. June 9
   597: Death of Columba, pioneer missionary to Scotland
   1834: Death of William Carey, father of modern missions

1911: Death of Carry Nation, temperance activist

6. July 9

    1838: Birth of P. P. Bliss, who wrote many songs, including "Wonderful Words of Life"

    1896: Birth of William Cameron Townsend, founder of Wycliffe Bible Translators

7. September 14

    407: Death of John Chrysostom, golden-tongued preacher

    1321: Death of Dante Alighieri, author of *The Divine Comedy*

8. November 4

    1740: Birth of Augustus M. Toplady, who wrote "Rock of Ages"

    1771: Birth of James Montgomery, newspaper editor who wrote "Angels from the Realms of Glory"

    1903: Birth of Watchman Nee, Chinese Christian author

9. December 5

    1791: Death of Wolfgang Amadeus Mozart, composer

    1848: Death of Joseph Mohr, Austrian pastor who wrote "Silent Night"

    1983: Death of John A. T. Robinson, English bishop who caused controversy with his book *Honest to God*

The 100 Most-Important Dates in Church History

Several years ago, I was involved in a project with Ken Curtis, founder of *Christian History Magazine,* to come up with this list. We surveyed the magazine's readers and an assortment of scholars, and then we wrote a book (with Stephen Lang) on our findings. Here, in chronological order, are the dates and events we came up with.

1. 64: The fire in Rome (sparking persecution by Nero)
2. 70: Titus destroys Jerusalem
3. c. 150: Justin Martyr writes his *Apology*
4. c. 156: The martyrdom of Polycarp
5. 177: Irenaeus becomes bishop of Lyons
6. c. 196: Tertullian begins to write Christian books
7. c. 205: Origen begins writing
8. 251: Cyprian writes *On the Unity of the Church*
9. 270: Anthony begins his life as a hermit
10. 312: The conversion of Constantine
11. 325: The Council of Nicea
12. 367: Athanasius's letter recognizes the New Testament canon
13. 385: Bishop Ambrose defies the empress
14. 387: Conversion of Augustine
15. 398: John Chrysostom becomes bishop of Constantinople

16. 405: Jerome completes the Vulgate
17. 432: Patrick goes as missionary to Ireland
18. 451: The Council of Chalcedon
19. 529: Benedict of Nursia establishes his monastic order
20. 563: Columba goes as a missionary to Scotland
21. 590: Gregory I becomes pope
22. 664: Synod of Whitby
23. 716: Boniface sets out as missionary
24. 731: The Venerable Bede completes his *Ecclesiastical History of the English Nation*
25. 732: The Battle of Tours
26. 800: Charlemagne crowned emperor
27. 863: Cyril and Methodius evangelize Slavs
28. 909: Monastery established at Cluny
29. 988: Conversion of Vladimir, Prince of Russia
30. 1054: The East–West schism
31. 1093: Anselm becomes archbishop of Canterbury
32. 1095: Pope Urban II launches the First Crusade
33. 1115: Bernard founds the monastery at Clairvaux
34. c. 1150: Universities of Paris and Oxford founded
35. 1173: Peter Waldo founds the Waldensians
36. 1206: Francis of Assisi renounces wealth
37. 1215: The Fourth Lateran Council
38. 1273: Thomas Aquinas completes work on *Summa Theologica*
39. 1321: Dante completes *The Divine Comedy*
40. 1378: Catherine of Siena goes to Rome to heal the Great Schism
41. c. 1380: Wycliffe oversees English Bible translation
42. 1415: John Hus burned at the stake
43. 1456: Johannes Gutenberg produces the first printed Bible
44. 1478: Establishment of the Spanish Inquisition
45. 1498: Savonarola executed
46. 1512: Michelangelo completes the Sistine Chapel ceiling
47. 1517: Martin Luther posts his 95 Theses
48. 1523: Zwingli leads Swiss Reformation
49. 1525: Anabaptist movement begins
50. 1534: Henry VIII's Act of Supremacy
51. 1536: John Calvin publishes *The Institutes of the Christian Religion*
52. 1540: The pope approves the Jesuits
53. 1545: Opening of the Council of Trent
54. 1549: Cranmer produces *The Book of Common Prayer*
55. 1559: John Knox returns to Scotland to lead Reformation there

56. 1572: St. Bartholomew's Day Massacre
57. 1608–1609: John Smyth baptizes the first Baptists
58. 1611: Publication of the King James Version
59. 1620: Pilgrims sign the Mayflower Compact
60. 1628: Comenius driven from his homeland
61. 1646: The Westminster Confession of Faith
62. 1648: George Fox founds the Society of Friends
63. 1662: Rembrandt completes *The Return of the Prodigal Son*
64. 1675: Philipp Jakob Spener publishes *Pia Desideria*
65. 1678: John Bunyan's *Pilgrim's Progress* published
66. 1685: The births of Johann Sebastian Bach and George Frideric Handel
67. 1707: Publication of Isaac Watts's *Hymns and Spiritual Songs*
68. 1727: Awakening at Herrnhut launches Moravian Brethren
69. 1735: Great Awakening under Jonathan Edwards
70. 1738: John Wesley's conversion
71. 1780: Robert Raikes begins Sunday schools
72. 1793: William Carey sails for India
73. 1807: The British Parliament votes to abolish the slave trade
74. 1811: The Campbells begin the Disciples of Christ
75. 1812: Adoniram and Ann Judson sail for India
76. 1816: Richard Allen founds the African Methodist Episcopal Church
77. 1817: Elizabeth Fry begins ministry to women in prison
78. 1830: Charles Finney's urban revivals begin
79. c. 1830: John Nelson Darby helps start Plymouth Brethren
80. 1833: John Keble's sermon "National Apostasy" initiates the Oxford movement
81. 1854: Hudson Taylor arrives in China
82. 1854: Søren Kierkegaard publishes attacks on Christendom
83. 1854: Charles Haddon Spurgeon becomes pastor in London
84. 1855: Dwight L. Moody's conversion
85. 1857: David Livingstone publishes *Missionary Travels*
86. 1865: William Booth founds the Salvation Army
87. 1870: Pope Pius IX proclaims the doctrine of Papal Infallibility
88. 1886: Student Volunteer movement begins
89. 1906: Azusa Street revival launches Pentecostalism
90. 1910–1915: Publication of *The Fundamentals* launches fundamentalist movement
91. 1919: Karl Barth's *Commentary on Romans* is published
92. 1921: First Christian radio broadcast
93. 1934: Cameron Townsend begins Summer Institute of Linguistics
94. 1945: Dietrich Bonhoeffer executed by Nazis

95. 1948: World Council of Churches is formed
96. 1949: Billy Graham's Los Angeles crusade
97. 1960: Beginnings of the modern charismatic renewal
98. 1962: Second Vatican Council begins
99. 1963: Martin Luther King Jr. leads march on Washington, D.C.
100. 1966–1976: Chinese church grows despite Cultural Revolution

PART 9

COMMUNICATION AND ARTS

Publishing

Ten Classic Devotional Books

1. *My Utmost for His Highest,* Oswald Chambers
2. *The Christian Secret of a Happy Life,* Hannah Whitall Smith
3. *Hinds' Feet in High Places,* Hannah Hurnard
4. *The Pursuit of God,* A. W. Tozer
5. *Morning by Morning,* Charles H. Spurgeon
6. *With Christ in the School of Prayer,* Andrew Murray
7. *Pilgrim's Progress,* John Bunyan
8. *The Practice of the Presence of God,* Brother Lawrence
9. *The Imitation of Christ,* Thomas à Kempis
10. *The Cost of Discipleship,* Dietrich Bonhoeffer

Twenty Christian Classics Written before 1700

1. *The Private Devotions of Lancelot Andrewes,* Lancelot Andrewes
2. *Confessions,* St. Augustine
3. *The City of God,* St. Augustine
4. *The Saints' Everlasting Rest,* Richard Baxter
5. *Grace Abounding,* John Bunyan
6. *Pilgrim's Progress,* John Bunyan
7. *The Institutes of the Christian Religion,* John Calvin
8. *Christian Perfection,* Francois Fenelon
9. *Devotions upon Emergent Occasions,* John Donne
10. *The Diary of David Brainerd,* Jonathan Edwards
11. *The Journal of George Fox,* George Fox
12. *The Secret of Communion with God,* Matthew Henry
13. *Poems,* George Herbert
14. *The Practice of the Presence of God,* Nicolas Herman
15. *A Shewing of God's Love,* Julian of Norwich
16. *The Imitation of Christ,* Thomas à Kempis
17. *Table Talks,* Martin Luther
18. *Pensees,* Blaise Pascal
19. *The Life of St. Theresa of Jesus,* E. A. Peers
20. *Letters,* Samuel Rutherford

Ten Persons in Pilgrim's Progress besides Christian

1. Worldly Wiseman
2. Porter
3. Piety
4. Talkative
5. Faithful
6. Money-love
7. Hopeful
8. Ignorance
9. Giant Despair
10. Apollyon

Twenty Religious Books Popular in Colonial America

1. *The Whole Book of Psalms,* Richard Mather, John Eliot, Thomas Welde (1640)
2. *Spiritual Milk for Boston Babes in Either England,* John Cotton (1656)
3. *Bay Psalm Book* (1665)
4. *God's Call to His People,* John Davenport (1669)
5. *The Day of Doom,* Michael Wigglesworth (1662)
6. *Meat out of the Eater,* Michael Wigglesworth (1670)
7. *Call to the Unconverted,* Richard Baxter (1664)
8. *The Practice of Piety,* Lewis Bayly (1665)
9. *War with the Devil,* Benjamin Keach (1707)
10. *God's Protecting Providence: Remarkable Deliverance of Diverse Persons from the Devouring Waves of the Sea,* Jonathan Dickinson (1699)
11. *The Baptist Catechism,* John Watts (1700)
12. *The Sovereignty and Goodness of God,* Mary Rowlandson (1682)
13. *A Token for Children,* James Janeway (1671)
14. *Alarm to the Unconverted,* Joseph Alleine (1672)
15. *The New England Primer* (1690)
16. *The Protestant Tutor for Children* (1684)
17. *Pilgrim's Progress,* John Bunyan (1681)
18. *Seven Sermons,* Robert Russell (1701)
19. *Husbandry Spiritualized,* John Flavel (1709)
20. *Memorable Providences,* Cotton Mather (1689)

Thirteen Christian Women Who Have Written Best-Sellers

1. Harriet Beecher Stowe
2. Grace Livingston Hill
3. Hannah Whitall Smith
4. Mrs. Charles Cowman
5. Janette Oke
6. Dale Evans Rogers

7. Elisabeth Elliot
8. Helen Steiner Rice
9. Catherine Marshall
10. Eugenia Price
11. Kay Arthur
12. Barbara Johnson
13. Hannah Hurnard

The First 10 Novels Written by Grace Livingston Hill

1. *The Story of a Whim* (1903)
2. *According to the Pattern* (1903)
3. *Because of Stephen* (1904)
4. *The Girl from Montana* (1908)
5. *Marcia Schuyler* (1908)
6. *Phoebe Deane* (1909)
7. *Dawn of the Morning* (1910)
8. *Aunt Crete's Emancipation* (1911)
9. *The Mystery of Mary* (1912)
10. *Lo, Michael* (1913)

Eight Nonfiction Books Written by C. S. Lewis

1. *The Problem of Pain*
2. *Pilgrim's Regress*
3. *Mere Christianity*
4. *Miracles*
5. *The Four Loves*
6. *Surprised by Joy*
7. *Letters to Malcolm*
8. *Reflections on the Psalms*

Ten Persons in C. S. Lewis's The Screwtape Letters *besides* Screwtape

1. Enemy
2. Our Father Below
3. Scabtree
4. Wormwood
5. Fr. Spike
6. Glubose
7. Toadpipe
8. Slubgub
9. Slumtrimpet
10. Triptweeze

Books That Have Shaped American Evangelicals

On its fortieth anniversary, *Christianity Today* mused about a score of Christian books in the last four decades that have had strong influence. (Article by John G. Stackhouse Jr., September 16, 1996.)

1. *Mere Christianity,* C. S. Lewis (1952), and other Lewis books
2. *The Meaning of Persons,* Paul Tournier (1957)
3. *Through Gates of Splendor,* Elisabeth Elliot (1957)
4. *Basic Christianity,* John Stott (1958)
5. *The Genesis Flood,* Henry Morris and John Whitcomb (1961)
6. *Interpreting the Bible,* Berkeley Mickelsen (1963)
7. *God and Other Minds,* Alvin Plantinga (1967)
8. Commentaries by F. F. Bruce and William Barclay
9. *Escape from Reason,* Francis Schaeffer (1968)
10. *The God Who Is There,* Francis Schaeffer (1968)
11. *Introduction to the Old Testament,* R. K. Harrison (1969)
12. *Dare to Discipline,* James Dobson (1970)
13. *Evangelism Explosion,* D. James Kennedy (1970)
14. *The Late Great Planet Earth,* Hal Lindsey (1970)
15. *The Living Bible,* paraphrased by Ken Taylor (1971)
16. *Evidence That Demands a Verdict,* Josh McDowell (1972)
17. *The Politics of Jesus,* John Howard Yoder (1972)
18. *Knowing God,* J. I. Packer (1973)
19. The *Holy Bible,* New International Version (1973)
20. *The Total Woman,* Marabel Morgan (1973)
21. *All We're Meant to Be,* Letha Scanzoni and Nancy Hardesty (1974)
22. *A Theology of the New Testament,* George Ladd (1974)
23. *Christian Mission in the Modern World,* John Stott (1975)
24. *The Battle for the Bible,* Harold Lindsell (1976)
25. *Born Again,* Charles Colson (1976)
26. *Discovering an Evangelical Heritage,* Donald Dayton (1976)
27. *God, Revelation, and Authority,* Carl Henry (1976–1983)
28. *Angels: God's Secret Agents,* Billy Graham (1977)
29. *Intended for Pleasure,* Ed and Gayle Wheat (1977)
30. *Rich Christians in an Age of Hunger,* Ron Sider (1977)
31. *Woman, Be Free,* Patricia Gundry (1977)
32. *Essentials of Evangelical Theology,* Donald Bloesch (1978–1979)
33. *The Authority and Interpretation of the Bible,* Jack Rogers and Donald McKim (1979)
34. *Whatever Happened to the Human Race?* Francis Schaeffer and C. Everett Koop (1979)
35. *Biblical Preaching,* Haddon Robinson (1980)
36. *Fundamentalism and American Culture,* George Marsden (1980)
37. *Between Two Worlds,* John Stott (1982)
38. *The Naked Public Square,* Richard John Neuhaus (1984)

39. *Power Evangelism,* John Wimber with Kevin Springer (1986)
40. *This Present Darkness,* Frank Peretti (1986)

Top 10 Christian-Book Publishers

In number of book titles published per year

1. Thomas Nelson (250)
2. Standard (150)
3. Baker (140)
4. Zondervan (130)
5. HarperSanFrancisco (125)
6. Educational Ministries (120)
7. Bethany House (112)
8. William B. Eerdmans (110–120)
9. Victor (100+)
10. (tie) Barbour (100)
    Liturgical Press (100)
    Tyndale House (100)

Publishers with the Most Best-Sellers

Publishers with the most books making the CBA top 10 between December 1994 and November 1995 in any of five categories: Fiction, Nonfiction cloth, Nonfiction paper, Children, Youth.

1. Multnomah/Questar (in various imprints) 30
2. Word 29
3. Bethany House 26
4. Tyndale House 26
5. Thomas Nelson 21
6. Harvest House 13
7. Zondervan 10
8. Crossway 9
9. Focus on the Family 9
10. Honor Books 7

Publishers with the Most Fiction Best-Sellers

1. Bethany House 16
2. Tyndale House 15
3. Thomas Nelson 7
4. Multnomah/Questar 7
5. Harvest House 4
6. Crossway 3
7. Multnomah 3
8. Word 3

The three previous lists came from *The Christian Writer's Market Guide,* by Sally E. Stuart (Shaw, 1996).

Eight Necessities of Good Fiction

1. An interesting plot that makes sense and stays on track
2. Real characters we care about
3. An environment (setting) that seems real
4. A sense of completeness and consistency
5. Skillful use of language
6. Conflict or tension between characters or possibilities
7. Surprises (without violating the story)
8. Respect for the reader (no condescending or exploiting)

Adapted from "Christian Fiction," by writer/editor Ellen Randall Dunn, *Regeneration Quarterly*, Spring 1996.

Favorite Novels

In its 1993 Book Poll, *Christianity Today* asked readers to name their favorite novel of all time. Here are the results:

1. *Pilgrim's Progress*, John Bunyan
2. The Lord of the Rings Trilogy, J. R. R. Tolkien
3. *The Brothers Karamazov*, Fyodor Dostoevsky
4. *This Present Darkness*, Frank Peretti
5. *In His Steps*, Charles Sheldon
6. The Chronicles of Narnia, C. S. Lewis
7. *Crime and Punishment*, Fyodor Dostoevsky
8. (tie) *Ben-Hur*, Lew Wallace
   Perelandra, C. S. Lewis
   Piercing the Darkness, Frank Peretti
   Prophet, Frank Peretti
   Till We Have Faces, C. S. Lewis

Book Topics Most Popular with Christian Publishers

1. Bible/Biblical studies
2. (tie) Christian living
   Family life
3. Prayer
4. Women's issues
5. Spirituality
6. Inspirational
7. Religion
8. Marriage
9. Current/Social issues

From *The Christian Writer's Market Guide, 1995–1996*, by Sally E. Stuart (Shaw, 1996).

The Christianity Today *Book of the Year*

Since 1990, *Christianity Today* has been surveying readers and experts to name a book of the year (plus winners in various categories). Here are the Overall Winners and Runners-up in each of the last eight years:

+ 1990: *Disappointment with God,* Philip Yancey (Zondervan)
+ Runner-up: *The Gospel According to Jesus,* John MacArthur Jr. (Zondervan)
+ 1991: *Dictionary of Christianity in America,* edited by Daniel G. Reid, Robert D. Linder, Bruce L. Shelley, and Harry S. Stout (InterVarsity)
+ Runner-up: *The Agony of Deceit,* edited by Michael Horton (Moody)
+ 1992: *Recovering Biblical Manhood and Womanhood: A Response to Evangelical Feminism,* edited by John Piper and Wayne Grudem (Crossway)
+ Runners-up: *Darwin on Trial,* Philip Johnson (InterVarsity); *Made in America: The Shaping of Modern Evangelicalism,* Michael S. Horton (Baker)
+ 1993: *Prayer: Finding the Heart's True Home,* Richard Foster (HarperSanFrancisco)
+ Runner-up: *Prophet,* Frank Peretti (Crossway)
+ 1994: *The Body,* Charles Colson with Ellen Santilli Vaughn (Word)
+ Runner-up: *The Message,* Eugene Peterson (NavPress)
+ 1995: *The Scandal of the Evangelical Mind,* Mark A. Noll (Eerdmans)
+ Runner-up: *The Soul of the American University: From Protestant Establishment to Established Nonbelief,* George Marsden (Oxford University Press)
+ 1996: *Not the Way It's Supposed to Be,* Cornelius Plantinga Jr. (Eerdmans)
+ Runner-up: *Evangelicals and Catholics Together: Toward a Common Mission,* edited by Charles Colson and Richard John Neuhaus (Word)
+ 1997: *Darwin's Black Box: The Biochemical Challenge to Evolution,* Michael Behe (Free Press)
+ Runner-up: *The Moral Vision of the New Testament: A Contemporary Introduction to New Testament Ethics,* Richard Hayes (Harper San Francisco)

Twenty-five Bible-Reference Programs for Your Computer

1. AnyText
2. Bible Companion

3. Bible Explorer
4. Bible Link
5. BibleMaster
6. BibleSource
7. Bible Windows
8. BibleWorks for Windows
9. CompuBible
10. Deluxe Bible for Windows
11. GRAMCORD/BibleWord Plus/acCordance
12. Logos Bible Software
13. macBible
14. Multimedia Family Bible
15. New Bible Library
16. Online Bible USA
17. Online Bible Macintosh
18. PC Study Bible
19. QuickVerse
20. The Bible on Disk for Catholics
21. The Holy Scriptures
22. Thompson Chain HyperBible
23. Ultimatum Bible
24. WordSearch
25. WordSoft

Ten Evangelical Magazines That Have Gone Defunct Since 1950

1. *Eternity*
2. *Christian Life*
3. *His*
4. *Sunday School Times*
5. *Christian Herald*
6. *Logos Journal*
7. *Our Hope*
8. *Fundamentalist Journal*
9. *King's Business*
10. *Evangelical Christian*

Former Editors/Staff with Campus Life Magazine

1. Harold Myra
2. Philip Yancey
3. Tim Stafford
4. Jim Long
5. Gregg Lewis
6. Steve Lawhead
7. S. Rickly Christian

Periodicals Whose Names Start with the Word Christian

Some of these actually start with *The*, but I didn't count that. And I may have missed some (but not many!).

1. *Christian Advocate*
2. *Christian American Newspaper*
3. *Christian Author Newsletter*
4. *Christian Baptist*
5. *Christian Bible Teacher*
6. *Christian Century*
7. *Christian Chronicle* (two of these!)
8. *Christian Civic League of Maine Record*
9. *Christian Communicator*
10. *Christian Community*
11. *Christian Composer*
12. *Christian Computing Magazine*
13. *Christian Counseling Today*
14. *Christian Country Research Bulletin*
15. *Christian Courier* (two of these!)
16. *Christian Crusade Newspaper*
17. *Christian Drama Magazine*
18. *Christian Edge*
19. *Christian Education Counselor*
20. *Christian Education Leadership*
21. *Christian Educators Journal*
22. *Christian Endeavor World*
23. *Christian Event Journal*
24. *Christian Focus*
25. *Christian History*
26. *Christian Home and School*
27. *Christian Index*
28. *Christian Information Association Newsletter*
29. *Christian Leader*
30. *Christian Librarian*
31. *Christian Library Journal*
32. *Christian Living*
33. *Christian Management Report*
34. *Christian Media*
35. *Christian Ministry*
36. *Christian Monthly*
37. *Christian Observer*
38. *Christian Outlook*
39. *Christian Parenting Today*
40. *Christian Reader*
41. *Christian Record*

42. *Christian Recorder*
43. *Christian Recreation*
44. *Christian Renewal*
45. *Christian Research Journal*
46. *Christian Response*
47. *Christian Retailing*
48. *Christian School*
49. *Christian Sentinel*
50. *Christian Single*
51. *Christian Social Action*
52. *Christian Standard*
53. *Christian Woman*

Periodicals Whose Names Start with the Word Church

Again, some start with *The*. And I suppose I missed a zillion church newsletters.

1. *Church Administration*
2. *Church Advocate*
3. *Church and State Advocate*
4. *Church and Synagogue Libraries*
5. *Church Bytes*
6. *Church Educator*
7. *Church Growth Network*
8. *Church Herald*
9. *Church Herald and Holiness Banner*
10. *Church History*
11. *Church Leader's Newsletter*
12. *Church Media Library Magazine*
13. *Church Music Report*
14. *Church Musician*
15. *Church of God Evangel*
16. *Church of God Missions*
17. *Church of God Progress Journal*
18. *Church of God Quarterly*
19. *Church Pianist*
20. *Church School Herald*
21. *Church Woman*
22. *Church Worship*

Awards of the Evangelical Press Association, 1996

Each year the EPA recognizes the best evangelical periodicals in various categories. Here are some recent winners of the Award of Excellence:

1. Christian Ministry: *Teachers in Focus* (Focus on the Family)
2. Denominational: *The Standard* (Baptist General Conference)

3. General: *A Better Tomorrow* (Thomas Nelson)
4. Missionary: *Leaders for Today* (Haggai Institute)
5. Newsletter: *Proclaim!* (Luis Palau Evangelistic Association)
6. Newspaper: *Minnesota Christian Chronicle*
7. Most Improved: *Christian Parenting Today* (Good Family Magazines)
8. Organizational: *New Man* (Promise Keepers)
9. Sunday School Take-Home: *The Lookout* (Standard)
10. Youth: *Clubhouse Jr.* (Focus on the Family)

Awards of the Evangelical Press Association, 1985

1. Christian Ministry: *Leadership* (CTi)
2. Denominational: *The Banner* (Christian Reformed Church)
3. General: *Christianity Today* (CTi)
4. Missionary: *TEAM Horizons*
5. Newsletter: *Spiritual Fitness in Business*
6. Organizational: *Worldwide Challenge* (Campus Crusade)
7. Sunday School Take-Home: *Sunday Digest* (Cook)
8. Youth: *Crusader* (Calvinist Cadet Corps)

Media and the Arts

Ten Places Where You Can Find a Gutenberg Bible

1. Bibliotheque Nationale, Paris
2. Henry E. Huntington Library, San Marino, California
3. British Library, London
4. Deutsches Buch und Schrift Museum der Deutschen Bucherei, Leipzig, Germany
5. National Library of Scotland, Edinburgh
6. University of Texas Library, Austin, Texas
7. Biblioteca Apostolica Vaticana, Vatican Library, Italy
8. Gutenberg Museum, Mainz, Germany
9. Biblioteca Universitaria, Seville, Spain
10. Biblioteka Seminarium Duchownego, Pelplin, Poland

Beloved Paintings of Christ

1. *Adoration,* by Gerrit van Honthorst (Dutch)
2. *Christ and the Doctors,* by Heinrich Hoffmann (German)
3. *Christ and the Fishermen,* by Ernst Zimmermann (German)
4. *Light of the World,* by Holman Hunt (English)
5. *Christ and the Rich Young Man,* by Heinrich Hoffmann (German)
6. *Christ's Triumphant Entry,* by Bernard Plockhorst (German)
7. *The Last Supper,* by Leonardo da Vinci (Italian)
8. *Christ in Gethsemane,* by Heinrich Hoffmann (German)

9. *Christ Before Pilate,* by Mihaly Munkocsy (Hungary)
10. *Crucifixion,* by Karl Heinrich Bloch (Danish)

Art Galleries That Display Art with Christian Themes

1. Biblical Arts Center, Dallas, Texas
2. Foxhall Gallery, Washington, D.C.
3. Eastbrook Gallery, Milwaukee, Wisconsin
4. Fred Jones Jr. Museum of Art, Topeka, Kansas
5. Gallery W, Sacramento, California
6. Genesis Art Gallery, Chicago, Illinois
7. Jubilee Center, New York, New York
8. La Band Art Gallery, Los Angeles, California
9. Museum of Contemporary Religious Art (MOCRA), St. Louis, Missouri

Paintings on the Teachings of Jesus

1. *Jesus in the Synagogue,* by James Tissot
2. *Sermon on the Mount,* by James Tissot
3. *Christ Preaching by the Sea,* by Heinrich Hoffmann
4. *Christ Preaching from the Boat,* by Harold Copping
5. *Teaching by the Lake,* by Fritz Von Uhde
6. *Christ and the Rich Young Man,* by Karl Von Gebhardt
7. *The Prodigal Son,* by Rembrandt
8. *The Lost Piece of Silver,* by Sir John Millais
9. *Christ and the Adulteress,* by Tintoretto
10. *The Sower,* by Jean-François Millet

Some Artists of Religious Works

1. Copping, Harold (1863–1932), England
2. Doré, Paul Gustave (1832–1883), Germany
3. Dürer, Albrecht (1471–1528), Germany
4. Hoffmann, Heinrich (1824–1911), Germany
5. Hunt, William Holman (1827–1910), England
6. Munkacsy, Mihaly (1844–1909), Hungary
7. Raphael, Raffaello Sanzio (1483–1520), Italy
8. Rubens, Petrus Paulus (1577–1640), Belgium
9. Tintoretto (1518–1594), Italy
10. Tissot, James (1836–1902), France
11. Uhde, Fritz von (1848–1911), Germany

Religious Paintings by Rembrandt

1. *David Presenting the Head of Goliath to Saul* (1627)
2. *St. Paul in Prison* (1627)
3. *The Prophet Jeremiah Lamenting the Destruction of Jerusalem* (1630)

4. *The Holy Family* (1631)
5. *Crucifixion* (1633)
6. *Christ Descending from the Cross* (1633)
7. *Abraham and Isaac (1634)*
8. *The Entombment of Christ* (1639)
9. *The Woman Taken in Adultery* (1644)
10. *The Adoration of the Shepherds* (1646)
11. *Supper at Emmaus* (1648)
12. *The Good Samaritan* (1648)
13. *Bathsheba* (1654)
14. *Return of the Prodigal Son* (1662)

Networking for Christians in the Arts

Organizations for support and fellowship

1. Artists in Christian Testimony, P.O. Box 1002, Rancho Cucamonga, CA 91729-1002
2. Associates in Media, P.O. Box 2014, Burbank, CA 91507-2014
3. Catholic Artists of America, Maria Regis Hall, Molloy College, 100 Hempstead Ave., Rockville Center, NY 11571-5002
4. Christian Artists Europe, P.O. Box 81065, Rotterdam 3009 GB, Netherlands
5. Christian Performing Artists Fellowship, 10523 Main St., Suite 31, Fairfax, VA 22180
6. Christians in the Arts Networking (CAN), P.O. Box 242, Arlington, MA 02174-0003
7. Christians in the Theatre Arts (CITA), P.O. Box 26471, Greenville, SC 29616
8. Christians in the Visual Arts (CIVA), P.O. Box 18117, Minneapolis, MN 55418-0017
9. Fellowship of Artists for Christian Evangelism (FACE), 1605 Elizabeth St., Pasadena, CA 91104
10. International Christian Dance Fellowship, 11 Amaroo Crescent, Mosman, NSW 2088, Australia
11. International Christian Media Commission, P.O. Box 70632, Seattle, WA 98107
12. National Association of Pastoral Musicians, 225 Sheridan St. NW, Washington, D.C. 20011
13. Upstream Arts Fellowship, 375 Colville Blvd., London, ON N6K 2J4 Canada

The Best Christian Films

1. *The Hiding Place*
2. The *Jesus* film (a worldwide phenomenon)
3. *The Cross and the Switchblade*

4. *The Gospel Blimp*
5. *God of Creation* (Moody Science)
6. *Mr. Texas* (early Billy Graham)
7. *C. S. Lewis: Through the Shadowlands* (BBC, before Hollywood made *Shadowlands*)
8. *Joni*
9. *Martin Luther* (BBC)
10. *A Time for Burning* (civil rights documentary)

. . . And a Few in Secular Release

1. *The Inn of the Sixth Happiness* (Gladys Aylward)
2. *Chariots of Fire* (Eric Liddell)
3. *A Man Called Peter* (Peter Marshall)

Thanks to Ken Curtis of Gateway Films/Vision Video.

Ten Secular Movies That Feature Ministers, Priests, or Nuns

1. *The Sound of Music*
2. *The Bishop's Wife*
3. *The Trouble with Angels*
4. *Agnes of God*
5. *Going My Way*
6. *The Bells of St. Mary's*
7. *Sister Act*
8. *Elmer Gantry*
9. *Leap of Faith*
10. *Dead Man Walking*

Seven Secular Movies That Feature Angels

1. *Carousel*
2. *Always*
3. *Angels in the Outfield*
4. *It's a Wonderful Life*
5. *Angel on My Shoulder*
6. *Heart and Souls*
7. *Michael*

Ten Secular Movies Based on Biblical Stories

1. *The Ten Commandments*
2. *The Greatest Story Ever Told*
3. *Ben-Hur*
4. *Jesus of Nazareth*
5. *Jesus Christ Superstar*
6. *Godspell*
7. *The Robe*

8. *Samson and Delilah*
9. *The Last Temptation of Christ*
10. *King David*

Note: I'm not vouching for the accuracy of all these movies, just that they're at least sort of based on biblical stories, OK?

Ten Secular Movies That Mention God or Heaven in the Title

1. *Oh, God*
2. *Oh, God, You Devil*
3. *Dear God*
4. *Agnes of God*
5. *Heaven Can Wait*
6. *All Dogs Go to Heaven*
7. *Days of Heaven*
8. *Heaven's Gate*
9. *Pennies from Heaven*
10. *Heaven Only Knows, Mr. Allison*

Ten TV Shows That Feature(d) Ministers, Priests, or Nuns

1. *The Flying Nun*
2. *The Father Dowling Mysteries*
3. *Amen*
4. *Christy*
5. *Highway to Heaven*
6. *Touched by an Angel*
7. *Little House on the Prairie*
8. *Dr. Quinn, Medicine Woman*
9. *Out of the Blue*
10. *Picket Fences*

Education

Bill Bennett's 10 Virtues

1. Self-discipline
2. Compassion
3. Responsibility
4. Friendship
5. Work
6. Courage
7. Perseverance
8. Honesty
9. Loyalty
10. Faith

From *The Book of Virtues* by William J. Bennett.

Members of ACCESS

ACCESS stands for the Association of Christian Continuing Education Schools and Seminaries.

1. Berean College (Assemblies of God), Springfield, Missouri
2. Columbia International University, Columbia, South Carolina
3. Covenant Theological Seminary, St. Louis, Missouri
4. Fuller Theological Seminary, Pasadena, California
5. Gordon-Conwell Theological Seminary (Ockenga Institute), South Hamilton, Massachusetts
6. Liberty University, Lynchburg, Virginia
7. Luther Rice Bible College, Lithonia, Georgia
8. Moody Bible Institute, Chicago, Illinois
9. Northwestern College, St. Paul, Minnesota
10. Prairie Bible College, Three Hills, Alberta, Canada
11. Reformed Theological Seminary, Maitland, Florida
12. Regent University (School of Business), Virginia Beach, Virginia
13. Southeastern Bible College, Birmingham, Alabama
14. Taylor University (correspondence), Fort Wayne, Indiana
15. Trinity Evangelical Divinity School, Deerfield, Illinois
16. Wheaton College Graduate School, Wheaton, Illinois

Why Students Like Christian Colleges

1. Christian values
2. A sense of community
3. Academic rigor
4. Personal attention from faculty and administration
5. Opportunity for leadership and service

Why Parents Like Christian Colleges

1. Safe, healthy environment
2. Care and concern for students
3. Spiritual development
4. Institutional financial aid
5. Source of lifelong friends

These two lists were taken from *Peterson's Choose a Christian College* (Bowker, 1996).

Why Parents Really Like Christian Colleges

I suspect these are the things parents aren't telling the pollsters.

1. Because they went there
2. So the kid won't join some cult
3. Because it makes them look like good parents in front of the other folks at church

4. So the kid won't take up bad habits like drinking, smoking, doing drugs, or cursing—at least not openly
5. Inbreeding

Members of the CCCU

CCCU stands for the Coalition for Christian Colleges and Universities.

1. Abilene Christian University
2. Anderson University
3. Asbury College
4. Azusa Pacific University
5. Bartlesville Wesleyan College
6. Belhaven College
7. Bethel College (Indiana)
8. Bethel College (Kansas)
9. Bethel College (Minnesota)
10. Biola University
11. Bluffton College
12. Bryan College
13. California Baptist College
14. Calvin College
15. Campbell University
16. Campbellsville University
17. Cedarville College
18. College of the Ozarks
19. Colorado Christian University
20. Cornerstone College
21. Covenant College
22. Dallas Baptist University
23. Dordt College
24. East Texas Baptist University
25. Eastern College
26. Eastern Mennonite University
27. Eastern Nazarene College
28. Erskine College
29. Evangel College
30. Fresno Pacific College
31. Geneva College
32. George Fox University
33. Gordon College
34. Goshen College
35. Grace College
36. Grand Canyon University
37. Greenville College
38. Houghton College
39. Huntington College

40. Indiana Wesleyan University
41. John Brown University
42. Judson College
43. King College
44. The King's University College
45. Lee College
46. LeTourneau University
47. Malone College
48. Master's College
49. Messiah College
50. MidAmerica Nazarene College
51. Milligan College
52. Montreat College
53. Mount Vernon Nazarene College
54. North Park College
55. Northwest Christian College
56. Northwest College
57. Northwest Nazarene College
58. Northwestern College (Iowa)
59. Northwestern College (Minnesota)
60. Nyack College
61. Oklahoma Baptist University
62. Olivet Nazarene University
63. Pacific Christian College
64. Palm Beach Atlantic College
65. Point Loma Nazarene College
66. Redeemer College
67. Roberts Wesleyan College
68. Seattle Pacific University
69. Simpson College
70. Southern California College
71. Southern Nazarene University
72. Southern Wesleyan University
73. Southwest Baptist University
74. Spring Arbor College
75. Sterling College
76. Tabor College
77. Taylor University
78. Trevecca Nazarene University
79. Trinity Christian College
80. Trinity International University
81. Trinity Western University
82. Union University
83. University of Sioux Falls

84. Warner Pacific College
85. Warner Southern College
86. Western Baptist College
87. Westmont College
88. Wheaton College
89. Whitworth College
90. Williams Baptist College

People

Ten Radio Pioneers in the Religious Broadcasting Hall of Fame

1. Clarence Jones of HCJB, Quito, Ecuador
2. Walter A. Maier, *The Lutheran Hour*
3. R. R. Brown, *Radio Chapel Service*
4. "First Mate Bob" Paul Myers, *Haven of Rest*
5. Donald Grey Barnhouse, *Bible Study Hour*
6. Richard M. DeHaan, *Radio Bible Class*
7. Theodore H. Epp, *Back to the Bible*
8. J. Vernon McGee, *Thru the Bible Broadcast*
9. John Zoller, *Christ for Everyone*
10. Myron Boyd, *Light and Life Hour*

Ten Honorary Members of the Evangelical Press Association

1. James Adair, longtime Scripture Press editor
2. Anita Bailey, past secretary of EPA, managed *The Alliance Witness* for years
3. Lester DeKoster, former editor of *The Banner*
4. Carl Henry, founding editor of *Christianity Today*
5. Gladys Peterson, Interlit editor for David C. Cook
6. Norman Rohrer, former EPA executive secretary who now "fires writers" with the Christian Writer's Guild
7. Robert Walker, longtime editor of *Christian Life*
8. Larry Ward, president of Food for the Hungry, former EPA executive secretary
9. Gary Warner, director of EPA for 14 wacky years, now teaches journalism at John Brown University
10. Sherwood Wirt, founding editor of *Decision* magazine

Ten Christian Athletes

Randomly chosen from the many.

1. Paul Azinger, golf
2. Michael Chang, tennis
3. Brett Butler, baseball
4. Evander Holyfield, boxing

5. Reggie White, football
6. A. C. Green, basketball
7. Michelle Akers, women's soccer
8. Dave Johnson, Olympic decathlon
9. Troy Kopp, arena football
10. Mike Gartner, ice hockey

My Favorite Christian Athletes of the Past

1. Bob Boone, baseball
2. Doug Collins, basketball
3. Bob Froese, hockey
4. Joe Gibbs, football coach
5. Bobby Jones, basketball
6. Bobby Richardson, baseball
7. Jim Ryun and Kip Keino, track
8. Stan Smith, tennis
9. Roger Staubach, football
10. Don Sutton, baseball

Full Names of Well-Known Christians Who Go by Their Initials

1. Clive Staples Lewis
2. Cyrus Ingersoll Scofield
3. Frederick Fyvie Bruce
4. Robert Charles Sproul
5. Frederick Brotherton Meyer
6. Aiden Wilson Tozer
7. Gilbert Keith Chesterton
8. Charles Thomas Studd
9. Wallie Amos Criswell
10. Amzi Clarence Dixon